The Crash Controversy
censorship campaigns and film reception

The Crash Controversy
censorship campaigns and film reception

Martin Barker, Jane Arthurs & Ramaswami Harindranath

WALLFLOWER PRESS
LONDON AND NEW YORK

First published in Great Britain in 2001 by
Wallflower Press
5 Pond Street, London NW3 2PN
www.wallflowerpress.co.uk

A catalogue for this book is available from the British Library

ISBN 1 903364 15 9 (paperback)
ISBN 1 903364 17 5 (hardback)

Printed in Great Britain by Biddles Limited, Guildford and King's Lynn

CONTENTS

ACKNOWLEDGEMENTS

This book owes a number of debts of gratitude. Firstly, to the Economic and Social Research Council for its grant award (Award No. R000222194), which enabled us to carry out the research. Any kind of media audience research is vastly expensive of both time and materials and is virtually impossible without this kind of funding. We are grateful also to the anonymous referees of our research who gave our proposal a fair hearing, both at its inception and in its outcome.

We owe a huge debt to our Research Assistant Jo Haynes, who tackled every part of the complex tasks of this research with professionalism, good humour and great intellectual skill. Without her care and understanding a good deal of what we have achieved would not have occurred. Thanks also to Iain Grant, who translated the French reviews for the research.

We record our thanks to Chris Auty, Co-Executive Producer of *Crash*; James Ferman, then Director of the British Board of Film Classification; and the many journalists who allowed us to interview them about their part in the controversy around *Crash*. We also record our disappointment that three key journalists, who had no hesitation in making large claims about the dangers of the film during the controversy, were unwilling to talk to us under any conditions about their views and their role in the controversy.

We wish to record our thanks to all those who took part in our screening. They met our requests with great courtesy and spoke to us with an astonishing frankness which helped enormously. We hope we have dealt fairly with all views of the film.

We are delighted that this book is being published by Wallflower Press, and we hope that it makes a contribution to their success.

1   One Big Controversy, Several Large Research Tasks

On 3 June 1996, the film critic Alexander Walker filed a report from the Cannes Film Festival. The piece was an outright assault on David Cronenberg's new film *Crash*. Juicily headlined 'A movie beyond the bounds of depravity' by a sub-editor at the London *Evening Standard*, Walker's attack provided the impetus for a year-long battle over Cronenberg's film.[1] It led to some 400 press reports on the film, much radio and television coverage, statements by politicians, and a host of other heated moments. It also led to the research project which this book relates.

Walker himself was clearly personally and morally affronted by the film. Normally an outspoken critic of censorship (he was a longstanding defender of Stanley Kubrick's *A Clockwork Orange* (1971), for instance), *Crash* offended something deeply in his Ulster protestant soul. For Walker, *Crash* was simply and repeatedly 'pornography', a film containing 'some of the most perverted acts and theories of sexual deviance I have ever seen propagated in mainline cinema'. To every possible defence of the film by its makers, Walker's response was: look at how debased the whole thing is. Look how 'overloaded with sex in virtually every scene' it is. The characters are 'defined solely in terms of their sexual obsessions'. The result: a film which 'pushes the envelope of sexual encounter farther than I remember seeing'. *Crash*, he concluded, 'is vulnerable on almost every level: taste, seriousness, even the public safety risk of promulgating such a perverted creed', whatever its pedigree and craftsmanship.

Walker himself never called for the film to be banned, but he undoubtedly set a wagon rolling. Within a short time, Nigel Reynolds of the *Daily Telegraph* had hinted at the need for a ban, but the serious demands for this would come courtesy of another Associated Newspapers title, the *Daily Mail*. Christopher Tookey laid down the position that was to dominate the *Mail*'s coverage, and to become the touchstone that many others – even his strongest opponents – found they had to respond to: *Crash* is 'the point at which even a liberal society must draw the line'.[2] Yet the most recurring quotation was that sub-editor's addition to Alexander Walker's original June 1996 article: *Crash* was a 'movie beyond depravity'. The very suggestive vagueness of this was its most potent force.

The Controversy and the Campaign

By any account this was an extraordinary controversy, even measured against previous campaigns against films or other media.[3] The *Mail* (whose campaign we analyse in some detail later) went so far as to door-step all the British Board of Film Classification's (henceforth BBFC) examiners, and run articles about their private lives. They also contacted every local authority[4] in the country with the aim of encouraging/persuading them to join Westminster City Council, an arch-Conservative council if ever there was one, who very publicly imposed a ban on the film, thereby denying it the normal West End opening. Forty councils asked for screenings before allowing it in their areas. In the end, only four other local councils – Cardiff, Kirklees, Walsall and North Lanarkshire – for differing periods banned the film, using their residual powers under the 1912 Act which established the BBFC.

To sustain its campaign, the *Mail* represented every expression of disquiet as an incipient local authority ban, their openly stated aim being to deny the film any significant circulation. For instance, the *Mail* reported that 'seven councils in Surrey have followed the lead set earlier this week by North Lanarkshire',[5] although not one of those seven subsequently enacted a ban. Virginia Bottomley, then Heritage Secretary in the Conservative Government, made a statement in which she too encouraged local authorities to use their powers to ban the film. It quickly emerged that she had not seen the film, and was acting under the moral promptings of the *Mail*. Various moral entrepreneurial bodies entered the fray. Mary Whitehouse, by now retired from active duty with the National Viewers and Listeners Association, spoke out on the need to make *Crash* a key issue in the forthcoming election. Other groups which, under most circumstances, the *Mail* would be unlikely to go near, now became righteous brethren. Islamic organisations, not normally among the *Mail*'s preferred moral opinion-leaders, received equal billing alongside other religious groups when they promised their organisations would picket any cinema showing *Crash*. At the height of its campaign, the *Mail* published a full-page call on its readers to 'boycott Sony'.[6]

Just about every local newspaper in the country joined in the debate, with a style of reporting which very quickly presumed that their readerships would not only have heard about the film, but would know the terms of the controversy.[7] Sometimes the local coverage was simply garish. Take as one example a tiny report which appeared in one very local paper: 'Certificate on way for *Crash*: It looks like this controversial violent thriller, directed by David Cronenberg and featuring graphic scenes of car accidents and violence, and starring Deborah Unger and James Spader as a psychotic couple, will be classified later this year. It has been revealed exclusively to the *Herald* that the British Board of Film Censors currently examining the film are cutting a number of scenes before they issue an '18' certificate in June or July'.[8] We would suggest that the most significant thing about this report is not the remarkable number of errors for such a minuscule article. Rather, it is that this paper thought it worth carrying, and making the daft claim to have an exclusive – and that the film was pre-defined not simply as controversial, but as 'violent'. This association with a generalised concern about 'violence' was also signalled by John Bell, chair of the licensing committee of Westminster City Council in giving the reasons for the Westminster ban: 'I cannot accept a film such as this. So much of this kind of violence is going on and we have had enough of it. Let us stop it'.[9]

It was this everyday presence of astounding exaggeration that makes the *Crash* controversy worthy of study. Yet the overwhelming presence in all this is the *Daily Mail*, which succeeded in turning its own crusade into a matter of national significance. The *Mail*'s tactics were to discredit the film's defenders at every step, sometimes with gratuitous venom. So, Carmen Menegazzi, London head of TriStar International, who were distributing *Crash* in Britain, was noted to be 'Belgian' while James Ferman, head of the BBFC, it was repeatedly noted, was 'originally American'. Bad guys could turn good if only they spoke with the *Mail*'s voice. One of the BBFC's tactics in arriving at a judgement had been to draw on the expert opinion of a QC (who remained anonymous) and a psychologist, Dr Paul Britton. When *Crash* was certified '18', the BBFC's accompanying explanation included a quotation from Britton in which he stated that there was no known fetishism to which the film might appeal. The *Mail* fulminated against the judgement, and against Britton: he was the man who 'masterminded the police operation against Colin Stagg over the Wimbledon Common murder of Rachel Nickell. He was heavily criticised when the prosecution collapsed. Last night his verdict on *Crash* was also under attack'.[10] Just a few days later, Britton issued a protest that his statement had been taken out of context – he had hated *Crash* and wanted it banned. Instantly, for the *Mail*, his status shifted. Now he was 'a leading clinical and forensic psychologist … a precise man. A scientist'.[11] The following day he became simply an 'expert witness'.[12] We shall see that the view his 'expertise' allows him to promulgate is an entirely speculative one.

The Questions of Crash

What do we need to ask about this extraordinary campaign? Why not simply see it as a sensationalist spasm, in which two incompatible sides went to war for a time? In the blue corner, the *Evening Standard* and the *Daily Mail*, whose champions Walker and Tookey would scream about a virtual end of civilisation as we know it, while delivering homilies on the 'luvvies' and 'liberal intelligentsia' who have lost the will to ever take a moral stance.

In the red corner, the opponents of censorship damning those who want to make judgements on their behalf; for instance, the local newspaper which spoke of the dangers of 'moral watchdogs', defended the 'rights of adults to choose' and called on local councillors to 'allow us to make up our own minds about *Crash*'.[13] We aim to show that there are a good number of questions which this account of the events must leave unanswered. Indeed we hope it will become clear by the end of this book that this account of the affair remains trapped unhelpfully in the surface of the events, and even makes it impossible to hear the distinctive voices both of those who loved and delighted in the film, and of those who loathed and despised it. Here are some 'starter' questions that we believe show the need to go deeper into the affair.

Why did the Mail campaign so vigorously against the film?

Consider the answers that have been, or might be, given to this question. The simplest is the cynical one which says that, with a coming General Election, which just about everyone was expecting the Conservatives to lose, the *Mail* – as the pre-eminent Conservative paper – was hunting an issue which might turn the tide. There are certainly some small indices of this, but actually this account has little travel. For a start, there were a good number of Labour spokespeople only too willing to join the anti-*Crash* camp. Mark Fisher (Labour shadow arts spokesman) criticised the Royal Automobile Club (RAC) for allowing that *Crash* might have some 'educational' benefit, saying, 'It is distasteful that the RAC is supporting the film. If there is one area of copycat behaviour it will be car crashes.'[14] One of the four councils ultimately to ban *Crash* in its area was the staunchly Labour council in Walsall. But more significantly, when the *Mail*'s campaign was at its peak, in editorial statements it took the opportunity to address Tony Blair as a possible incoming Prime Minister and to ask him, in tones suggesting that he might well agree, if his commitment to 'family values' should not lead him to reform the BBFC – one of the *Mail*'s more general goals in the campaign.

More widely, a number of commentators have begun to take note of the rise of the *Mail* as the spokesperson for 'middle England'. After the success story of the *Sun* from 1970 onwards, which has been widely documented,[15] the emergence of the *Mail* as, firstly, 'Thatcher's paper', and then more widely as the newspaper to articulate an aggressive and campaigning English moral vision is one of the most important stories of the contemporary press.[16] This moral vision covers everything from Britain's place in Europe and the World, to matters of the family, education, sexual life and the manners of the young – all addressed through a 'restatement' of some central values. The *Mail*'s campaign against *Crash* is a good index of this, and to understand it purely cynically misses out the edge of real conviction and anger which pervades its writing. It might thus allow us to address questions such as these: what is the content of this 'middle England' ideology? How does it connect issues together? And in what ways was it influential?

Why Crash? Why was this film deemed so provocative?

There is no shortage of cases of films, or television programmes, or video games and so on, that have from time to time provoked moral outrage in the press, and among various pundits. Yet the outrage provoked by *Crash* went beyond most other cases we can think of. There seemed to be some quality in the film which, whether in the circumstances of the late 1990s or for more general reasons, marked it apart.

It is not our task to offer some alternative account of *Crash*. We are primarily interested here in how *others* understood, analysed, or responded to it, whether implicitly or explicitly. For this purpose, the moral denunciations of Julian Brazier MP, on behalf of the Conservative Family Life Association, are every bit as interesting as Derek Malcolm's careful film-critical evaluation or those of the four academics who analysed the film in the journal *Screen*. This is because, as we will show, all of them in different ways incorporate into their accounts of the film a shadowy 'figure' of an audience who *might* see the film and get the message of the film that each writer finds there.

Still, there are things to be said about *Crash*. First, a minimal account of its narrative: *Crash* follows the lives of a couple, James and Catherine, whose sex life is precariously kept alive by extra-marital encounters, always wondering if 'maybe the next time' will bring sexual satisfaction. Following a car crash in which James is injured and hospitalised, they encounter a group, led by a weird but weirdly fascinating character Vaughan, who find sexual gratification through recreating famous crashes, attracted by the risks and scars that crashes cause. Drawn increasingly into the experiments, James and Catherine are drawn into a spiral of traffic and sexual involvements that come closer and closer to risking their lives.

The film ends with Catherine being driven off the road by James. As she lies shaken but apparently uninjured, James begins to make love to her, whispering, 'Maybe the next time'. Of course a good deal of the controversy did not concern the narrative details so much as the explicit sexual encounters of the film, which include a number of (ambiguous) rear-entry sex scenes, two homoerotic encounters, and several involving fascination with wounds and damaged limbs.

It is necessary to draw out some features from this, in order to be able to understand people's responses at all. Three seem central. Firstly, the film seems to defy categorisation. Not one person writing about it was able to say 'this is a typical...'. It was not even a typical Cronenberg movie, for those who were willing to approach it from that angle. J G Ballard himself, a strong proponent of the film of his novel, put it like this: 'Crash is not a conventional film, there are no conventions Crash is relying on'.[17] We are convinced that this anti-formulaic quality in the film explains the extremity of many responses – people were simply confused, and surprised, by what they saw.

Secondly, it is a very self-conscious film. Crash was very evidently formed out of a combination of the visions of J G Ballard and David Cronenberg. Here was a film designed, for good or ill, to embody a philosophical position. In the very many interviews which accompanied the film's release, both in Britain and elsewhere in the world, Cronenberg enunciates a clear intent which, he argues, is embodied in the film. In one interview, Cronenberg discusses a suggestion that was put to him by an American agent, who wanted to propose the insertion of a voice-over commentator who could be a 'voice of comfort and to explain the film to everybody'. Cronenberg said no – and shortly thereafter changed agent. The reason was that he wanted what Ballard identified as an 'absence of a moral frame around the film'. Cronenberg positively wanted audience uncertainty and self-scrutiny. Crash declined to render a judgement on the characters and behaviours it showed.

One particular aspect of the film recurs in those interviews, and constitutes our third feature: the opening. In just about every interview which Cronenberg gave about the film, he talked about the opening three scenes, and relates a response he had at one pre-release screening. Here is one version of this:

> The film begins with three sex scenes. For most people that means it is a pornographic film; they've never seen a movie that began with three sex scenes before. And instead of watching to see what I'm really doing with that, they just react the way they normally do – which is to switch off and wait for the movie to get going – but it doesn't get going because the sex scenes are the movie, so if they resist watching them for narrative, for character development, for the texture, for other things which are there – they don't get the movie. I had little screenings of the film – my version of the Hollywood test screening ... I just showed it to some friends and people; and I got a card that said 'a series of sex scenes is not a plot', and my reaction to that was 'why not?'[18]

This refusal to provide a traditional narrative seems to have provoked viewers, whether towards favouring the film, being bored by it, or hating it.

Defenders of the film

This book does not in some simple sense 'take sides'. Although individually we would probably be seen as having 'liberal' views on censorship, we do not agree fully among ourselves over, for instance, what kinds of representation of sex we feel comfortable with, or would want to associate with, and so on. But more importantly, in researching the *Crash* controversy and writing this book, we have deliberately sought to set aside our own responses to *Crash* and to ask: in what terms and drawing on what wider ways of talking and thinking (discourses, as they are often termed) did both attackers and defenders of the film articulate their views?

Take an example. In one of his quite frequent returns to *Crash*, Alexander Walker took aim at the film's defenders. He noted how often they used one word to describe the film:

> The word 'cool' has been the one most often bandied about by the defenders of David Cronenberg's film about a coven of degenerates who top up their fagged-out libidos with the thrill of car crashes. It's one of those words suggesting the users have freed themselves from most inhibitions – especially the elitist one of making moral judgements about other people.[19]

Walker was right about this: it was indeed a common move among *Crash*'s defenders to call it 'cool'. Yet it is doubtful that they would recognise themselves in the remainder of the paragraph – any more than Walker would see himself in their counter-descriptions of him and Tookey as puritan, arrogant, and censorious. In fact, from the 'third-party' position we aim to try to sustain in this book, we would begin from the fact that here we have two languages which in an important sense are unable to understand each other. Yet they are neither disconnected nor equal, as we will try to show. We see the word 'cool' as performing another function altogether – one which reveals a great deal, in fact, about the power that the *Mail* acquired. For a time, the *Mail* became a dominant definer of things such as *Crash*, to the extent that people seeking to challenge the *Mail*'s hegemony had to define themselves in opposition to its terms. Although the *Mail* did not, as far as we can see, ever use the term 'hot' to describe *Crash*, in various ways they set up claims that the film was *dangerous-because-arousing*. To call it 'cool', in that case, was to mark off a space around it, for defence. But that raises an awkward question: what if this rhetorically achieved space itself collided with the way ordinary viewers who did enjoy it experienced the film? It also raises other questions which outrun the limits of this book: for instance, how exactly did the *Mail* achieve the feat of setting the terms of the debate, when it lacked the power to block the film itself?

What impact did the campaign against Crash have?

One common, cynical comment we frequently met was that the makers and distributors of *Crash* were in reality only too pleased to see the controversy – it was all just free publicity for the film. It certainly is not unknown for producers to play to the gallery, and hope to coin it on a frisson of excitement. Chris Auty, the Co-Executive Producer of *Crash* firmly believed otherwise; he worried that the campaign against *Crash* scared many people away from seeing it. And certainly its British box office was well below its takings in most other European countries – a fact that the *Mail* was happy to claim as a small triumph for itself. Claim, counterclaim, engendering public cynicism: in all this, perhaps the only question that can sensibly be asked is, how do we examine the impact of these kinds of debates on people's interest in seeing a film?

Where is the 'viewer' in all this?

One aspect of the controversy which repays close attention is the way in which both sides draw on and refer to 'figures' of the audience. Of necessity, it seems, as they make their respective cases about the risks, harmlessness, or positive benefits of the film, commentators have to incorporate claims about what the 'audience' is like, how they are likely to respond, and how the film might potentially involve them. This is such a powerful component in all such arguments that we will spend a little time on this.[20] Consider, for instance, this *Western Daily Press* editorial:

> Ram-raiding and reckless driving by youngsters for the fun of it are already endemic throughout the country, with a particular West Country favourite being a game of chicken in which the drivers of stolen cars signal they are going in one direction before going in the other. When it is a fact that scenes of violence or depravity from other films have produced real-life copycats it is not being sensational to suggest this one's lethally reckless driving for sexual thrills, fetishism, voyeurism and sadomasochism could prove the latest game for some lunatic West thrill-seekers.[21]

The elemental components of this need to be laid out. First, an item of behaviour shown in a film is abstracted from its context there, and 'named' ('lethally reckless driving') as a thing in its own right. It is then linked to a piece of real behaviour which at best is loosely similar, and is feared. It does not matter if several pretty unrelated behaviours are lumped together here (ram-raiding and reckless driving do not obviously belong in the same register). The film, with its named behaviour, can then be treated as a potential cause of the real, feared behaviour. To complete the picture, it is necessary to paint a portrait of a possible audience who *might* see the film, an audience which is somewhere between immature, bad and mad ('some lunatic West thrill-seekers'). The resulting argument can be made all the stronger if those making it can call on a shared assumption that the sheer act of *showing* the behaviour, that it will be *seen*, is itself dangerous. And indeed it is the case that a widespread unspoken premise in British cultural thinking is that to show something is *per se* to encourage it. This is the most widespread, 'commonsense' claim about how films might work on audiences.

Slightly more sophisticated readings upgrade the understanding about *how* the unit is shown in the film, using expressions like 'entertaining', 'gratuitous', 'making attractive'. But as before, the arc from film to audience is completed when a putatively vulnerable/corrupted audience is mentioned as likely to see it – their weak egos, or incomplete moral conditioning means that they are most likely to be successfully invaded by the film's 'message'. This whole argumentative package can, in practice, be condensed into a very few words, as in the following: 'I am extremely worried about the impact it might have on 18 or 19-year-olds who think themselves very clever and tend to like fast cars' (Ann Barnes, Westminster Labour Councillor).[22] The irreducible minimum is that notion of a 'possible impact'. These two words are effectively unchallengeable because they are virtually without substantive content. What *kind* of 'impact' on which *actual* audiences? The idea, the words, are pure rhetoric, and all the more effective because of that.

Assertions of this kind abounded in the debate over *Crash*, in, for instance, the statement issued by Westminster Council to explain its ban. It argued that the characters, by being made 'sexually attractive, independently minded, interpersonally powerful, effective and tenacious' were being 'depicted as attractive role models'. So the behaviour is not dangerous for the majority, who would be 'likely to reject the message of the film', but for a minority who might drift to Westminster and be 'exposed' to the film there, because of its place in London:

> The Sub-Committee is concerned that immature persons and the physiologically vulnerable who do not have firm moral views would well be adversely affected by the film and we are especially concerned that those who have a predisposition to anti-social behaviour will be encouraged in their beliefs. A view which is supported by the views of Dr Paul Britton.

The end clause is an interesting addition; it signals a wish to bring in a scientific supplement to give substance to the moral concerns. Then listen to how Britton himself expounded the idea:

> Young people, and those whose moral and philosophical systems have not yet matured, or who are particularly impressionable, are much more likely to be influenced by the moral vacuum associated with the sexuality shown by the main characters. This is significant because sexually inexperienced people may look to the main characters as role models.[23]

An array of unsubstantiated claims is assembled in here, without which his position is peculiarly empty.

Yet critics of the film are not alone in these tendencies. Equivalent counter-assertions can be found among *Crash*'s defenders. Here is how Chris Auty argues the case with Westminster Councillors in defence of *Crash*. Comparing the film favourably with *Showgirls* (1995) and *The Lover* (1991) for amounts of nudity, and with *Heat* (1995) and the *Die Hard* (1988, 1990, 1995) series for amounts of violence, he proceeds to argue that what it shows it clearly does not recommend: it is 'painting a disturbing world … it clearly warns us *against* dehumanisation, *against* a society drifting into affectlessness'.[24] A 'message' is again found, and is presumed to be readily noticeable by 'ordinary' viewers of the film. The increased sophistication mainly lies in the assumption he is making that a film cannot be dissolved into units of shown actions or events – it matters *how*, and *in what contexts*, those actions and events are shown. This same move can be found in the BBFC statement explaining its decision to grant an uncut '18' certificate to *Crash*, but this time with the added: 'Rather than sympathising or identifying with the attitudes or tastes of the characters in the film, the average viewer would in the end be repelled by them, and would reject the values and sexual proclivities displayed'.[25] What is fascinating is to see the ways in which debates around a film like *Crash* could turn on these abstract entities. Here is Christopher Tookey, not directly responding to the BBFC's case, but nonetheless countering one abstraction (the 'average viewer') with another:

> I've never argued that normal people will see *Crash* and be inspired to engineer pile-ups on the M25. *Crash* is a landmark in pornography because it will encourage those who have a sadistic sexual bent (or discover that they have one as a result of seeing this film) to feel that they are not alone, that attractive people feel the same way and that no significant harm will come to others as a result of sado-masochistic acts.[26]

Not the 'average viewer', then, but another figure, the 'potentially sadistic viewer'. It is important to see that these 'figures' must be made up of several components: the powerful message; the viewer, with weaknesses or dangers; and some resultant 'harm'. Take one element away and even the most intense dislike of *Crash* fades from danger into taste-difference. Here is how one newspaper did just that with Tookey's 'figure'. In a strange editorial, the *Daily Telegraph* argued that however vile *Crash* might be, *The English Patient* (1996) should be seen as much worse because it would make most audiences cry, and care. Therefore it 'could do more damage to the nation's moral health than *Crash*'. The *Telegraph* had that same 'figure' who would enthuse about *Crash*:

> The film *is* disgusting, debauched and depraved. But it has an '18' certificate and most adults, having read a newspaper or listing magazine, will decide it looks repulsive. Those drawn to the film: sexual voyeurs, sado-masochists or people looking for the thrill of the new, will know what they are in for.[27]

Thus knowing, less 'harm' would be done. Yet with *The English Patient*, 'knowingness' was supplanted by the vulnerability of involuntary emotion. Thus could Tookey's judgement be undone – without a trace more or less evidence in either direction, because these debates are not *about* evidence.

The prevalence of these 'figures' set one of our key research tasks. Is it possible to do better than this? Can research give us knowledge that goes beyond this succession of *ideas* about audiences; guessed at, putative, or invented viewers? Could research reveal how audiences *actually* experience the film; how those who derive pleasure and satisfaction from it differ from those who dislike and withdraw from it? This was the most important task we set ourselves when, in early 1997, we began formulating our proposal to research the controversy. In June 1997 we put in a proposal to the Economic and Social Research Council for a year-long project to explore five areas:

- What was the nature of the public debate about *Crash*? What discursive repertoires were used?
- Through what journalistic practices did these views come to predominate?
- How did these relate to the patterns of press coverage of *Crash* in other countries?
- What impact did the British controversy have on ordinary viewers?
- What different viewing strategies among ordinary viewers went along with liking and approving of the film, and disliking and disapproving of it?

Three months later, we heard that our proposal had received support. How we went about doing the research to answer these questions, we explain in our Methodological Appendix at the end of this book. What we found, and the evidence which grounds our claims, follows.

2   Reviewing the Press

The *Crash* controversy featured in just about all broadcast media: newspapers, television, radio, magazines. But it was first and foremost a creature of the Press. Here, the story was told that *Crash* was coming, and was dangerous. Here, the foundations and main shapes of 'public opinion' were laid down. In this chapter we review the nature of Press responses to *Crash*.

Ordinarily, when journalists write reviews of films, they do so with two things balanced in their minds: their personal opinion on the film, and their sense of who the readers of their publication are. From our interviews with journalists, we learnt a good deal of the normal dynamics here.[1] Readers do not want to be told too much, so a self-denying ordinance operates on 'giving away' too much of a film. But they do like, in general, to gain a sense of the reviewer's opinion. Yet that only works if they feel that the reviewer belongs broadly to the same cultural universe as they do. So journalists told us that they work with a general sense of the kinds of readers they are speaking to.[2] Personal preferences therefore are moulded, either by not reviewing films that would be a long way out of the register of likely readers, or by writing in the guise of 'if this is the kind of thing you like...'.

However, *Crash* was anything but ordinary, and therefore reviewing it took on other purposes; and of course a very large proportion of the coverage was not in the form of reviews – *Crash* passed over into the sphere of 'news' (important events, controversies, public policy issues). Knowing how to write about it became a matter of more than personal opinion. For a few people writing reviews, there were editorial requirements. It is rarely the case, we sense, that journalists are expected to take a 'party-line' on a film, but with *Crash* this clearly happened in some cases. More significantly, we believe, reviewers felt the need to write about the film by reference to the controversy. Repeatedly we were told that it was difficult not to write about *Crash*, even if the film was almost certainly outside their readers' likely viewing, or even if it was not being shown in the immediate area, but also difficult to write about it without making reference to the claims and language of the *Mail*. This did not at all mean that reviewers felt that they had to *agree* with the *Mail*, but as we will see, it did in significant ways shape the way the film was dealt with.

This might seem a very obvious point to make, but in fact it has quite wide ramifications, once carefully considered. To feel constrained to write about *Crash*, and to write about it by reference to the *Mail*'s account, is to agree to a certain definition of the 'terrain of debate'. What do we intend by this idea of a 'terrain of debate'? This concept invites an examination of the relations among different responses to, for example, a film. It invites questions such as: how far are individual responses shaped by their acknowledgement of other, perhaps different ones? Is there a hierarchy of responses, such that one, perhaps, sets the terms of reference which the others, in being formulated into words, have to take account of (by agreement, qualification, circumvention, or direct disagreement, for instance)? We aim to show that the *Mail*'s account of the film became the dominant and defining account in the British debate, to the extent that those seeking to defend the film – even if they were writing for audiences who would not normally encounter, let alone agree with, the *Mail*'s version – still wrote with an eye to that account. The effect of this was that the British terrain of debate over *Crash* was markedly different from that which we found when we compared British responses with those in France and the USA. With caution because of the limits to our evidence, we suggest that there were, in effect, distinct national terrains of response – an idea we explore later.

The *Mail*'s account, first. We saw in Chapter 1 the general character of its campaign against *Crash*, but here it is necessary to go deeper: what language was used, what assumptions were made, and what broader ideological positions were being invoked?

Walker, Tookey and the Daily Mail

We begin with Alexander Walker's original article, as this became the touchstone for many – partly, of course, because of Walker's own status as an elder statesman of film reviewing and author of several highly regarded books on Hollywood cinema. Walker opened his long (around 1,000 word) review with a prediction that *Crash* was going to test Britain's censors, and public tolerance, to the limit. He queries how it is possible for people with the pedigree of Cronenberg, and his cast, to have become involved in such a monstrous film:

> To explain why means describing some of the most perverted acts and theories of sexual deviance I have ever seen propagated in main-line cinema. *Crash* takes place among a group of people, urban sophisticates, so morally exhausted, so remote from reality, that they need to invent a series of sexual perversions merely to keep their feelings alive. The form this takes is bizarre. It involves deliberate participation in car crashes, all engineered to top up their libido by courting injury, mutilation, sometimes death.[3]

Walker dismisses any defence that this is a 'cautionary tale', pressing the case that even to conceive such characters and tell such a story is 'immoral by any reasonable standard'.

As already noted, Walker was not responsible for the headline with which his account became associated. The text of the original article, though, is hardly less forthright. *Crash* is described as 'in effect, if not in intention, movie pornography' which 'left many hardened film-goers at the Cannes preview feeling debased and degraded'.

There had been many challenging and difficult films before, but this one was different. It crossed a line, for Walker, because the characters in the film 'push the envelope of sexual encounter farther than I can remember seeing or hearing in a film intended for public screening'. Walker seems to have been particularly disturbed by the rear-entry sex.

Yet all this, although important, does not quite explain his vehemence, sufficient for him to name *Crash* as possibly the most corrupt movie ever made. Something in the nature of the film hit Walker, a filmically highly experienced person, very hard. It is only possible to guess in part what this was, but there are two clues, one of which is important in light of the subsequent career of his claims. Walker hints at a parallel between the characters and the likely viewers: 'The characters are defined solely in terms of their sexual obsessions. The normal world outside is simply used for the fetishistic opportunities it offers.' As the characters, perhaps so the audience.[4] He talks of the film delivering a 'sensory overload'. Walker is claiming, in effect, that the film had moved out of the realm of the representational. It – and its potential audience – were positively drowning in excess. He shows no interest in the usual claims of possible copycatting which would feature in the articles by Christopher Tookey in the *Mail*. For Walker, the problem of *Crash* is its proximity to an amoral intelligentsia.

How any of this might be true is unexplained, but we get a tiny indication in something he says, which in subsequent repeats gets slightly edited. Aside from the headline, the most quoted sentence from his article was the claim that '*Crash* contains some of the most perverted acts and theories of sexual deviance I have ever seen propagated in mainline cinema'. From almost all subsequent uses of this, two words disappear: '... and theories'.[5] What might those two words mean, given the context of the rest of his argument? A number of possibilities suggest themselves. He might most obviously be referring to the moments in the film where particular characters talk about the potency of sex – Vaughan's assertion, for instance, that car crashes should be thought of as 'fertilising' rather than destructive; or perhaps the talk-dirty scene, in which Catherine, being made love to by her husband James, arouses herself by fantasising out loud about what sex with Vaughan would be like. He might, at a next level of generalisation, be drawing from *Crash* a proposition that the central characters are just driven by desire, but see the pursuit of sexual pleasure as the *point* of their lives. In either case, in those two small words is an admission that *Crash* is a film, and that is not a trivial statement. Walker understands that narrative film works in particular ways. To be the vehicle for a theory of sexual deviation, a film must either place it in the hands of one or more of its favoured characters, or else embody such an idea through an act of filmic enunciation (through practices of camerawork, editing, point of view, *et cetera*). Yet this suggests a primarily *cognitive* evaluation of the film, which is flatly contradicted by the unavoidable sense that Walker was *deeply disturbed* by *Crash*. He does not just disagree with a message he sees the film as promulgating; he hates what he feels it does to him, personally. This is an unresolved mix of disagreement and dislike. Whether because a review does not have the length to allow its full expression, or because Walker could not have done so (his subsequent contributions add nothing to this), we cannot say.

In the hands of Christopher Tookey and the *Daily Mail*, this relative complexity, along with those two words, all but vanishes. The series of lead articles by Tookey and others descend to adjectival disgust. *Crash* is now simply 'offensive', 'sick', 'perverted', 'filth'.[6]

Using the full might of the random hypothetical, Tookey stormed at *The Telegraph*'s Barbara Amiel, who had advised Virginia Bottomley not to get so heated over *Crash*.[7] Tookey listed a series of (supposed) copycat crimes of various natures and then added: 'joy-riding, ram-raiding and reckless driving by the young are already social problems. Cronenberg's reputation as a cult horror director might tempt many more to seek out this movie than would normally be attracted to a boring, repetitive art-house film'. The poverty of this kind of argument is astonishing. And it is worth noting the difference from Walker, for whom *Crash* was definitely not boring – it was overwhelming.

Beyond these kinds of specious claims and adjectival sermonisings, the *Mail*'s arguments are conspicuously thin. Like an exhausted general rallying troops, a great deal of its case depends on quoting yet another person saying how 'perverted', 'filthy' and 'obscene' the film is, and that now is the time to 'draw the line'. If only they shout long enough, surely our side will see the need to fight on! Two premises underpin the rallying call.

First, without one step that is as common as it is illogical, none of their claims could stand up for one instant. It is the claim that what to 'us' is bizarre, revolting, disgusting and depraved might be to 'them' a turn-on to something they would never have dreamed of on their own; and the worse it seems to 'us', the greater the danger it might get to 'them'. Indeed, the *Daily Mail* even delighted in its refusal to give any further arguments. In response to the BBFC's arguments when announcing its classification decision, an editorial declared: 'All the psycho-babble in the world cannot refute the simple fact: The film is sick. It should not be shown.'

The second step is to treat *Crash* as a symptom of a universal moral decline. One article by Bel Mooney, who wrote specially for the *Mail* on this issue, particularly illustrates this. In a full-page assault, Mooney takes as given that *Crash* is an agreed problem – her comments on the film are limited to two paragraphs out of fifty-six. Instead, she issues a challenge to 'liberals'. Once upon a time it was possible, if not necessary, to stand up for total 'freedom of expression'. But now, the world has become such an unpleasant place that it is time to make a different stand:

> In recent years I have felt myself to be increasingly at odds with many of my peers over an issue of huge importance – one of the most vital issues we have to confront today. I am talking about the limits of freedom of expression. About whether we shall allow our society to be corrupted by a handful of people who believe that there are no boundaries to what the screen should show or the writer describe. Over many a dinner table I have argued that unless people like myself take a stand against the seemingly endless downward spiral of sex and violence in books, film and on television, the world that I was born into will disappear forever, and we shall allow our children to inherit a moral vacuum, not a civilised community.[8]

This style of argument takes the film as a symptom of something much larger. It fits the attack on *Crash* into a much wider ideological project. The enemy now is 'liberalism', an 'anything goes' society. It also points the finger – it is time for former liberals to stand up and be counted. Not to do so is to condone evil. It reads the world as a whole in one mode: the 'endless downward spiral', the 'end of civilisation as I have known it'. And most importantly, it has an enemy: the 'intellectual establishment'. The article marked a meeting point between a certain style of liberal, anti-porn feminism and the populist conservatism of the *Mail*. The result is a general charge laid against the middle-class establishment. At their door lies the blame for this general decline of standards.

The most striking thing in all the *Mail*'s articles about *Crash* is the virtual absence of argument. Repeated tirades are packed with adjectives, and warnings of doom. Given this, we must ask how the *Daily Mail* could have such an impact. This is a serious, not a rhetorical question. There is a total absence of evidence or argument in the *Mail*'s coverage, a wholesale presence of moral screaming.[9] Why didn't others, including other journalists, just mock? In the next section we examine how other newspapers dealt with the film.

The Crash debate in the British Press

Among the more than 400 articles about *Crash* which we examined from national and local press and magazines, there are substantial differences. Yet in one respect there is virtual unanimity: *Crash* is marked as 'controversial'. News coverage in local papers often turns on whether there might be a local authority ban the film. National news coverage spotlighted various results of the *Mail*'s campaign, such as the many assertions of its harmfulness, the challenges to the BBFC, and in particular the actions of the few local authorities who banned the film for a time. The question which underpins news coverage is: how much of a danger is *Crash*? But what kind of danger? How is the film perceived and understood?

A useful way in is to look at the criteria through which reviews were organised. Reviews are, of course, a special kind of writing. They are places within a newspaper where opinion is often allowed free run. There is less likely to be editorial pressure to express a particular view. But reviewers do more than give personal responses to a film. They also generally write with an eye to the kind of reader they are addressing. For example, how knowledgeable about films in general are they? What interests in film and cinema are they likely to have? What kinds of discussions and debates might they have been privy to? While these considerations tend to make the character of much film reviewing more 'local', there are factors which tend in other directions. Films reach localities on the back of national distribution systems, and national marketing and publicity. These intrude very directly into the routines of reviewing journalists, in the form of Press Packs and Electronic Press Kits, screenings for journalists, director and star interviews, and other means by which distributors try to drum up interest in their films. Reviews are also constrained by many other factors. Most newspapers have very limited space allowed for reviews overall, and there may be competition from other new releases. In some cases, films are absorbed within a general category of 'Leisure and Entertainment', a siting which may press reviewers to measure films against a 'popcorn' criterion – is this a good 'Friday Night Out' experience?

However, other things also become relevant on those occasions when films become the subject of debate outside the arena of films, stars and cinema. Most commonly, perhaps, this is where films are judged to offend against morality. Yet there are other possibilities. *Schindler's List* (1993), for instance, occasioned a good deal of discussion which entered the fields of historical memory, of education, of racism and anti-semitism, and so on. *U571* (2000) produced furious arguments about Hollywood's rewriting of history. At such moments, reviews are very likely to carry traces of the terms of reference of these broader debates. These are our interest here, inasmuch as they can reveal the broad character of the British debate about *Crash*.

An important clue emerges when we examine how different reviews in Britain presented the narrative of *Crash*. Take, first, Nigel Reynolds in the *Telegraph*. Reynolds disliked the film intensely, but did not want it banned – that would be to give it an undeserved importance:

> *Crash*, the movie, has no plot. It has an idea, or possibly several. Central is a group of emotionally dysfunctional adults who are so bored by normal sex that they seek their thrills by crashing cars and watching people being maimed. After a crash, they have sex.[10]

This is the sum total of the narrative for him. There is no need to say more:

> The film is morally vacuous, nasty, violent and little more than an excuse to string together one scene after another of sexual intercourse. I totted up 16 such scenes – on the back seat of cars, on the front seat, in wrecks of cars, in a car wash – before I stopped counting.

Crash is thereby reduced to a list of its incidents, each counted and given a mark for level of disgust. But Reynolds' denial that there is a 'plot' does not mean that events do not have a cause-effect sequence – clearly they do for him. 'Plot' has to be more than a list of linked events. A film must have a moral point. Notice the interesting elision in one sentence: 'The film has so little merit, so little reason, it adds so little to the sum of human knowledge, condition or entertainment…' From 'merit' to 'reason': Reynolds makes an argument that *Crash* does something worse than failing. It *pretends* to morality. Therefore the film was a test-case for Parliament:

> Time and again Parliament and Mr Ferman have made it clear that while it is difficult to stem Hollywood's daily diet of sleaze, porn and punch-ups they will not tolerate scenes promulgating the idea that violence can lead to sexual pleasure.

'A daily diet of sleaze, porn and punch-ups': this is markedly tabloid writing, and very readily connects with the *Mail*'s complaint that *Crash* is a symptom of overall moral decline. Yet Reynolds shows no sign of taking the *Mail*'s route towards demanding a ban on the film. The reason for this perhaps emerges four months later in a *Daily Telegraph* editorial. Commenting on the BBFC's eventual decision to classify *Crash*, the editorial restated Reynolds' dislike: 'The film *is* disgusting, depraved and debauched. But it has an 18 certificate and most adults … will decide it looks repulsive. Parents should ensure that their children do not sneak past the ushers. Those drawn to the film: sexual voyeurs, sado-masochists or people looking for the thrill of the new, will know what they are in for'.[11] *Crash* thus dismissed, the *Telegraph* declares its real film fear: *The English Patient*. Precisely *because* it is 'cinematically wonderful', 'likely to become a classic' and makes audiences cry, 'it could therefore do more damage to the nation's moral health than *Crash*'. The list of crimes the *Telegraph* attributes to *The English Patient* is long: immoral, implicitly condoning euthanasia, treachery and adultery, setting the shallow demands of the individual above the greater good, and more. But the difference clearly is that *Crash* will be seen as perverse, according to the *Telegraph*, while *The English Patient* looks beautiful and makes people feel good. It is a difference in broader ideological frames which leads to the difference in the two papers' conclusions.

The manner in which the film's narrative is retold gives pretty immediate access to the judgements that will ensue. Take this review from a local newspaper, by Maria Croce:

> James Ballard and his wife Catherine are already leading pretty unhappy lives, having affairs, chasing fulfilment. Then James crashes his car and feels drawn to the widow of the other driver who dies in the smash. They meet weirdo Vaughan who introduces them to a strange group. This obsessed bunch have waved goodbye to their no claims bonuses as they embark on a rather bizarre and dangerous quest for sexual kicks. They're either having sex in cars, watching re-enactments of famous crashes like the one that finished off James Dean or they're glued to videos of dummy test smashes.[12]

Croce did not much like *Crash*, but equally did not like the campaign against it. Her way of riding these twin responses is to re-present the film in terms of its *outlandishness*. The characters, their motives and their actions are all too weird to be taken seriously! From this position the judgement about this film is one of *disappointment*: 'After such a battle against censorship it's a shame the film isn't a bit more interesting.'[13] She thereby locks together her general anti-censorship feelings with a dismissal of the film.

Strongly positive reviews were few and far between in Britain. One of the strongest was Lesley Dick's in the film magazine *Sight and Sound*. Written from America, the review does nonetheless directly address the British context of reactions.[14] Right from the outset, Dick posits a series of negative judgements, each of which is something which critics such as the *Mail* have claimed as its dangers:

> This film turns its medical gaze on an obsession, and it does not seduce us into partaking in this obsession, it does not invite us to identify with the obsessed, indeed it refuses to provide us with those narrative trappings like motivation or personality which would allow us to identify in any conventional sense. Not a pornographic text ... *Crash* is rather a text on pornography, a cool, detached look at sexual obsession itself.[15]

This strong use of negatives is a rebuff to already circulating claims. Dick then retells *Crash* in a way that allows it to express symbols:

> The opening of *Crash*, in a light aircraft hangar, sets the terms of the film's proposal of sexuality as an encounter of bodies and technology. Catherine, in high heels and straight skirt, presses her magnificent breast up against a plane, before being fucked from behind by some anonymous man. I was irritated by the Victoria's Secret-style satin bras that kept appearing until I got the technological parallel: the gleam on the protuberant satin like the skin on the bulging wing of a car or nose of a jet.

Crash has a 'proposal' which she had to 'get' by catching hold of its 'parallel' – her personal reaction, with all its ambiguities (unproblematic acceptance of 'anonymous fucking', aesthetic admiration of her 'magnificent breast', knowing irritation at the 'Victoria's Secret satin bras') had to be superseded once its overall import was reached. The narrative is incomplete until a viewer reaches the plane of metaphoric readings. This allows Dick to come to a very positive reading of the film which in the end integrates those many personal reactions: 'The sexual obsession in this movie is idea-driven, and while it presents an unutterably bleak and dark view, it also allows for a vein of wit that occasionally comes forward into outright comedy.' From this basis, she can conclude that the film is brilliant and 'brave', precisely *because* it allows its audience no hiding place – it confronts them with the very things that make them uncomfortable.

In these three (we believe, typical) cases we can see that narrative or 'plot' means incompatible things, and associates with very different judgements on the film. This is surely interesting in itself, but given the dispute of *Crash* we are particularly interested in the relation between the three interviews. The central connection is via something almost taken-for-granted in the *Mail*'s attacks, and which is then acknowledged in other reviews by their feeling the need to say the opposite. Again and again in reviews that distance themselves from the *Mail*'s position, we find the proposition that *Crash* was 'too cold' to be influential. Croce: 'The sex scenes are cold and the crashes are brutally realistic and not glamorised. [...] This is just a clinical study of sexual obsession.' These very qualities make it end up 'dull', and therefore incapable of influencing anyone. This is the position taken by the President of the BBFC, explaining the Board's judgement on the film:

> *Crash* ... had been condemned in advance, because of excessive violence. Actually, there was little violence in the film. It was also diagnosed as glorifying depravity – a depravity where sexual excitement was linked to car crashes and the pain and injury resulting from them. In this case, the description of the depravity was accurate enough, but so far from glorifying it, the film stood back in icy astonishment at the desperation of a tiny minority who needed such stimuli to generate even a spark of human, sexual warmth.[16]

Lesley Dick takes this one step further by *celebrating* the coldness. She variously called the film 'cool', 'detached', with a 'medical gaze':

> *Crash* is a brilliant, brave film – non-narrative, anti-realist, cool as a cucumber, it sticks to its conceptual guns, refusing to situate the audience comfortably, calmly bringing forward a celebration of sex and death, as if for our consideration. It is this very calm – the stylisation, the use of tableaux, the emptiness of the characters – that makes the film so disturbing, witty, and dispassionate, as it studies an obsession that is itself shocking and necessarily as obsession must be, a little dull.[17]

This style of defence is to be found very widely in reviews, often in association with the slight sense of irritation which Croce evinced. As one further illustration, consider the *Scotsman*'s review, headlined: 'Crashing bore is all talk, no action.'[18] This already suggests a sense of let-down, a disappointment verging on blame that *Crash* ought to have been more troubling, more 'action'. The first sentence confirms this: 'Without the hype, *Crash* would be a low-key art-house film that few people would recommend to their friends.' Dalton calls the film 'cold', 'emotionless', and 'stilted'. There was 'nothing attractive about the characters', and their coming together is 'bizarre and unbelievable'. He concludes with the following series of negatives:

> The film appeared to make no big statement about society's obsession with sex and car crashes. It certainly will not entice people to go out crashing cars for sexual gratification. I don't think audiences will empathise with the characters – or want to go out and emulate them.

This effectively refuses both the *Mail*'s propositions and what it conceives as the alternative: a 'message-driven' film verging on documentary.

As a rhetorical trope these kinds of response may have been fairly effective, but an important consequence needs noting. By insisting that *Crash* is 'cold, therefore safe', these retorts were implicitly allowing the counter-proposition that if the film *had* been arousing, it would have been dangerous. Much can be packed into the terms 'cold', of course. Among our audience it was sometimes used as a term of criticism, that the sex in the film lacked emotional involvement, and was therefore 'cold'. But that is to make coldness a criticism. When it functions as a *defence* of the film against the *Mail*'s claims, its opposite is an implied but never-stated 'heat' of arousal. The terrain of debate, thus, was set from elsewhere. The status of this claim is curious: it is so deeply embedded in British filmic culture that the *Mail* never needed to say it directly – it did not need saying that arousing an audience's senses and emotions is 'obviously' risky. We will see in a moment that the French reviewers, at least, will have no truck with that notion. And in Chapters 5 and 6, we will see that the notion of *Crash* as a cold, unemotional film found no favour with its greatest enthusiasts among our audience.

More than 400 articles appeared; a mix of news, reviews and editorials. In the vast majority of them, the terms of reference through which the film is debated are those proposed by the *Mail*: this film is controversial in the extreme; have film-makers gone too far this time, in proposing an association between sexual arousal and mayhem on the roads?; is 'art' just an excuse?; don't we all know that films can be particularly dangerous? Politicians from both main parties colluded in accepting this agenda, often accepting even the *Mail*'s conclusions. Film professionals and academics were astonishingly quiet in the main. A quite specific way of talking about *Crash* predominated in Britain, whose power very much lies in its ability to seem the *only* and the *obvious* way to discuss it.

The Crash debate in the French Press

How unique to Britain was this controversy and the associated terrain of debate? Cronenberg himself often commented that he found the British hostility towards *Crash* a 'peculiar' phenomenon, not repeated elsewhere. We were unable to study the reaction right across the world,[19] but we did compare in detail the reactions in Britain with those in France and the USA. Consider France, first. Here, too, there were positive, ambivalent and negative responses, but they were framed quite differently. For a highly positive review (and there were many more than in Britain), consider Gérard Lefort's. Here is his account of the narrative:

> Through the lens of a story of a troubled couple, the film lulls us with a moral tale: once upon a time there was desire. James Ballard and his wife Catherine are seeking an identity they can no longer find in an unbridled sex life in which the pleasures of adultery, secretive outings for a furtive screw, nevertheless leaves them imprisoned in the sadness of the flesh. Only a massive accident can reorient their disoriented lives. On the road, this happens physically when James' car collides with another, driven by Dr Helen Remington. As Cronenberg films it, in slow motion, the time of the accident is a kind of extra time, which becomes an important event in James' life (and contaminates his loved ones) precisely because in this time, nothing moves any more, as if turned to stone by the atomic explosion of the event.[20]

From the outset this account of the narrative is permeated with philosophical language: 'desire', 'identity', the 'sadness of the flesh'. To Lefort, and to a good number of other French critics, Crash was exciting precisely because it combined the heights of philosophy with the 'baseness' of sexual arousal: 'You come away from this film with your head filled with mad ideas and your pants filled with extraordinary itches'. But this review goes one stage further, and articulates an idea about *films in general*. Films are not mere shadows on the screen. They are like difficult friends, who will insist on asking awkward questions of us. Lefort parallels the 'orgies in the head' with the 'genital orgies', calls Crash a 'magnificent inquest on our desires and the abysses they open beneath us', and ends with this remarkable panegyric:

> Crash looks at us as we, disturbed and excited at the same time, perceive its extraordinary images. But it also happens that, as we are watching it, we attract its attention, so that it turns its beautiful eyes towards us and considers us. Crash is a chat-up film that chats itself up, which is to say that you have to struggle to deserve it.

This kind of language for discussing film is almost incomprehensible in a British context. It is to treat films as live entities, capable of challenging and provoking. We owe them something, and they repay by making us look at ourselves in dark but necessary ways. They achieve this by doing exactly that which British film culture cannot conceive: working on us simultaneously hotly and coldly, appealing both to mind and body, to erotic, emotional and imaginative impulses. For French enthusiasts, Crash was one hot movie.[21]

Revealingly, hostile French critics accept large parts of this philosophy of film, but just see Crash as not meeting these criteria adequately. Here is the narrative account of one of the strongest critics, Marie Queva:

> In Crash, then, everything begins with an accident. A car, belonging to a producer of commercials with a pressing but exhausted sexuality, crashes head-long into a couple's car. The producer is seriously injured. The husband dies from the impact. His wife is in shock, but seeks consolation in the arms of her

husband's killer. From this, the producer rekindles his love life with his own wife, who is left out of the complex and futile games in which her husband is embroiled. Henceforth, their three lives will be tuned to the frequency of automobile accidents, in a whirlwind of new sensations tied to the violence of the traumatic shocks suffered by the road's victims. The more violent the crash, the more desire is intensified; the more conspicuous a victim's scars, the more excitement rises. Mutilated flesh becomes an object of pleasure, while the automobile chromes and leathers are promises of thrills to come. Bumper to bumper, driving at insane speeds, the protagonists flirt with death to the point of orgasm. [22]

Unlike the hostile British critics' claims that there is 'no plot', this review recognises a powerful narrative thrust. Indeed it seems a quite positive acknowledgement. What, then, does Queva dislike or disapprove of in the film? She concludes her quite short review by damning *Crash* as 'a rather dismal little porno flick'. But this is not because of some dislike of explicit sex – it is because, in her view, *Crash* never quite lifted itself into the sphere of the metaphysical: 'The love scenes between Rosanna Arquette and James Spader cannot be taken seriously as they grow ecstatic over each others' scars. It is impossible to forget this and become involved in a metaphysical reading of the story.' It is because it is 'flat' and *not* titillating that the film fails. In a sentence that bears setting alongside British reviews, she concludes that Ballard's novel has thus become 'no more than a succession of cool and pretentious scenes'. Here 'cool' has become a term of abuse!

The majority of French reviews were enthusiastic about *Crash*; a few were condemnatory. We did find a few which neither praised nor damned *Crash*, but one notable feature of them is that, unlike the clearly positive and negative reviews, they are very short. This makes analysis a little difficult – unless brevity was simply a function of space constraints, it is as if the reviewers really see it as not worth the trouble. They are like a brief note so you can know the film is there if you like that sort of thing. Even in these, there are marks of the difference with the French. One is that, in the midst of damning, there is the faint praise for the potential of the 'auteur' film-maker. Auteurs pursue visions, even if they may be strange:

Obsessions, phobias, metamorphoses, ambiguous parapsychological phenomena and sexual violence, identity crises, drug hallucinations, biological deformities, transformations of living beings into machines; ask Dr Cronenberg for what you have not imagined.[23]

Cronenberg, for his French critics, has to be reclassified as the *wrong kind* of auteur, as in this one-paragraph snort of dismissal:

The Festival finally has its controversy. David Cronenberg's *Crash*, presented to the competition on Wednesday, was profusely booed. Unjustly. *Crash* inspires more laughter than outrage. What's it about? The injured only come when they're driving and crashing into other cars; naturally, in this play of car crashes and tampons [*auto-tampons*], they are covered in pink scars and metallic prostheses. *Crash* is not a case for the vice-squad, but it is about screws. Seeing

Rosanna Arquette with both legs cramped in metal frames trying to get under the steering wheel so as to be better able to make love is a perfect moment. It whines, grates and bursts with the heady vapours of *meaning*. Cronenberg, once a cult director (*The Fly*, *Rabid*), is now just an ass of a film-maker, and a maker of ass films.[24]

Crash is not meaningful enough, and its effort to achieve meaning produces the 'whining' and 'grating' which marks the film for this reviewer. As a result, Cronenberg is no longer a proper auteur, he is an 'ass'. But even so, no case emerges from this that would help the moral vice-squad in Britain who pursued the film – the judgement must still be an *aesthetic* one.

The Crash debate in the American Press

In the United States, the response to *Crash* was different again. If in Britain the hub around which reviews of all shades turned was the shared proposition that if the film aroused, it was dangerous; if in France that hub was the proposition that cinema's job is to arouse us at simultaneous sensuous and metaphysical levels; in America the shared terrain was differently defined. It appears to have turned around the category-proposition of 'art-house'. 'Art-house' designates a *kind* of film, with its own circuits of production and distribution, and its own audiences. Originating in the late 1960s to accommodate European films gaining an increasing audience, especially among students, the category combines two things in particular: an expectation of riskier (especially sexual) content; and a more philosophical approach to film-making. The third element, a feeling that there is an 'author' speaking through the film, preceded the effective growth of this market, with its origins in the film-theoretic work of Andrew Sarris, among others.[25]

How is this tendency displayed within American reviews? The signs can be detected within this narrative summary in the *Miami Herald*:

Based on J G Ballard's quasi-science fiction novel, it's a story about people who like to re-create famous automobile accidents and have sex in cars. They think of screeching brakes and metal tearing into metal as a 'liberation of sexual energy'. They get turned on by the idea of dying 'with a force that's unavailable in any other manner'. And they love to ogle snazzy motor vehicles: for them, a trip to a Mercedes-Benz dealership is the equivalent of Spanish Fly. OK, so on premise alone, it sounds pretty ridiculous. But the movie is something else, strange and disturbing and obscenely beautiful. It's hot, too: here, for a change, is a movie about sex that is really, truly erotic. It's just not the kind of sex you'd describe as 'normal' – which is what gives *Crash* its subversive edge.[26]

Rene Rodriguez's review nicely acknowledges that there are two distinct ways in which *Crash* can be understood. If you are within the first mode of response, *Crash* will seem ridiculous. What makes the difference is to perceive *Crash* filmically – in which case it turns from 'cold' to 'hot' ('it radiates a cold heat') and becomes 'subversive'. And this is precisely *through* being that combination of 'strange' and 'disturbing' and 'beautiful': 'it's frightening … because it gets so deep under your skin'. This is a quality Rodriguez is happy to choose for himself, although he recognises that this may not be the case for others, more content with mainstream or 'traditional movies':

> *Crash* doesn't work like a traditional movie: It's practically plotless, and its characters remain as impenetrable to us as they do to each other. The film is more of a mood piece, and what tone that mood takes depends greatly on the viewer's own sensibilities. Some will find the film repetitious and pointless; others will find it weirdly beguiling, a cerebral film about sex on wheels. Count me among the latter. [...] *Crash* is some kind of freaky classic. Fans of the offbeat, start your engines.

This is a particularly clear expression, it seems to us, of the characteristics that arthouse films are supposed to offer, and the status that this kind of cinema has – a matter of choice and sensibility, off-beat, provocative. The absence of 'plot' is not a barrier to the film's meaningfulness, it merely requires that it be approached differently. Heat (erotic pleasure, emotional involvement) is produced by the (cold) distancing that is achieved by focusing on its filmic qualities. These allow it to interrogate us and our world, to be 'subversive'. It is against just such claims that those who disliked *Crash* in the US also measured it. For instance, here Stephen Hunter. Seen on its own, the following narrative summary might sound similar to, say, Nigel Reynolds:

> Derived from a 1973 novel by British sci-fi bad boy J G Ballard, it basically watches as an upscale Toronto couple, used to life in the sexual fast lane, allows itself to be seduced by the force's darkest side. The Ballards, James and Catherine, drift into a culture that finds sexual stimulation among the smeared flesh, bent metal, shattered glass and bones and stench of octane and blood that attend an automobile catastrophe. That's it: car crash = sex. Duh.[27]

Hunter definitely loathed *Crash*, calling it 'rancid, putrid, offensive'. His long review explores the narrative of the film in some detail, describing it as an induction into a 'wacky world of crash fetishists, a small band of mutants, most of them crash survivors, who appear to worship at the altar of crippled flesh and crumpled steel' (something he is positively unwilling to attempt, having himself recently survived a major crash). All this could have appeared in any hostile British review. But there is another current, one which allows (even in the middle of intense dislike) that there might be another way of watching, in which the film is a 'troubling threnody' – not the kind of language the *Mail* will be likely to allow to sully its critique of the film! To watch it this way, 'it's definitely for graduate students in this area'. And Hunter is able to deal with *Crash* in these terms. His critique of the film is not just that it is horrible, but that it is not as subversive as it seems:

> Yet the secret arc under all this voluptuous carnage happens to be an arc of healing. Cronenberg isn't really as brave as he thinks, even if he never averts his gaze from suffering. Slice away the bent metal, and the movie is about a marriage repairing itself. Despite the proclamations of radical avant-gardism and sexual outréness, underneath one discovers a tepid little bourgeois feel-good drama about a Mr. and Mrs. re-inventing their sex life.

In America we find, as this example suggests, the continuous presence of a way of thinking about films which is hardly available in Britain, and here only within a self-enclosed academic world of film analysis. In small but effective ways, 'art-house' cinema has carved for itself a right to its own language and criteria, in parallel with its small but significant successes in gaining and holding on to specialist cinemas or even dedicated screens within multiplexes.

Conclusion

This suggests three quite different terrains of debate: each of the three countries whose reviews we examined appears to have had a different set of parameters within which evaluations of *Crash* were made. In all three, we found examples of positive, ambivalent and negative reviews, but *why* and *how* they are so judged significantly varies. Yet to people in each terrain these seem just the obvious way to talk about *Crash*.

This fact, in turn, suggests the possibility of a new approach to the idea of a 'national film culture'. In current literature, this has been used largely as a way of thinking about characteristic traditions of film production, and about the ways in which films in different countries provide a commentary on the nature, and even a resource for the formation, of 'national identity'.[28] Our research suggests that a fruitful line of enquiry could take researchers in a rather different direction: to ask whether there may be characteristic ways of understanding and responding to films within different countries. Such an enquiry might ask, for example: What are films allowed to be and to do? What role are they perceived to fulfil within different national cultures? What relations are they conceived to have with other parts of people's lives, as individuals and as members of their community? How are films conceived to touch and affect people? Many of these questions will be explored in the final chapter.

We must be cautious about what this chapter can claim to have achieved. Space limits have restricted the amount of detailed analysis we could give even to the materials where we can be sure we have a large proportion: the British press coverage. In the cases of France and America, we know that we have only a selection of the press coverage, and even of published reviews. There may still be a virtue in making quite a strong claim which can then be critically examined by other people.

Our claims here further depend on the concept we have deployed, of a 'terrain of debate'. This concept owes a good deal to two sets of ideas. It grows in part from Michel Foucault's notion of a discourse as a field of knowledge and power which, in the very act of 'knowing' its object, creates the space for counter-knowledges. This important idea has been widely used in an indicative way, for example in showing how the category 'homosexual' produced by medicalising knowledge simultaneously produced a ground from which those so named could demonstrate the 'naturalness' of their state. But to our knowledge, it has not been much used as the basis for systematic study of other cultural fields. The second source is the idea of a 'discursive repertoire' developed by discourse researchers. There, it refers to the resources which speakers draw upon which they do not originate, but which provide them with the bases for making culturally valid argumentative moves. But researchers such as Michael Billig have largely used this idea as a means of investigating particular contexts of talk.[29] They have not in the main sought to determine, within a field of talk, what are the limits, hierarchies, dependences and conflicts that speakers observe and acknowledge.

It is not difficult to see why people might shy away from this. To make this move, a number of conditions would need to be met. In the first place, it depends on having good reason to suppose that one has a sufficiently enclosed body of materials, a distinct field. Otherwise, the materials would constitute simply a collection, rather than a linked body. Then, one has to be confident that one has access to a secure sample across that field. If not, one would be trying illegitimately to draw conclusions from an unreliable range. Finally, one has to be sure that analysis reveals sufficiently strong traces of these relationships to be able to 'map' the discursive state of this field. For these traces mark the ways each piece is responding to others around it. With all the caveats that this generates, in the case of our British materials we believe that our analysis does genuinely point to some significant findings. Our French and American materials are less sure on all three grounds. Their main function, therefore, is to help by comparison to point up how very particular and peculiar the British response was to *Crash*.

In Britain, it seems, we still have the narrowest and most morally-restrictive view of films and what they may do, of many countries. This is not simply a matter of (as has often been commented on by critics) Britain having the strictest and most invasive forms of film censorship in Europe. It also has to do with the terms within which people feel able to debate films, their meanings, their pleasures and their roles in people's lives in the public domain. What is particularly perturbing is the ease with which and the extent to which, in this recent period, the numbing commonplaces of the *Mail* have been able to dominate any situation where a film became a topic of public debate. How has this been achieved? We return to this question in our concluding chapter.

3   Expecting the Worst

In setting out to explore the different ways in which audiences made sense of, and responded to, *Crash*, we were of course attending to reactions to a very controversial event. The various vehemently argued reviews and news stories which surrounded the film's release marked this as more than 'just a film'. It was a political event, and one about which it was quite hard for people not to have some view. We need to ask, therefore, in what ways the controversy had framed people's expectations of the film. What had they expected the film to be like? And what responses did they expect in themselves to seeing it? How far was the predictive picture they developed of *Crash* a version of what the *Mail* said the film was like? If we could answer these questions, we would be able to see what part the controversy played in shaping prior orientations. But then another set of questions would arise, about the ways in which people moved from their initial expectations towards making sense of the film when they eventually saw it. Would it be possible to discern the effects of the controversy on the final estimations people made of *Crash*?

Many writers have shown that interpretations of films do not merely depend on a straightforward relationship between the filmic text and its audience. In all kinds of ways, seeing a film is a social event. This means much more than that people very often go to the cinema in company. It includes the way people choose the right kind of cinema to see a film, the way they discuss it before going and afterwards, and – more trickily – the way their actual watching is permeated by learnt and shared ideas and assumptions, wishes, hopes and fears that arise from their social history. Particularly relevant at this point, though, is Thomas Austin's demonstration that audiences' responses are a function of their meeting with marketing strategies, with materials such as posters, trailers, interviews and reviews, as well as news features.[1] Austin explored the ways different audiences were prepared for viewing the controversial sex-thriller *Basic Instinct* (1992). In his case, one strong response among young men was that they were 'desperate to see it'. The film became almost a rite of passage, a proof that you had been there, done that, and thus entered a kind of adulthood. Yet his research reveals a problem which we also encountered – that people do not make some clear distinction between information about a film which comes from the makers, and that which comes from elsewhere (reviewers, critics, *et cetera*). We had, therefore, not only to ask what information about the film people had gleaned before they saw it. We needed, as far as we could, also to find out what people had done with that information: who had they talked with, how did they feel about what they learnt, and how did it all eventually affect the way they watched and responded to the film?

The controversy would not be for everyone their only source of information on the film. We needed to know whether people had read J G Ballard's book, on which the film was based. Or, how much might they know about the film from specialist sources (say, information from other countries where the controversy hardly occurred), or from knowing about Cronenberg as director, and having seen his previous films? Because of the intersection of all these, we are dealing here with something which we sense is highly individuated – particular intersections of prior knowledge, moral convictions, taste preferences, awareness of previous encounters with materials like these – all of these involving combinations of knowledge and affect. A good deal of this chapter, therefore, looks at the nature of *individuals'* relations with the controversy. We will be able to draw out some significant patterns, in particular about the way in which people used the term 'violence' as a bargaining chip.

One important factor that emerged early was that for many people our screening was an opportunity. It would 'allow them to make up their own minds'. They 'wanted to see for themselves what the fuss is all about'. They could 'judge for themselves'. This motivation is very commonly there, regardless of whether people were eventually positive or negative about *Crash*. It may be that this is in part an expression of a distrust of authority: who are these people to tell us if something is good or bad, moral or immoral? A democratic urge to form their own judgement, and not to trust 'experts' surfaces quite often in both the questionnaires and the interviews. However, to suppose that this suspicion inoculates people against being influenced by the campaign and the controversy would be a mistake. We begin with some short examples of the ways in which our interviewees acknowledged the force of the campaign to set up expectations:

V   Well I think, just to correct you, I did go with expectations that it was going to be quite shocking. I did expect something quite major from it, I suppose. [Interview 19]

S   I did have expectations. I thought it was going to be, because I heard about like the uproar I thought oh, I was expecting it to be really controversial and really shocking and umm, bascally as I said before I didn't find it that way. [...] And I spoke to a couple of my colleagues about it just because they knew I was going, umm and then to people in the faculty, but I just explained to them basically that I didn't find it at all upsetting or, you know, it didn't sort of bother me in the least.

D: Personally I didn't know much about it at all ... I'd read about it in the papers and I'd been watching film, Barry Norman on TV. And, and I was interested in seeing it. I think that was it, I don't think I would have been so interested in seeing it, if it hadn't caused all the controversy actually. Because I wanted to decide for myself.

JA *Right. So based on what you did know, was the film as you had imagined it would be?*

D Partly. Umm, I, I, I didn't think it was shocking at all. I thought it was an interesting film, I didn't find it shocking. [Interview 22]

E I'd heard stuff about it ... err, people being inflamed about it. I'd listened to *Kaleidoscope*, I actually had a little list of words, things like dehumanising, degrading and all that sort of thing, which I ... I wrote down from what people were saying about ... hello, this is this guy saying this, you know. I don't think I've been ever to a film that was disgusting and degrading and [indistinct/laughter]. And I'd quite like to go, you know, see what all the fuss is about. [Interview 7]

DA I knew, I hadn't actually read any reviews but I'd heard other people talk about umm ... it's quite controversial ... and, it's sort of from what I'd heard about objectifying, umm, sex ... or people getting into sex through car crashes or car crash victims. And so that's what I went with the expectation of. [Interview 9]

P I hadn't read the book or seen the film before. I'd heard somebody talking about the book and, I think, I think he described it as one of the most unpleasant things he'd ever read. [Laughs] Which at the time made me think well I'm not going to see the film then. I'm not that keen on horror and, sort of visceral films. But, interested in the debate about censorship I suppose and particularly, the sort of the furore over *Crash*, and I was interested to see the film for free and talk about it. And, I suppose the ... I suppose in the end it wasn't as bad as I expected it to be. [...] I thought there was probably going to be sort of more actual blood and gore. And in a way although there were, there were crashes, umm, accidents and people were injured, you couldn't see a lot of the actual metal ripping flesh or anything like that which would have been very unpleasant. So I think I actually enjoyed it more than, more than I was expecting to. [Interview 11]

There are evident relationships among these responses. *Crash* was expected to be 'major', shocking, very gory. But that does not mean that people will actually *experience* it in that way. Does this mean that these expectations are then irrelevant to the experience? Definitely not. Consider first one interview, with two young people who did in fact have other kinds of knowledge about the film. Their discussion of *Crash* and their expectations of it reveals a great deal.

Helen and Michael very definitely liked and approved of the film. Helen, who was familiar with Cronenberg's *Videodrome* (1983) and *Dead Ringers* (1988), considered him to be preoccupied with 'machinery and bodies and stuff'. She had already seen *Crash* before she came to our screening. Her motive for seeing it was exactly the one we have already mentioned: 'I wanted to know what all the fuss was about, I have to say'. This, coupled with her strong general anti-censorship views ('I don't have objection to much ... as long as there's no sort of snuff involved'), might lead one to expect her to show little if any influence from the campaign. Actually, her responses reveal a more complicated situation. The controversy surrounding *Crash* had led her to expect 'something violent and pornographic, and I didn't think it was either':

I thought it was a very calm film in that respect, umm, although quite intense at the same time, and I thought that the sex ... I thought ... I was expecting the sex thing to be more ... pornographic. I'm not sure exactly what ... and I was expecting the violence to be perhaps a bit gorier, but I didn't think that either of those sort of issues ... I thought [laughs], 'what's all this about?' [Interview 1]

Helen is aware of having to make distinctions which could be considered 'dodgy'. She searches for words that capture what the film actually felt like to her. But even though she watches this kind of film regularly – it is her preferred kind, as opposed to Michael, who watches action movies, blockbusters, anything – she doesn't have a ready alternative language to that of the critics:

> I just remember, a vague memory of the sort of controversy that was going on. I don't really remember reading huge amounts. I remember the first thing I heard about it was a reading in *The Face*. They were showing a cult party, a party where they had sort of re-enacted all this sort of crazy stuff, with chainsaws slicing up cars and all wearing some kinky bondage gear ... all a bit silly [laughs]. And then there's the controversy thing, and I kind of ... as much as I'm sort of interested in it, you know, 'what's the latest censorship debate?' ... I kind of just think I really don't want to hear because it's just going to be another waste of time thing, that you know ... I just, I can't imagine that I, I can't imagine that it could be that bad, really. I didn't know anything about the book, anything about it at all. It just sounds quite laughable, 'what are you doing?' you know, and there's parts in the film where you laugh, I think.

Her mechanism of self-defence ('it can't be that bad...') did not give her an alternative account to the *Mail*'s. Instead it went along with just a generalised scepticism towards the press, and a generalised defence of viewers. Speaking of those who criticised the film, she said: 'I find it quite condescending. It doesn't credit the public with any intelligence'. Again, in a more extended answer:

RH What do you think of the people who have different reactions to the film from those that you have?
H   I think they are ... I think I'd think that ... maybe they were missing something. Although I don't think there was a huge big crushing message underneath it, but I think that maybe that they weren't fully thinking about some of the things that were involved, you know, for example, this the sort of social context that these people were sort of being framed as being in. I think that ... I think that maybe they thought that if it was a dangerous film, that they're sort of underestimating the audience, really. And I think you know, it's just fiction. It's just fiction [laughs].

Yet by the end of the interview, and perhaps partly through encountering Michael's more committed views, Helen begins to evolve a wider-ranging account, one which positions *Crash* within an entirely different language:

> Almost it's like a really subtly sort of anti-establishment sort of film in a really ... in a really kind of strange way. But it's not perverted. I mean ... it might ... I think, that's another dodgy word to use, it's definitions again. But yeah, it's a very ... it's a strange thing that they get off on but it's not real ... I think that

the underlying thing, I would I suppose if I was gonna be really sort of left about everything, I would be saying yeah it's a kind of anti-establishment, it's got anti-establishment themes running through it.

This is to arrive at a position from which it would be possible to challenge very directly the language of the controversy, because she would have a whole different perspective on what one asks about a film. But as can be seen it is only just emerging in her views, even by the end of the interview. But a prescient sign of this move comes when her thinking about the film and the controversy it generated completes a loop, so that the film becomes a commentary on the very reactions which the *Mail* typifies. She begins from remembering her own reactions after seeing *Crash*:

H   It was the Showcase. I went with two of my friends who are also quite into Cronenberg, and they knew a bit about it ... and we got in the car on the way home and it was really strange. And I felt really strange from, erm, the sort of the familiarity I had with traffic. And we were pelting down the motorway thinking this is really strange ... we're going really fast [laughs]. Which was quite odd, you know, I was ... I did feel ... some films leave you in a really different state of mind, and it left me sort of, erm, thinking about how much we take for granted, which I think is something ... something that film does really in a way.

RH *Yeah, things seemed a little bit clinical. OK. What kind of things do we take for granted that that film actually ...?*

H   The automobile. The speed that people go at, and umm, the vulnerability of your body, I think. And that was one thing that I kind of get really quite worried about, when people respond to a film like that in that way, because it seems that, ahhh, it's hard to say. It seemed that the way that Vaughan and the others were dealing with, umm, the things they were doing, were responding to a society that had forgotten about its biological make up and its vulnerability. And then you have that exact same society and that exact same mind-set responding to that film and kind of completely missing the point. But yeah, I think that's what's been taken for granted.

'You have that exact same society and that exact same mind-set responding to that film and kind of completely missing the point'. From this standpoint, the claims of *Crash*'s critics change from being possible truths into evidence about their own inability to see things. Michael is more of a Cronenberg fan who had actively sought out material about the controversy, wanting to engage with the debate. Unlike Helen, Michael has a relatively well-developed position with regard to the controversy. And whereas Helen is weary of judgements in the press, he takes a more definite moral stance about the rights of the film viewer to 'make up his/her own mind'. Reports and reviews in the press are for him unnecessary and in some cases 'fascistic' interventions into the pleasure of watching a film, and their evaluations of *Crash* and its audience particularly distasteful.

I remember just what the *Daily Mail* said. People were going to get into their cars and crash into walls or something, just to get pleasure or something

... Because if you read the articles, they're first of all paranoid, and second they were close to fascism at some points. 'Whoever goes to this cinema is a perverted person', or something. You know, it should be like, 'I should let him decide', or something like that, you know. I just ... I just couldn't understand why, what was it that disturbed him so much?

Michael's assessment of the controversy and of the stances of the *Daily Mail* and the like verges on a critique of right-wing mentality. They illustrate a particular kind of scaremongering which extrapolates from film to make pronouncements on society as a whole.

You know, newspapers always invent, and television invents stuff, facts, no, not facts, invent stories. So I don't know if there was anything else to talk about. You know, it's like always the media's kind of tactics, you know, 'our society is going down', you know, 'corruption, crime, we're gonna be destroyed', or something like that. It's not going down, it's been always like that, umm, so it doesn't seem strange that they did it. It seems strange that they do it with this one. Because in my point of view there wasn't anything that you actually ... oh there wasn't that many injuries ... or it wasn't that provocative or offensive, I think.

It is not only in his evaluation of the press that Michael has an alternative stance. He also links Cronenberg with David Lynch, seeing in their work the emergence of a certain type of film-making.

M I remember hearing last year about *Crash* and hoped to see what was going on, so I just bought some newspapers on the way back home so I read all the stuff about it then. [...] And besides, of course I've liked him before. Apart from the usual one which is *Videodrome*, I've watched *Scanners* [1981], and *Naked Lunch* [1991], and umm, *Shivers* [1975], *The Fly* [1986].
RH It sounds as though you like Cronenberg?
M Oh I like ... I like ... one of my favourites, I think. I like him, I like David Lynch, things like that. So yeah, I like Cronenberg's stuff. And I had friends who had seen it, and I heard positive and negative reactions. Some of them had told me 'it's great. It's excellent stuff', some others said, 'no, I just laughed'. So I didn't really know what to expect.

This blurring of boundaries between Cronenberg and Lynch is intimated again in Michael's discussion of the controversy:

Oh I wasn't shocked or something, err, because I knew what kind of films that Cronenberg makes. It's the same thing that happened to me in October when I went to see *The Lost Highway* [1997] by David Lynch.

His prior orientations thus include both this knowledge of Cronenberg as well as his grouping of his films with Lynch's in an incipient, 'things like that' near-genre. Not only in the content of their films, but also in his own response to them, Michael finds similarities between the two film-makers. They are both thought-provoking, different from others, and court controversy. To these he adds his contentment to listen to opposing views from friends. The combination of these with his personal certainty that the newspapers conspire against a film like this left him in a contented suspension of expectations.

If these cases are at all typical, it seems as if an important variable in deciding how far people would be influenced by the rhetoric of the film's critics is their holding views *by means of which the claims against the film are turned into symptoms*, rather than being possible truths. The very forcefulness of the claims is thereby turned against their speakers. It is important to recognise that reactions such as these to prior orientations could not determine whether people would like or approve of the film itself. That is a further and separate step. A good illustration of this is Tejinder, who disliked *Crash* quite deeply, and found it intensely disturbing. Even knowing this, she could reflect back on the way she had responded to the controversy:

> I had actually been quite aware of the media hype around it, I mean, it was a David Cronenberg film, and that was quite special because he hadn't done one in a long time and ones he'd done previously like *Videodrome* were very strange. That really appealed to me. Umm, most of the people that were in it were a strange collection of actors. I kind of read about that, so it was interesting but also all the hype about it being very violent, very sexually evocative, and also the whole censorship debate, so I was quite aware about that as well. [Interview 26]

For Tejinder, the fact that it was Cronenberg made it 'special' because it was a long time since his last movie, is more crucial than the 'hype' generated by the controversy, which she characterises as 'very violent and very sexually evocative'. Significantly, she acknowledges Cronenberg's different style of film-making – 'strange' – which is important to her enjoyment of his earlier films such as *Videodrome*. In other words, this 'strangeness' is generally an important and likeable feature of his films. Her initial expectations were shaped by her prior knowledge, and she was thus *prepared* to watch a 'strange' film. That allowed her to distance herself from the campaign against it:

> Oh I wasn't, I wasn't worried about it at all. I just kind of, I felt, 'Oh here we go, this is another evocative film', so I was going to go to it anyway. This certainly wasn't going to make me more excited or put me off it. I just think, as a discussion, that other people who are probably not very objective but just think, who aren't going to go and see it, anyway, it doesn't matter.

That did not mean she went without expectations – she had some highly specific ones, based on her knowledge of Cronenberg's previous films. But when she actually encountered it, a personal element kicked in, which made the whole experience deeply uncomfortable for her:

> It's really strange because I don't know that I had any preconceptions of it. I knew it would be dark. And I knew it would be in a way quite minimalist because that's what I think David Cronenberg's films are like. And I also [laughs], I also expected it to have quite a umm, how do you put it? Explicit

special effects, because he seems to do that. It's very gory. He's into sort of manipulating flesh and that's, and I kind of thought this is going to be a disturbing film. But it was actually a lot more uncomfortable when I saw it. It was actually really disturbing, I didn't anticipate so much. I mean, I honestly believe that it's a good film, I just didn't enjoy it. I didn't, I didn't like it, but I didn't think it was a bad film. [...] As I mentioned earlier the fact that it was a David Cronenberg film, I've watched a lot of his previous films, found them disturbing as well, but really enjoyed them.

What we might learn from Tejinder's very ambivalent response – admiring the film in some ways, but finding it uncomfortably disturbing in others – we return to in later chapters. In other cases, people evince a definite wish to show that they weren't influenced by the controversy, yet end up showing in an important way that they were. An interesting case in point is the interview with Stella and Stephen, both Dislike/Approve. Stephen first:

> Yeah, I'd heard about it through word of mouth, really, and I saw a review by Barry Norman talking about it and umm, the controversy around it made me sit up and take notice and want to see it. But I never actually got around to seeing it actually, at the time. But then I saw your project, I thought I'd like to see the film because I hadn't seen it and then. But I didn't really know how explicit it was, you know, sexually or how, how bad the violence or whether it was just a combination of the two, I had no idea. I was going to see it pretty blind. [...] No, I didn't, I didn't have any expectations. I like to think I went in there wanting to let the film do the talking and let the film, umm, I didn't really have any preconceptions. I didn't go in there thinking, you know, how horrifying that they could make a film on that subject? [Interview 23]

This self-presentation of open-mindedness in itself is perfectly genuine, and it does indicate that for Stephen at least the *content* of the claims against *Crash* was not influential – he would not go into the cinema saying, 'This should not be allowed on screen'. Stella, his co-interviewee, gives her account slightly differently, although the consequences come out much the same – she was neither going to allow the controversy either to stop her seeing it for herself, nor was she prepared to trust the (to her) clearly exaggerated account in the press:

> I'd read bits and pieces about, and they wanted to censor it and everything. Umm, how bad it was, and I was thinking, 'well, what could possibly be that bad, that they want to cut bits out and everything, and not let us see it?'

That precisely allows another area of influence to operate. When they discuss together their own assessments of the film, the role of the controversy emerges quite clearly:

Sa I think it was too hyped for me I was quite disappointed because I thought, 'ooh it's gotta be something beyond my imagination here', and there wasn't. And I found the people all boring.
Sn Yeah, and I think actually, I think that the film benefited a lot from the

controversy actually, as a film. I don't think umm, I don't think as a work of art, as a craft it umm, merited the exposure obviously that it got. I think actually the controversy helped the film because it wasn't, I don't think it was a particularly good film. It was an interesting idea, but not particularly well...

Sa If I hadn't heard about it at all and then went and saw it I might have thought, 'oooh!', but no, I thought, thinking about it later I don't think it was. I think I find *Casualty* more sick [laughs] to be honest. But for a regular weekly spot for that to be on and people sit there watching *Casualty* every week and watching blood pouring out of everyone's jugulars, and accidents. I think that's more sick in a way, feeling the need to watch that every week. This is like a film, a one-off type thing, 'yeah, let's go and see it and see what it's all about'. I think that is pretty normal, to do that.

Their assessment of the film is in light of the weight of expectations that had been put upon it. And they just did not rate it, in light of these. It is interesting to see how the film ends up carrying the can for the criticisms it received – under the term 'exposure' comes both publicity *and* criticism, marketing *and* controversy. Stella's final self-absolution, that her wanting to see it is no judgement on her (compared to those who watch *Casualty* regularly) closes the loop again, albeit in an entirely differently way than Helen (above).

What we see in all the above individual cases is a real complexity in the role that the controversy played in people's thinking. Never absent, but rarely directly determinant, it functioned quite variably to shape expectations, but it never directly controlled people's reactions to the film itself. What it could do, on occasion, was to so overload the film with expectations that *Crash* could not survive the demands made of it – perversely, especially where those demands were that it be thoroughly pornographic, gory, and awful.[2] The best 'defences' against being overwhelmed by the *Mail*'s rhetoric seem to have been to have a broader view of the world which could see their claims as symptoms of a misreading. Even better was to have an alternative language through which the film should be viewed. That would not make one *like* it, necessarily, but it made it more approachable.

Appealing to 'violence'

What happened with those who lacked this alternative language? Something which surprised us, and required our close examination, was the extent to which people felt impelled to discuss *Crash* in terms of 'violence'. Anyone who has seen the film will have difficulties finding much which could be called 'violent'. All the sexual scenes are consensual, although it is true that one scene (the car-wash scene) carries implications of 'rough sex' – see Chapter 4 for a discussion of audience responses to this. The car crashes have a strict factuality about them – there is no trace of the exaggerated slow-motion emphasis with which car chases are usually presented in mainstream Hollywood movies.

But in significant ways, many people felt drawn to the language of 'violence' in discussing *Crash*. It seems important to ask why, and indeed in a number of the interviews when we encountered this talk we did directly ask people what they meant by this. The results were interesting.

In a recent book, David Morrison and others present the findings of a research project which asked how people arrive at a judgement that something on screen is 'violent' or not.[3] Working in ways comparable to our research, they conducted in-depth interviews with a wide range of people, ranging from 'hard cases', that is, young men with an interest in and attraction to violence, to women with children and with a general dislike and fear of violence. Morrison *et al* did use one special research device productively; they allowed groups to re-edit the various materials they showed them, so that they could determine the point at which their judgements changed. What their research shows is that judgements about 'violence' are never simple quantitative measures. Rather, in different ways all their groups operated by a combination of 'primary' and 'secondary definers'. Primary definers of violence are 'drawn from real life, and what is deemed violent on screen is the same as what is deemed violent in real life' (1999: 6). The key here is that something is called 'violent' if it breaks codes of conduct which people recognise as shared and appropriate: social rules of the groups to which people feel they belong. Secondary definers determine the degree of violence which people perceive, according to how 'real' they believe the screen presentation to be. The kinds of thing which come into play here are things such as the degree to which the violence appears threatening, how graphically (for example, length of shots, or use of close-ups) it is shown, and how close to people's own lives the situations, story-forms *et cetera* are felt to be. This work is very important in being among the first to till the previously unbroken soil of the meanings of 'violence' to actual audiences.[4]

Morrison's findings will not apply without remainder to our study, not least because of the strong evidence we have that our audiences were not able to respond to *Crash* purely, or even primarily, through their own communities of response. The weight of the *Mail*'s campaign was such that at the very least people's expectations were heavily over-determined in advance. How else should we understand these responses? Earlier, we quoted Helen's bemused recognition that there was a mismatch between her expectation of 'something violent and pornographic' and her realisation that 'I didn't think it was either'. This is largely repeated in the following responses from Deborah and Sunny:

JA *What kind of expectations did you go with? What had you already heard about it?*
D I had expected it to be controversial because of the reviews I'd read, that was my expectation. And I knew it had sex and violence ... well I thought it had violence in it, although I didn't think that when I saw it, but I was told it had lots of sex in it, and it was depraved, and so that's what I expected.
JA *So, it was unexpected in that that wasn't part of what you expected? That was a surprise?*
S That was a surprise, yeah, I think. I don't think it's a straightforward sex and violence movie. [Interview 2]

Again, the mismatch is very striking, but several further things are equally as interesting here. First, note Deborah's realisation that she had *thought* she 'knew' – a word implying confidence in the truth of the claim – that *Crash* was 'violent'. She has had to undo that knowledge retrospectively. Second, to judge it in these ways is already to know the morality of the outcome – it would have been 'depraved'. So the terms 'violence' and 'sex' come freighted with implications, even as they appear descriptive. And that is the third component to show here: the *ordinariness* of this judgement, even at the point where it proves unreliable. So, to Sunny, there is a category that *Crash might* have fallen into, but in his view did not: 'straightforward sex and violence movies'. We argued that the evaluation of films is deeply imbued with 'figures' of the audience, and that the figure which claims about 'violence' carry with them is of a vulnerable/corrupt person for whom 'violence' becomes the message of the film, to be enjoyed. We can see how this arc is closed, again with great 'ordinariness', in another person, Tim's, response: 'I'd read about the film, just read about car crashes and people getting off on the violence basically...'. To 'get off' on the violence is to be attracted to it for its own sake. What is striking is how this language is transferable with the remainder between a supposed description of the *characters* and of the *audience*.

Yet of course these people are good examples of those who would estimate that they had been deceived by the controversy, since they ended up enthusiastic defenders of *Crash*. Therefore, after seeing the film they would refuse to continue to use the word 'violent' to describe it. Not so some others, who still wanted to name *Crash* in this way. What did they mean when they called *Crash* 'violent'? Here is the response of one person, Horst, who fell strongly into the Dislike/Disapprove category:

> It repels me and simply because of the violence. The senseless violence from my perspective. I do not think that err ... you can be as err ... ruthless to other human beings by simply saying OK, we kill them ... we kill them just for the heck of it. That is just totally alien to me, and err ... that's what I rejected in the film. [Interview 7]

Horst displays very clearly the negative side of Morrison's processes of judgement. He has a general concern about 'ruthlessness' between humans, perhaps not unconnected with his sense of being German and indeed a researcher on 1930s fascist film, and experienced the film as challenging that in him. Naming it as 'violent' and simultaneously 'senseless', making it thus killing 'just for the heck of it', puts an explanatory shape on his rejection of the film. There is a clear sense in this that the 'violence' of the film is as much in what he feels it is trying to do *to him* as in what the characters might be doing to each other. The same can be seen in a second exchange, involving Marilyn:

JA *But would you like to say more about the violent aspects of the film because you were mentioning violence as well? Which aspects did you find violent, what are you saying when you say it was violent?*
M   Well, what I'm meaning by that is that people actually get cut up, I mean there is, there is damage, bodies are in the process of, there will be, in fact I actually can't remember because I'm getting confused to some extent with 'sick' but there is, and again I can't find the right words really, but there is a sort of scarring, the damage, there's a violence against the physical body, which, and, and also the metal, the fact that that, that, what is there normally is a sort of sense of security in a car but actually, potentially, you know that metal that same metal, it could be going, it could be whipping right through you and, and also you could be that somebody else is actually almost responsible for your

death there's the potential there could be, they may be drunk and they may not be but, but, but, I mean it's almost, like, war on the motorway. [Interview 15]

There is little doubt that Marilyn is here struggling to say what she meant by 'violence'. Queried as to its precise meaning for her, she has difficulty spelling out what had seemed easy to say via the term 'violence'. She becomes aware that she is sitting on the boundary of making what would be essentially a judgement of taste ('I'm getting confused to some extent with "sick"'). And her eventual clear statement could just as well be a *defence* of the film – that it is wickedly effective at making at least this viewer horribly aware of the dangers of cars, of the mortality and vulnerability of human flesh in the face of tough metal, and that other people on the roads may be fatally careless. *Crash*, by the end, sounds like a road-safety film!

There is more to be said about the way the concept of 'violence' functions within our audience's talk, and we return to the topic in Chapters 7 and 8, when we investigate the argumentative structure of those who were opposed to, or ambivalent about, *Crash*. Yet we have said enough here to make the point that this concept, 'violence', functions simultaneously as a piece of concealed rhetoric, a resource in thinking and argument whose attraction, but also whose risk, is the speedy combination of description and judgement it proffers.

4   Talking About Sex

It was unquestionably the sexual content of *Crash* which made it controversial. Therefore in this chapter we focus on analysing the range of ways in which our audience talked about the sex in the film. Central to the public controversy was the degree to which the sex in *Crash* could be considered obscene, or likely to deprave and corrupt. It was framed by the anti-*Crash* crusaders in this way because these are the criteria used by the BBFC in their processes of classification and censorship. The BBFC bases its judgements on a combination of two things:

a) prevailing public opinion about what should remain 'outside representation' (obscenity).
b) expert advice on what the likely effects of watching films will be on particularly vulnerable members of the audience who are susceptible to harm.

The other key factor in the controversy was the designation of the film as 'pornography' by the anti-*Crash* campaigners, who argued that it should therefore be denied general distribution. 'Pornography' as a term mixes legal and classificatory definitions with moral judgements on its makers and users. In dealing with this attribution, press commentary included speculations on the intentions of the film-makers. Was the film meant to be arousing, and if so did it work? Were their intentions venal and therefore to be condemned? What other motivations might they have had? These debates provided a framework to our audiences' responses.

Our interview questions encouraged people to talk both about their general attitudes to sexual representation in film, and also about their more specific responses to *Crash*, and to specific scenes within it. In talking about the film, then, our interviewees covered a wide range; they discussed what is shown, how it is shown, what the intentions of the film-makers were, and what effect it had on them; they also argued about what effect it might have on other people and whether it should be shown or not. To analyse this range of talk, we used NUD*IST [see the Methodological Appendix] to collate and then to classify into sub-groups all the sections of the transcripts which we had coded as 'sex talk'. The advantage of this is that the patterning of responses is made easier to discover; the disadvantage is that the sections of text become increasingly divorced from the discursive context in which they were generated. We needed therefore to go back to the individual interview transcripts to place the fragments of text back in their context in order to go beyond seeing just a mass of different responses.

The way in which people talk about sex is highly dependent on context. This might have proved an obstacle to our research, but in some ways the formal research context appears to have given people permission to talk about their sexual responses in ways that would normally be inhibited except amongst very close friends. Yet it would be naïve to think that everyone was being totally open, or even could be, about their response to the film's sexual imagery. We are capturing simply what people were prepared to say in the social context of these interviews. This is the limit of our ambition. We do not have access to any unmediated evidence, whether physiological or psychological, which would allow us to measure people's levels of emotional and physical arousal as they watched. We can only investigate what people were prepared to say about it afterwards. Inevitably, then, what we are analysing is the social mediation of sexuality through discourse, and this is something which may change over time.

We wanted to do more than analyse our audience's responses in the terms set up by the controversy. Awareness of the details of the controversy was confined to a minority anyway; by far the greater proportion of our interviewees just had a general sense that the film was controversial and therefore a heightened expectation that it would be shocking in some way. Rather, we wanted to see what range of discourses people had available to them, and how they used these to state and account for their responses to *Crash*. A useful beginning is to see how different people described their reaction to the opening scenes, and to ask what this might tell us about the emotional and cognitive processes at work in those first few minutes: What has lingered in the mind from these opening encounters with the film and the kind of response they elicited at the time? How did people draw conclusions about their meaning? What prior experiences did they use in order to make sense of what they have seen? When expressing judgements about these scenes, what kind of moral or ideological discourses did people draw on?

The question of the opening scenes arose spontaneously in twelve of our interviews, without our directly asking about them.

Three Opening Scenes

Crash opens with a three-scene sequence: in the first, Catherine is leaning against the nose of an aeroplane in a hangar, being entered from behind; then, James, in an editing suite, is interrupted while having sex with a work colleague on the table; finally, James and Catherine on their balcony look out over the city while they recount these experiences, and James enters her from behind. Cronenberg frequently commented on how audiences find this opening difficult to read (see Chapter 1 for an illustration of this) – a series of sex scenes like this would usually only occur in pornography. Yet various things (the slowly tracking camera in the first scene, for example, or the lack of explicitness in the way these scenes are shot) alert viewers to the problem of simply assigning the film to this genre. This poses a question that the audience must answer before they can decide on what the sexual activity might mean. Compare the reactions of these two groups who used the opening sequences to place the film generically:

A   It started off with, umm, I think the woman having sex on the aeroplane when they're going round. And after that, it was very, I found it very predictable. And, ... nothing sort of, umm, how do I put it ... it just got boring to me, to be quite frank with you. Yeah. Umm, I just couldn't have seen no point whatsoever in making a film like that.

P   I don't know, I don't think it contained ... a higher value message of sort of road safety or anything like that. It wasn't about that, was it? As I say, it was neither fish nor fowl, it was neither pornography or it was some perversion over injuries sustained in road traffic accidents. I mean as you say it started off with the wife having sex in an aeroplane, in a hangar. And her husband having sex with one of his staff in the film studio. And I thought, well here we go, then. And then they discuss it, don't they? [Interview 10]

Alan and Peter use the opening scenes to try to work out what genre it belongs to. Peter implies that the opening had led him to classify the film as pornography ('And I thought, well here we go, then'), a genre he had wide experience of watching from his previous job in the Vice Squad. Yet he soon realised his mistake – it didn't deliver on its promise. That is, it failed to arouse – 'it certainly didn't do anything for me'. Even worse, by combining sex and crashes in one film, it violated for both of them their sense that these are subjects which can only be made intelligible within their own proper genres. In combination, they become disgusting. It is a violation of their principles of classification. Or as Peter says, 'it's neither fish nor fowl'. They might not like pornography, but at least they know what it is, and how they are supposed to respond to it. Because *Crash* does not fit their previous experience of watching sex scenes on film, they are unable to see what the point might be. Paradoxically, Alan also describes it as predictable. This is a way of expressing his reaction to the repetitive quality of the narrative which failed to engage his interest in the way he expects in mainstream entertainment film. For these two viewers, then, the film's uncertain generic identity makes the sex scenes pointless and boring, and it is a short step from there to condemning them as gratuitous.

In contrast, we can see in the following a more positive response to the difficulty in placing the film generically:

A   Well, the huge undertone is sex. In the hangar, the guy started to have intercourse with her, and then there was a cut to a scene of him ... doing some film-making, and he's making love to a woman in an editing suite, so there's obviously a huge sex thing, the link is sex, I suppose. I found it interesting, I mean that's why, I like the extremes, I like the fact that it was, you know, and I suppose because it's taboo in this country, sex is a bit taboo still, isn't it? We've come a long way from what we used to be. But it is still, still you know, a bit... [Interview 16]

Here, the fact that there are several sex scenes in a row at the start is attractive because it is breaking the rules of mainstream film – it signals a transgressive film which is a category Alex and her husband (whom we interviewed together) coin to describe their own film tastes. They later suggest that the BBFC should have a new classification, SXT, standing for 'Subversive Taste'. It does not therefore bother them that they cannot fit the film into an established genre; it is their role to work out for themselves what the film might be about and why. Alex concludes from this sequence that the film must be *about* sex rather than merely showing sex; and it is their task to discover what the film is saying about sex, by drawing out what each of the sex scenes might mean, even though this is difficult for them.

Genre is not the only categorising that is taking place as viewers respond to these opening scenes. They are also interpreting the sexual activities in relation to their own experience and codes of sexual behaviour. We can see this in the very different interpretations of the opening scenes made by the following interviewees:

JH *Would you regard the sex in the film as quite violent? You just mentioned the violent sex scenes. Would you describe it like that?*

T   Well it's like, a person like me could see rape there, it's very violent. Because I mean although the portrayer was obviously a great lover of sex, umm, she didn't have, it wasn't love at any time, I don't think. And I think that the opening scene where she was in the air, I mean, that was more or less a straight rape scene. Umm, and again if you think about the very ending scene, where she's lying on her back [indistinct], with for some reason, and perhaps I, I don't know why she didn't have any other clothes on but, because I can't remember why she took them off, although she didn't have them on the first time, but if, as was inferred he was having sex there, again that was a rape, as far as I'm concerned. It wasn't, umm, it was just sex for sex's sake. And of course that's the whole point, sex for sex's sake. [Interview 14]

We do not find out anything from Tony about how he arrived at this conclusion, why he decides that these scenes are showing 'sex for sex's sake'. Perhaps it is the infidelity of the two central characters which convinces him that there is no love between the sexual partners. He goes one step further and classifies it as violent sex and therefore rape. Again he moves straight to these conclusions without elaborating on the reasons why. So we are simply left with the connections he makes between sex for sex's sake, violent sex, and rape. All of these are on the wrong side of a boundary which divides sexual behaviour of which he approves from that which he condemns as morally wrong on the basis of the presence or absence of love. The next example shows a quite different set of evaluative criteria in use:

JH *What about you, Marilyn, how did you feel about the characters?*

M   I certainly remember the opening shot. I thought that was deeply powerful. I thought that was absolutely brilliant. I mean, I felt the sex was interesting, it was kind of, you know, it was a bit like, OK sex in phone boxes, sex in whatever, but, but sort of in that kind of environment I thought, you know, that straight out this is what the film, it kind of set the scene for me anyway. And umm, it was because I've always been in love with great big American cars, I mean I used to, I have yeah, I used to have a great big barn, I was going to fill with cars a bit like that, so I've always been deeply in love with the kind on postcards, you know, with the chrome and the, the slight curvature you know, although I don't own them, I kind of umm, sort of I have a relationship with these. So, so I thought that the opening scene was it, if they could have sustained that throughout the whole film, I would have been, you know, much more impressed. [Interview 15]

Marilyn found the opening scenes powerful because she finds a match between the film and her own sense of the erotic potential of metal and machines, an attraction which she describes as 'love'. Although this is in answer to a question about characters, she has no memory of the characters, just the objects in an environment. She finds the surface of the machines erotic, and she is content to find them erotic, to the extent of upgrading her responses by calling them 'love'. There is no sense here that she judges sexual behaviour according to normative criteria, rather this is presented as a matter of personal taste and lifestyle. This is part of a wider attraction to the urban environment in which the film is set, which she comments on later in the interview. She enjoys feeling a sense of distance from other people in their anonymity. Yet her acknowledged personal pleasures and fascinations provide a template against which the film still manages to fall short – if only it had had more of this!

For Stephanie, this sense of distance from the characters is a barrier to any enjoyment of the film:

JA *So you thought that particular couple were sad?*
S   Sad, empty, flat. Umm. Yeah really, I just found them sad. You know all the things that happen to them, the whole thing was … you know what I mean … something like they screwed leaning over, what was it, an aeroplane wasn't it?
JA: *At the beginning, yeah.*
S   So what? What a lot of fuss about, you know, where you do it. Lots of people do it in lots of different places. She chose an aircraft hangar over a, over an aircraft itself. Fine, if you've got that sort of money. [Interview 27]

The classifications Stephanie makes are of people, rather than of sexual acts. She is scathing of moralists who make a fuss because of a narrow view of the sexual acts which can be shown. That these characters are so preoccupied with sex makes them uninteresting, just as the moralists who make a fuss about the film are overvaluing its importance. It is the film's failure to be truly shocking; its mundanity that she condemns. Having sex in an aircraft hangar is no different from the kind of sex she herself has experienced. She is divided from these characters by a lack of empathy with their moneyed lifestyle rather than because of their sexual behaviour.

From this brief analysis we begin to see how and why people's reactions to the sexual behaviour depicted in the opening scenes of *Crash* differed. The differences depend on a complicated process of interpretation and classification which calls on a number of things. Even Alan and Peter's reactions, apparently the simplest, involve complicated use of their prior knowledge of 'pornography'. The complications include that people's prior experiences always come freighted with things to be avoided as with Tony, or to be desired as with Marilyn. They embrace people's wider sense of what is or should be allowed, as with Alex. They also include people's personal – including physical – response to the sex scenes; to admit that the scenes might be sexually arousing can be difficult. Thus we can see how people's responses to *Crash* turned to a great extent on their feelings and beliefs about the proper place of sex, and sexual desires, in their own life as well as more generally.

The differences also depend on the salience that categories like 'pornography' have for them. Such a category is not simply a label to be applied to things which are perceived to meet the descriptive criteria. In its classic meaning, 'pornography' carries a judgement on the user – to admit to being aroused by pornography is to admit a weakness. To say that you like it is even more problematic. Judgements which follow from these interpretations therefore depend on what relation people have to the moral and ideological codes which govern sexual behaviour in both the representational and social spheres. Whether they consider themselves, in retrospect, to have enjoyed the scenes seems to be closely bound up with what kind of judgements they have made about them. It is impossible to say which precedes the other.

Yet it throws an important light on the status of these judgements if we see how one other group assessed the opening scene. For them, the fact that they were three sex scenes was not the prime consideration – the sex was a symptom of something more important:

J   I like the thing you said about this alienation thing [indistinct] … how many people do you meet, how many people meet through dating agencies [indistinct] and how lucky they were that they did meet through a dating agency or something like that. Because everyone just works, works and in these lovely jobs, as you said, [indistinct] a high salary, but what's there? What have they really got? It's all materialistic in that sense. There's no…

JA   *So, alienated in the sense of what? You're all using this word alienated.*

J   Alienated … alienated … I … was there … alienation was the motorway going up like that. They lived in a high-rise, they were looking out at their balcony, alienated from … everyone's at a distance of it … everything.

JA   *So it's about distance?*

J   Distance within … between people.

S   It did seem to be that way, didn't it.

D   But they're actually performing very close things, weren't they, at the same time as being alienated.

S   But then again, even when they were like, you know, err, locked in each other's arms or whatever else they were … they sort of seemed not … not together really. Not even on the same wavelength [indistinct] when they were even … like the times when he and his wife were having sex in their marital bed, presumably, I don't know, I sort of felt that she was far away and he was here … yeah it was pretty much about spaces between people, but I don't think that the film was saying that people in general were like that. I think that it was maybe sort of trying to say that [laughs] some people may be like that or maybe you maybe think that some people are like this … or … I don't know, it would be interesting to read the book. [Interview 2]

Sunny, Deborah and Joe perceive the sexual encounters as something to be measured against another criterion: what they might be saying about the overall quality of human relationships. Indeed, they hardly notice that the scenes to which they are referring are at the opening of the film – for their purposes they become embraced into an understanding they have of the film as a whole. For these three, then, 'sex' is not a thing to be assessed just in itself. Challenges over the 'explicitness' of sex scenes, for instance, miss the point, as would claims that a scene was 'sex for sex's sake'. It is the capacity of the sexual relations to talk about something *other than* sex which matters. This reading of the scene should remind us that the treatment of 'sex' as a thing-in-itself, with special, separate standards applied to it is not a truth of nature but a product of particular beliefs and discourses.

Coercive Sex

We saw, in the previous chapter, how 'violence' was used by some among our audience as a borrowed concept which helps end argument. The idea of sexual violence, however, carries particular force in British contemporary culture, and indeed is one of the key criteria used by the BBFC. What was it about *Crash* which made some of our viewers judge its depiction of sexuality to be violent? How did they read the power relations involved in the sexual encounters shown? Where people considered it violent, often the reason given at the most general level was that a film which linked car crashes and injuries to sexual arousal is by definition linking violence to sex. At a more detailed level, particular scenes were analysed to establish the degree of violence and coercion involved. Signs of violence and coercion towards women were inferred from the sexual positions shown, and especially the preponderance of scenes in which Catherine is being entered from behind. These scenes were read as lacking intimacy, as being cold and emotionless, because there is no eye contact and the angle of their heads often accentuated the degree to which the characters were looking out and away from the other person. Catherine, also, bore an impassive expression on her face all the time. Is this a sign of her powerlessness, that she is being used for sex that has no emotional significance, and which at its most extreme could be interpreted as rape? Or is it indicative of an equal ability to enjoy impersonal sex, a sign of her sexual freedom? This was a matter of debate amongst our viewers.

This ambiguity is acute in the car-wash scene when Catherine emerges with bruises following a rough encounter with Vaughan in the back of the car. This scene attracted considerable discussion, spontaneously arising in thirteen interviews. It was a scene which made a number of people, especially (but not only) women, uncomfortable. But although there are signs of violence, the bruises, it is less clear whether this should be interpreted as coercive sex. Indeed, some – including some women – marked the scene as particularly memorable. It was read as an overt metaphor by some people (for example, Angela [Interview 16]) – the car wash was directly sexual, the soaping was ejaculatory. Others (both women and men) simply marked the scenes as particularly 'good', 'amusing' or even 'realistic'. A clear example of this is Helen:

H   The scene with the crash with, erm, James Spader/Holly Hunter's crash really stood out because it seemed to represent everything that the film was about, almost? Because they crash and there's no slow motion and there's no, like, replay and the next thing … they just crash and it happens like in seconds and then there's just that silence like straight afterwards. […] Well yeah, it's just like a kind of a drama at the same time as there being a kind of lack of drama, in the actual crash, it's the sort of, it's just those moments afterwards that … that … I mean I've never been in anything that dramatic but oh, but … you know, it just seemed like so powerful, and it was those moments of sort of capturing that that seemed to be part of the deal with the.. with the sex thing. And then there's the scene in the car wash as well which I thought was really intense ... and really good. [Interview 1]

Helen's delight in the scene is linked to her seeing the scene as one component – indeed, not perhaps the central one to her – in a sequence. Together, this connected series of moments became 'powerful' and 'intense' to her.

In the other direction, some marked this scene as one that left them distinctly uncomfortable. Vicki was one of these. Her explanation is interesting:

In the car wash ... I obviously sort of like didn't, that didn't like sort of get absorbed into my head. [...] And umm, the next time she has intercourse with James, she was just lying there as though she was really quite disturbed by the, everything that had happened, like she'd suddenly turned cold. And I found that quite, in fact that's the only bit I found really disturbing to be honest. Because after that she was quite cold. I mean I suppose I didn't like to see that, but that was, I suppose I wouldn't want to, I'm not sure I'd want to cut that out the film, because that was one scene that was actually quite interesting as well. [Interview 18]

Vicki's refusal to let the scene into her head was reinforced by seeing Catherine go so 'cold' in the next scene. So although overall she was very critical of the film, in fact this was one scene which by its very troubling intensity rescued itself, and was worth keeping. Something of the same uncertainty is present in these comments from Della:

D   And I thought the woman's, umm ... it was like she'd been raped. I thought it was very realistic. All the bruises, and she was lying there very still. And I thought that was a good reaction. That was quite a realistic reaction, I thought.
JH: Through the car wash trauma?
D   Yeah. And it also showed the fact that she wanted him, she wanted him obvi-ously. And she wanted sex and she was like, and she thinks of the smell of leather and everything like that, but the reality wasn't as she thought it was going to be, I don't think ... I don't think she enjoyed it, by her reaction at the end, although she got into it with what's his name, her partner. [Interview 9]

This scene had the most impact on Della. She tries to imagine herself in Catherine's place and measures her reactions against what she imagines her own would be; she assumes that Catherine is disappointed, that the sex didn't give her the satisfaction she was expecting.[1] She describes it as 'a rape scene' despite Catherine initially wanting it. It left her with a whole lot of sexual images in her head ('It leaves a bad energy') which she wishes she could get rid of because they make her feel unwholesome. Her arousal is an involuntary response which goes against her ideological position on porn images: 'Whether it's a good thing or not depends on all these different arguments and all that exploitation stuff.' This leads to her linking her response to the way that 'Gossard bra adverts on the back of buses exploit women', using the kind of feminist critique which condemns the way in which women are photographed as 'objects to be looked at' irrespective of whether it is in adverts, mainstream films or porn. Yet at the same time, she allows another side, that the character in the film did want sex with Vaughan, and her response to it all going so wrong is 'realistic'. But there is a hint in her answers that 'realism' may not be that attractive to her, even as she acknowledges its force. Even as she recognises that there may be positive qualities, she makes clear that it is not a positivity she herself is attracted to:

JH So which bits would you say were the violent bits in the film?
D   Well there's the car wash bit I, the, the sex generally wasn't good sex. I mean it was good in the fact that it was erotic or it got, or they came or whatever, but it wasn't good in the fact that there was no love there was no compassion.

Good sex is not 'good' for her if it involves no compassion. In the next example, a group of two men and one woman who is married to one of the men, we can see Alex tentatively marking out her difference from the men as a woman viewing violence. They consider cinema to be an imaginative space for the playing out of fears and desires which would be too risky in real life, as a catharsis which might pre-empt potentially dangerous impulses. Alex is always more ambivalent about this than the men in her group. If they are wrong she, as a woman, has more to lose. We quote the exchange at length:

A   Violent sort of sex, from a rape point of view or, sort of, umm, just general violent type of sex, I would not choose to watch. But I am not saying that there aren't people out there who may get off on it or sort of enjoy it or whatever from a sort of, you know, umm...
D   Yeah but you'd rather let someone watch violent sex or rape in sex or whatever sort of sex, watch it, come out there, enjoyed it and then go out, than do it to someone.
A   Oh of course, one sort of does, but then I also think on the other side that maybe it is semi making it acceptable...
D   I have no problem with violent sex if that is what the storyline was actually about, if that is what the whole crux of the, the, the film was. And I don't think I can watch violent sex and feel comfortable about it. Perhaps it is because I recognise something within me as a human being that is potentially there. And all these things you can talk about...
A   I mean I'm coming at it maybe from the female point of view ... the vulner-ability...
D   I appreciate that, yeah.
A   Sort of, it is the male type of thing.
D   There's a difference between violent sex within a programme that is there to, to, to progress the story line, and violent sex that is there for the purposes of the viewer to get off on it, and that is objectionable.
A   Yeah, but because everything is acceptable and everything we should be allowed to see, like you were saying 'what, everything?', and I said yes. So I'm just saying sort of from my point of view, maybe from the female side of it, you know, the violent sex and sort of you know umm out of control for me and things like that, and I would feel uncomfortable going to see it or choosing to go and see it or whatever. So it is something that I would not go and see.

D But you didn't feel uncomfortable when Vaughan in the back of the car...

A No, because as far as I'm concerned like you said, she was goading it on, wasn't she so...

D She is mentally sort of...

A That is it. You know, it was something she was attracted to, so sort of, when she got, you know, beaten up and sort of you know, when you next see her all covered in bruises...

D On the bed and like, sympathy, let me have it, I just think, no, you are basically being provocative in the car and, you know, that is the situation.

A You asked for it, and that is what you, that is what you go so.

JH *Do you think there was any violent sex in Crash at all?*

D I suppose the violent sex was when it was Vaughan and her at the back of the car.

JH *In the car wash scene, yeah.*

D But it wasn't, I mean I don't know, was it that violent or more ... just frenetic sex that happened?

A It wasn't offensive.

D I think it was probably the most violent sexual scene, but it wasn't offensive. [Interview 16]

By the end of this exchange they are all in agreement about this scene, and Alex's general points about not enjoying watching sexualised violence have been tested against this borderline case in *Crash*. Yes, it is violent sex in that it involves physical injury, but, no it is not coercive and therefore it is acceptable. Her more generalised solution to reconciling her libertarian position on censorship with her own discomfort with watching coercive sex is to turn it into a question of personal choice to not watch it rather than a matter which requires external regulation. To arrive at this position, she has had to let go of her tentative worry that showing coercive sex has a more general ideological effect of making it more acceptable. In other group contexts she might well have chosen to pursue this argument further but in the face of Darryl's certainty her own hesitant doubts are sidelined.

This emphasises two things at least. First, it is an important reminder that 'opinions' are not fixed entities. Second, it shows the impact that relatively organised and coherent discourses can have, in allowing people to 'make a stand'.[2] In the section below on Art Cinema, we will see that Alex had access to another discourse which allowed her to turn in yet another direction.

Crash and 'Pornography'

The fact that *Crash* was defined in advance as 'pornography' by the campaign against it had far-reaching consequences for the ways in which people experienced the film, and the criteria they used to evaluate it. Pornography has its own generic conventions and pleasures with which our viewers were, to varying degrees, familiar and whose defining feature is its supposed singular aim to produce sexual arousal. *Crash* could be named as 'pornography' because of the amount of sexual activity in the film and because of the degree of explicitness with which it is shown. How did our audience respond to this widely-known categorisation?

One common reaction among our audience was that the hype had led them to expect more explicit sex than was actually there: 'There was more sex in *Boogie Nights*' [1997], complained one of our interviewees. Another, an enthusiast for the film, observed that 'that was one of the things I disliked about the film rather than one of the things I liked, was the fact that they weren't prepared to show'. To use the category 'pornography' means that people may feel cheated if it is not 'explicit' enough. Even some who disliked *Crash* strongly made this case – for example, Patrick:

> It's a bit like the way they portray shops on TV, you know, when someone goes into a shop to buy something you never see the money change hands, do you? You don't really see the whole thing. [Interview 17]

Those who did regard *Crash* as pornography were likely to describe the film as nothing but a series of sex scenes. Ines: '*Crash* didn't make me think of anything, it's just like … this is two hours of sex, it's boring.' [Interview 3] It was gratuitous sex, 'sex for sex's sake' which marked the film as pornography more than anything else. Where *Crash* was regarded as meaningless or pointless, there was no other reason for the sex than titillation and therefore it was pornography. What it did associate with was a condemnation of the film's makers – they had made it for dubious motives. Harsh judgements are made about the film's director. He is despised for his venal motives. He deserves to be pilloried although he doesn't deserve all the attention he is getting as a consequence, which will simply allow him to make more money out of the film. Kenneth: 'To my mind it was just another attempt to make money by approaching the public in that angle'. [Interview 18] Cronenberg and the other people involved in the film's making and distribution turn into a generalised corrupt 'they', as in Peter's remark that:

> It just seemed to plumb the depths of depravity. Umm, I'm sure if they could have thought of a third element they could have thrown in, they would have done. [Interview 10]

An associated recurring cause of complaint was the narrative structure of the film which was considered too repetitive. It created boredom rather than arousal because it failed to match the usual process of anticipation and suspense accelerating to a narrative, and sexual, climax; instead it offered an evenly paced series of sexual encounters which didn't offer the increasing levels of explicit display which the genre usually delivers.

> There's nothing erotic about them. I mean they were just there. And it was just continuous really, wasn't it, it was a sex scene and then a little break, something else happened and then sex between two different people of the same group, and, once they'd finished all the permutations of the group. [Interview 20]

Sue's complaint catches hold of an ambiguity in many responses to 'pornography'. 'They' were motivated simply by a low desire to 'get it all in', to make sure every permutation of sex was included. This made the result simultaneously arousing (bad, 'pornographic') and boring (bad, poor movie-making).

The issue of whether *Crash* was arousing produced some very contrary responses. On the one hand were some for whom the sex scenes in the film were so weird and impossible that they couldn't possibly arouse. For some, the association with car crashes was the overriding force. Stephen [Interview 23] put it thus: 'I mean, I've had car accidents before and it really is scary, and the last thing that comes to mind is feeling sexy. Definitely.' He was not alone in this, although – as we will see in Chapter 6 – there were contrary responses. A comparable reaction is the comparison made by Tony between his own experience of disability and the portrayal of Gabriella having sex with James in the car show room:

> I mean, I'll tell you about disabled people in a minute as such but, but to portray a, a girl in callipers, and full-length callipers who wears them as if they were actually more welded to her body, she couldn't take them off, I mean it was quite ridiculous, because if she really wanted to indulge in sex, umm, they are metal, so she could have taken them off. [Interview 14]

Stephen's and Tony's reactions are illustrations of the ways in which personal experience can debar participation. What is not so obvious is why it should lead to condemnation. It may be that an ambivalent response makes this more comprehensible. Della [Interview 9] had had relatively limited experience of sexually-charged films. When asked what films she would compare *Crash* to she says: 'I don't know – how about *Emmanuelle* or something like that?' *Emanuelle* (1974) is notable as the first soft porn film to get a mainstream release in Britain, a marker perhaps that Della has very little experience of seeing pornographic films. Her reaction to *Crash* was doubled: 'I don't think it's aimed at me particularly although it is erotic. I mean just like any porn's erotic, porn does work, it turns you on, that is why it is there'. At another point in the interview she labels it 'sort of S&M' and decries its lack of tenderness; she describes the calliper scene as appealing to people who are into 'heavy duty sadism'. The film is aimed at 'people who are into specialist sex', not people like her. But that may be precisely why she found her experience of the film disturbing. She found it erotic at times, almost against her will because she was also nauseated by its 'violence' and 'brutality'. For her, therefore, the film encourages self-disgust, 'because I'm sitting watching this film and getting turned on by bits of it, other bits are disgusting me, but it's all part of the same spectrum really.' 'It leaves a bad energy' which she wishes she could get rid of because it makes her feel unwholesome.

Della's response points up something important, that it is very hard in our culture to see sexual preferences as a matter of choice, or personal taste. They always seem to come freighted with moral judgements. This is surely the reason why it is hard for Stephen and Tony, or many others whom we interviewed, to say 'It didn't personally turn me on, but that's just me'. The most readily available alternative to 'pornography' is the category of the erotic. This is a less easily defined category and more easily has positive connotations for some people. It is both broader and more personal, which enables viewers to discuss their responses and in particular the nature of their engagement with the sex in the film in terms of their own pleasure. What followed from evaluating *Crash* as pornographic or as erotic, or even as a combination of these? Again our findings are complicated. For example, Diana:

> Yeah I found *Crash*, umm, not very erotic at all. And umm, I think that's probably what I'm looking for in film, an eroticism rather than sex pure and simple.

Umm, I find that umm, the films that are on general release by my standards are very cold, and if they just concentrate on the sex act usually from a male perspective, and they're totally boring. But I would like to see more films that were made different, did have a lot of sexual content in them, in an erotic way. [Interview 15]

Here we see a distinction being made between sex and eroticism and a sense of disappointment that *Crash* did not deliver the pleasure Diana had hoped for. The eroticism of mainstream films lacks passion and the sex in pornography is too male-oriented. For Diana, at least, there is an implied new ideal: a women's pornography – an idea that significantly undoes the implications of standard ideas about pornography as exclusively male. The elusive combination of sex and eroticism for women viewers is, however, found in *Crash* for the following group of four women. Lindsey:

Well I just thought it was umm, I mean, it was slick soft porn, I thought really. But I don't have a problem with that, yeah no, I thought it was very well done. I like the imagery even right from the opening titles, the sort of twisted metal, I thought that was done very well. It could have been in poor taste, the whole thing, specifically the subject matter like sort of about the wound and stuff, actually that was very well done. And it was funny, umm, which was what I liked about it. I wasn't expecting to, to find it so sort of ... You know you couldn't compare it to, you know, most people's idea of porn. [Interview 12]

For Lindsey and the other women in this interview, defining *Crash* as porn did not prevent their finding it erotic and pleasurable. (Kelly: 'It is one of the most erotic films I've seen for a long time'. Lindsey: 'Yeah'). Where it differs from porn (as we show in detail in Chapter 5) is that it is well done and more complex than is usually the case. It is thereby possible for the film to be both arousing, thought-provoking and engaging at the same time.

But again this seriously undermines the standard distinction between the pornographic (visual, explicit) and the erotic (emotional, meaningful). Mary from the same interview:

If you just filmed them talking about it and not doing it, it wouldn't have had the same effect. And that was what you would have had to done, I think, I mean it was about their sexual relationships and you're gonna have to have sex scenes in it. And you know, vivid, graphic ones really. He used it as art, I don't think it was just soft porn just to get you up, it was there to make you think. [Interview 12]

For many others, though, pornography remains a negative term associated with illicit activity, moral degeneracy and cultural debasement. Therefore to define *Crash* as porn is to condemn not only the film but the people who enjoyed it. They would not therefore want to be considered part of the target audience for the film. Yet even here we find a recognition that, however much a person might dislike and disapprove of pornography and its users, they exist, and maybe even have the right to their pleasures. Alan, whom we heard above, makes this acknowledgement:

I mean everyone's entitled to their own views but umm, they must be a bit sick. Umm, I wouldn't want to be associated with it myself and the people that like it, I'd rather know of them, but no, not know them. [Interview 10]

Our research has taken a snapshot of some contemporary reactions to 'pornography', and they suggest that its previous supposedly clear and obvious meanings are undergoing change and challenge. The experience of watching *Crash* produced for many a collision. Was it 'pornography' when it lacked many of the supposed qualities of pornography? What did it mean for a film to be arousing, when one might not like being aroused by it? What is the relationship between showing something and involving us in it? The disturbances – mental, emotional and physical – these brought with them seem integral to people's responses to *Crash*. For some people, the erotic and the pornographic are mutually exclusive, others use them in combination. For some people, the attribution of either judgement is a function of how 'explicit' sex is, for other people it is a function of how well executed and narratively meaningful the sex is.

Recently the BBFC has begun to reconsider its position on the availability of explicit sexual materials in this country, partly as a result of the decisions of its own Appeals Committee which has overruled its objections to classifying explicit films for sale in Sex Shops.[3] This increasing fluidity around the meanings, inclusiveness and 'harm' of pornography is very evident in our audiences.

Crash as Entertainment Cinema

Most people go to the cinema to be entertained. This statement is true, but it conceals as much as it reveals.[4] A wide range of genre films are available at the local multiplex to cater for variations in taste, which signal through their genre a characteristic use of textual conventions with their associated audience pleasures. At a more general level, mainstream cinema is premised on a broader set of expectations about storytelling, and emotional engagements that have been established through the global dominance of Hollywood films. These mean that for many people films are assessed against these criteria, although they may not obviously be appropriate to a film like *Crash*.

The notoriety of *Crash* and its availability on general release in multiplex as well as art-house cinemas meant that mainstream criteria about what counts as a good film could easily come into play. Whilst *Crash* was often praised for its cinematography and remembered as a series of arresting images, it was in its storytelling and its character portrayal that disappointment was centred. Where the film failed to live up to these expectations, its poor quality in comparison to Hollywood provoked the worst condemnation of a night out at the cinema. It was boring. It was the film's failure to integrate the sex scenes into a meaningful plot or to provide characters with whom the audience could feel empathy which produced this effect. *Crash* was a film whose point they could not fathom nor did they care enough about the characters to bother. *Basic Instinct* (1992) was the most frequently cited mainstream film for comparison. Alan, whose primary relation with *Crash* was shaped by his job as a policeman (see Chapter 7), still used *Basic Instinct* as his measure:

I think I'd class it with, umm, *Basic Instinct* with Sharon Stone. When that first came out there was, umm, there was talk about it, but well I've seen the film and there is a storyline to it and it didn't disgust me in any way, you know, and I think I've watched it twice now, umm, but I think there was sex in that and a lot of talk about it, but it didn't disgust me like this film did. [Interview 10]

The lack of a proper 'storyline' made the whole film pointless and the sex unmotivated. As a consequence, for some, but not all of these people, the sex became 'gratuitous' and provoked disgust.

For others it was simply dull because there was nothing to think about. Nor was there anything to feel. They just felt distanced and emotionally disengaged: 'it's just sex, not sexual relationships' [Linn, Interview 3]. Out of this disengagement came a propensity to find the sex ludicrous rather than erotic because of a lack of empathy with the activities displayed. Rose:

> And the bit that made me hoot, with all the women who didn't even know each other had this, sort of stick their hand into their bra and pull out their [voices drown the next few words], at the end, like it was a trifle on a plate and that really made me roar because I'm sure there's not a woman in Christendom would ever do that. [Interview 20]

There were people for whom the film's difference from Hollywood was its great strength, as it provided an exploration of sexuality which mainstream conventions preclude and was therefore more satisfying entertainment as a consequence. These people were often highly critical of the ways in which Hollywood films represent sexual relationships, and as we can see from the following examples, who use the same criteria as those who condemned the sex in *Crash*...

For being pointless – Tim:

> I find the sex much more annoying in some Hollywood films, when it serves no purpose ... it seemed to serve a purpose in this film. [Interview 24]

For being unrealistic – Nicholas:

> One thing, I did almost chuckle, was the sound effects during the sex scenes because after all sex is not like Hollywood, umm, there is not this like great swelling orchestra music as soon as people get naked. [...] There is this rosy coloured glow about sex that is portrayed through, umm, a lot of film and TV and it does give, it just gives a very poor preparation actually and perhaps you could find that ordinary sex is rather disappointing, so you go off looking for that Hollywood sex, there's no other word for it, and it doesn't exist and so you carry on looking and, you know, trying very odd things as the people in *Crash* do. [Interview 30]

And for lacking emotional engagement – Patrick:

> I know that there's conventional ways of what you're seeing that is considered sexier. I remember that film of, is it *Basic Instinct*? With Sharon Stone. That

was seen as a very sexy thriller. And I didn't think it was. I just thought it was a cold film, you know. [Interview 17]

Mainstream cinema's promise to entertain is not simply about the film itself; it is also about the pleasure of a night out at the cinema as a social occasion. The extent to which a film can enhance or detract from these social pleasures is an important criterion of evaluation. Very different kinds of experience might fulfil this expectation for different viewers, and our interviews included questions designed to discover what people generally enjoy as a night out at the cinema in order to compare it with their evaluation of seeing Crash. However, the experience of watching Crash as part of an invited audience taking part in a research study is a very different experience from the usual practice of cinema-going. Comments about the effect of the occasion on people's reactions to the film include those who found the perceived seriousness of our screening an impediment to their enjoyment. There was in these people a greater sense of self-consciousness about their reactions which prevented the kind of escape into the film, a losing of self-consciousness, which formed an essential part of their pleasure in cinema-going.

We can take Milly as an example of someone for whom the film did not work as an enjoyable night out, despite appreciating some of its good qualities, which she defines as technical:

I like the lighting and the mood of things, it was very dark, umm, most of it, which went with the mood I think and I don't think I was taking much notice of the music, but now that I think about it, umm, the music that was running through it was very appropriate and worked technically, so yeah technically it was a really well made film. Umm, but content wise I'm still at a bit of a loss.

Its repetitive narrative structure puzzles her and in the end makes her bored because 'it started to get a bit predictable'. Yet above all it was the distance she felt from the characters which was the greatest obstacle to any enjoyment in the film:

I like going to see films where I feel drawn into it and I feel like I make a connection with the characters, but I just, I had no feeling of that at all watching Crash. The people in the film, the characters in the film to me were very two-dimensional and I think that's why I didn't get any kind of connection with what was going on, and also the sex in the film seemed not to be about people in relationship with each other... [Interview 31]

Yet she concedes that if she had seen the film at a different time in a different context she might have responded very differently. She had come straight from work as an advisor in a sexual health clinic.

What I was seeing on the screen with a lot of the sex that was in the film was something like I said before didn't seem to be about people connecting with each other and yet what I spend all day doing was counselling people about real relationships and real sexual encounters and so that may well have influenced how I felt about the film to be perfectly honest.

The film was both too close in subject matter but too distant in values for it to be either an escape from, or validation of, her everyday experience. Milly is a keen cinema-goer and her tastes in film are eclectic:

> I'm trying to think what I've seen recently, umm, films like the last thing would have been Jack Nicholson in *As Good As It Gets*. That kind of film. I like comedies, I like things that make me laugh, I like good drama, I like the occasional Schwarzenegger movie and I don't like horror films particularly. I quite like art-house films and I'll go and see most things, to be perfectly honest.

What she chooses to see depends on her mood. She uses cinema to take her out of herself and her immediate context:

> I mean in a sense it's social, but I quite often take myself to the cinema which I like the sort of solitude of it. I like going and spending two or three hours in a dark room, just kind of being and nothing else and not thinking about anything else, just kind of getting sucked into whatever the film is about, and I like watching films that have something to say, that might challenge me to perhaps think about things or see things differently, and sometimes if I'm feeling pissed off then I'll just go and see a film that I know is going to make me feel better, that I'll go and have a laugh or whatever.

Crash neither gave her anything to think about nor did it work as emotional therapy.

In contrast, another young woman in her twenties, Stephanie, managed to overcome the 'serious' context of the screening and enjoy the event as a social occasion and as a 'laugh'. She went with her boyfriend and together they decided that it was not a film to be taken seriously – it was pure entertainment with no relation to reality: 'If it was real it would be sick'. She implies that this is an attitude to film which is more common among younger than older people, so she thinks it is aimed at young people under thirty:

> Anyone who was older or more serious wouldn't, you know, would find it difficult or wouldn't enjoy it or would see it as rubbish. I just see it as, like junk movie, like junk food, like junk movie. [Interview 19]

Yet she recognises that it is not a mainstream film (because of its content). It is almost as if she has decided to treat it as an 'entertainment film' so as to be able to enjoy it:

> Because I took it as complete entertainment, no reality to it, umm, it's fine it's then harmless, do you see what I mean? But if I thought it was portraying reality, then I would have a real problem with it ... if it was real then it's another ball game.

She had no established view of Cronenberg as an 'auteur', nor had she read any of the press coverage of the controversy, so she had no prior reason for approaching the film as 'art'. Nor does she feel she needs to in order to justify its sexual content against charges of pornography. *Crash* was not explicit enough to qualify. She did not feel disturbed by the film: 'it just didn't touch me that way. It just didn't bother me at all'. It made her laugh, especially the scene in the car showroom: 'it was absolutely comical, we just cracked up'. She explains her reaction as 'like going on a fairground ride', and it was thrilling in that way. She did not find it boring because she took the repetitions as an essential part of the film's exploration of the characters' obsessions, 'so I thought their lifestyle was boring, not the movie'.

Constructing the film as pure entertainment seems to have enabled her to fully appreciate the experience after the event. This response emerged subsequent to the screening because it depended on a series of social encounters, whereas the screening itself denied that sociality and that interpretation because it was an occasion imbued with seriousness and regulatory constraints, made even more so by her role as an administrator in the Faculty running the research. Stephanie's enthusiasm for the film increased once she had had a chance to talk to her boyfriend about it and they had found mutual ways of identifying with it. She also used other social encounters to define herself against, namely her ridicule of some older women she had overheard in the toilets after the screening; their disgust helped to construct the film as addressed to young people, a category in which she included herself.

> 'Pure pornography' [she is reporting some older womens' overheard talk] – and that's what made it even funnier for me, if you see what I mean. I was just cracked up because they were like 'shock, horror!' you know.

As far as she was concerned, it is not pornography at all.

There is some contradiction between her insistence that the film is 'ridiculous … so far away from reality, and I didn't think it was serious' and the degree to which she and her boyfriend *did* take it seriously enough to talk about it 'in depth', and also the fact that they found elements in the James/Catherine relationship with which they identified ('You know, there are certain bits of the movie that we identified with, because we know each other … we identified with aspects of people's relationships within our relation-ship … we sort of put ourselves in that scenario.') However, she distances herself from the particulars of the *Crash* scenario and the links being drawn between the sexual drive and death. She describes the ending as very weak, a cop-out; the idea that Catherine is seeking death does not fit in with her way of reading the film as a light sexual thrill.

These cases illustrate a general problem with 'entertainment'. While it clearly includes, for many people, a demand for certain kinds of characters and of narrative development, these tend, for some, to go a further stage – to a demand that in *being* 'entertaining', films are not *more* than that. The demand for strong narrative is so that they can lose themselves in a film, and not have to worry about its relations to the world beyond. It is *only* a film. Stephanie is unusual in having been able to recruit *Crash* to this purpose.

Crash as Art Cinema

People who did have experience of films outside the mainstream and who responded to *Crash* on those terms were generally more positive about the film, although there were exceptions – particularly those whose point of reference for 'quality' viewing was British social realist films, often signified by the figure of Mike Leigh. What these viewers did have in common was an orientation to the film which assumed that the sex did have a meaningful conceptual purpose, even if they might not be quite sure what it was in this case. Art cinema is differentiated from entertainment cinema by an assumption that the film is motivated by a director who has 'something to say', who is driven to make the film for other than purely commercial reasons of wanting to make money out of it. The chance to read Ballard's book or to see more of Cronenberg's films are mentioned as opportunities to explore the film's meanings in greater depth. The film is assumed to be the product of a director's personal vision and artistry so that part of these viewers' interpretative activity is to look to the director as a source of meaning to try to fathom his intentions.

Surprisingly few of our audience had read extended reviews of the film in specialist film periodicals or lengthy interviews with Cronenberg in the quality press, so their knowledge of his intentions had to be derived either from deductions drawn from watching the film, from knowledge of his previous films, or from short quotes circulating in the mainstream press.[5] Indeed, it was a minority who identified the director by name; more often it was a more general figure of 'the director' who was invoked as the source of meaning, whether it was to vilify or to admire him.

One effect of the attempt to get at the meaning of the film through the author was to personalise the film to the extent that the film's themes were taken as an expression of Cronenberg's own sexuality and desires, with the characters merely a vicarious stand-in for the director's sado-masochist propensities. Marilyn:

> I also had a sense that it was an expression of Cronenberg's own sort of SM, yeah I presume his sexual practices, if you like, are quite well reflected in the film, you know, it was. Well, you know, the whole thing about the callipers for instance. I mean if in fact you, umm, I didn't feel they were really needed for a real injury. I felt it is a bit like if you tie, if I have handcuffs on, it's not that I actually need to have handcuffs on, I'm doing it because it is, you know, it's all about giving up power or equally I might be wearing some sort of callipers, which suggest injury, but I might not be injured. And I think that that in itself is quite interesting. There is a sense in which we all felt, well I know I felt safe in that environment, voyeuristically enjoying the idea of, the idea of something that you can go like that in a car towards that, knowing you might be killed, sorry no you wouldn't get me doing that, but, but to actually, umm, entertain the idea, to have the thought is, is, is in itself quite pleasurable. So I felt it came from Cronenberg, I felt it was made because he's into that kind of, umm, sex, those sorts of sexual practices, that is what I think. [Interview 15]

Marilyn's 'expressive' approach to interpreting the film is offered as a possibility by our next example, where Alex and Darryl debate the meaning of *Crash*. Darryl is determined to find a meaning in the film, because it would allow the film to be a weapon against the 'Christian puritanism' which he disliked, but he is unsure how:

> I mean the interesting thing to me is, the film-maker, he made it for what reason? To push the boundaries of your mind or what, his own subjective reasons, his own exorcism of his own feeling or what, for what reason did he make it? Just to

push people's mind open a bit more that sex is not, sex is anything, do whatever you want, should never be dirty. But we have a Christianity sort of Church of England upbringing and loads of taboos, baggage on us that we look at it, think it's, you know, it's, it's rude, it's dirty to do it in the car, whatever. I don't know what he was, was he, what what boundaries is he trying to push, what was the reason, is anyone, has he written anywhere why he's made this film or what he's trying to say?

Darryl's problem is that he is not sure *how* to find the meaning he believes *must* be within the film. In a subsequent exchange, he debates this with Alex whom we met earlier:

D I thought what was the whole point of the film, I thought, have I missed something, have I, am I, have I actually missed the point here? Is it some sort of, like, metaphor for something in human society as it is today and I'm just not picking it up.
A That's what I kept thinking, that I was not picking up.
D Because I can't believe that a film that had such, a film that had such controversy, that I got to see and came away and thought, what was all that about? [laughs].
A Is that our narrative mind? Should we not actually view it as in conceptual art, when going through it? It is what it is and come away and that was it. Perhaps you know, we're looking to see too much into it, I don't know. We're trying to understand everything in life all the time, put it into physical, I don't know.
D Yeah but to me such a strong film, the director has obviously had to have a point to it, I mean he wanted to make this film, he chose to make this film, I haven't read the book, but... [Interview 16]

Between them, the two explore how it might be possible to find meanings which elude them, but which they are both sure are there.

A Yeah I wasn't, I found enjoyable but I didn't think he pushed it far enough and there's scenes where it's all, like, sexuality and sort of like, cars in the distance all running like little running along, like it's semen or something running somewhere and it's, it's all sexually suggestive, and then there's the violent scene which is quite, I suppose you could tell if it's gratuitous-seeming violence against a woman, which is the car-wash scene and there's the classic soap pouring down the window, we know what that means. No I just, I don't know I, I wasn't quite sure what what's he saying here I don't know what he's actually saying I mean, everyone knows that people, there's a connection isn't there with sex and death. [...] But I just wondered, what he's trying to say, is he just trying to push our boundary and our mind a bit which wasn't, to me it didn't push many boundaries at all.

Alex sees that it might be possible to 'read' the film quite symbolically, but to do that she feels she needs some confident insight into the director's mind. If that were there for sure, then the meaning of the car-wash scene might change again.

Darryl meanwhile was not sure whether they are 'making love' on the embankment at the end. This denotative query is picked up by the other man in the group, David, who questions the term 'making love' as compared to 'having sex' and they start to compare sex scenes which were 'just sex' and those which involved an emotional engagement between the characters.

D   Obviously the death thing was in there, but also what was the situation at the end after when she smashed down on the verge and they went there and he lay down, did he make love, did they make love there and then or something this whole near death thing and this? I don't know what the situation was, then the film ended. I don't know if we were meant to think they were making love and because they got such a heightened thing over this, I wasn't quite sure. He just lay down, didn't he, and sort of behind her I can't remember.

Dd I don't, I don't know, I didn't think that, I didn't think that there was so I didn't think they were so, umm, aroused by what they had just done that they had to have sex, but to me that wasn't it. It certainly had, they had, yeah you said make love I would, interesting you say that because I would have said had sex, because in that situation were they making love or...?

D   No, having sex was the guy with the scar in the car, that was just gratuitous sex, wasn't it? He wasn't taking any interest in her whatsoever. But then again I think...

Dd He was, the other woman at the back of the car was subjected to sex. That was different from the embankment after the crash at the end.

D   She was subjected to sex. But she also sort of played the whole game towards the sex thing. She'd, you know, she'd got in the back with him and everything. So you know it's ... I don't know you can analyse these things, it's like art isn't it. Someone looks at half a fish or half a cow in a tank and thinks God, how horrid a cow in a tank how horrendous ... Yeah it's quite different, oh its definitely different, yeah it's got something you know.

Their attempts here to classify the type of sex that was being represented in different scenes is not to draw moral distinctions between good and bad sex, although the woman in the group had tentatively done this in relation to the car-wash scene, but rather as a strategy to get at the meaning of the film. They have already decided that the film was about sex and it was about a 'near-death thing' but they were still having trouble connecting it together in a coherent way.

Often when the meaning of the film remained elusive it led to charges of failure and pretentiousness on the part of the film-maker, that is, it was poorly achieved art which promised more than it delivered. 'I don't think it was made clear, and I'm not stupid' [Interview 9]. One of the obstacles to the film gaining acceptance as achieved 'art' amongst its British audience is the lack of any cultural tradition for taking sex seriously as a 'proper subject' for art film. Indeed, a popular conception of 'French cinema' in Britain is that it is soft porn thinly disguised by pretentious plots. What is missing in British intellectual traditions is any history of exploring sexuality and desire at a philosophical level of enquiry in the way that is commonplace in French theory. Comparisons drawn between *Crash* and other art films tended to reveal an assumption that sex in art films is there for a humanist purpose of revealing character and inviting emotional involvement rather than being an exploration of sexuality *per se*. For example, Graham drew on his own viewing history:

> Can I just say that I wasn't put off by the amount of sex necessarily in ... the last film I think I saw before *Crash* was *Breaking the Waves* (1996) which had far more explicit sex in it than did *Crash*. Indeed the men got their clothes off as well as the ... err ... the women, which was noticeable in *Crash*. And ... but ... their ... the sex was part of the story and one could identify with the woman victim in *Breaking the Waves*, in a way which, err ... got one emotionally involved. *Crash* just seemed to be a group of err ... actors and actresses who'd got together for their own mutual self satisfaction. [Interview 6]

But the primary example is *The Piano* (1993) which acts for many as a kind of touchstone for film eroticism at its best, although connections might also have been triggered by the fact that Holly Hunter was in both films. Patrick, for instance:

> And the film *The Piano*. There were a couple of sex scenes in *The Piano* which I thought were quite powerful actually. And it took me by surprise because it wasn't sold that way. It wasn't just like a peasant-lady angle. I just thought the sex scenes were done quite well. You know the seduction and ... I thought it was quite powerful. [Interview 17]

For people who evaluated the film in positive ways, *Crash* had a point to it and they enjoyed trying to find it. This was surmised to be an exploration of the boundaries of human sexuality and representation, the relation of sex to death and the relation of bodies to machines. Being able to see the point of it was related to emotional as well as intellectual arousal. They felt powerfully engaged, fascinated, gripped, and this was not cancelled out by moments of disgust, boredom and perceived coldness in the characters' sexual relations to each other. For those who found the film fascinating because of its difference from the mainstream, the difficulty of working out what it meant and what the sex in the film was for, and why it was bound up with crashes, is what made the film powerful – worth the effort of trying to reconstruct its meaning after the event. It was, in these cases, a film which lingered in the mind as they worked through the meanings it held for them. This could happen even where they quite intensely disliked some aspects of the film.

Conclusion

This analysis shows how cognitive processes of classification affected the way in which the audience experienced and evaluated *Crash*. These cognitive processes are not distinct from their emotional responses but are two sides of the same coin; enjoyment or disgust are produced through the maintenance or transgression of existing classifications and the boundaries they depend on. These processes begin in anticipation of seeing the film and affect people's expectations of what they will see and the kind of pleasures or discomforts it will bring them. In the case of *Crash* the classification of the film as controversial and pornographic in the public debates about the film competed with the more usual classification of Cronenberg films as art and therefore only to be enjoyed by the cognoscenti. This was an unbalanced conflict, given the force of the *Mail*'s critique of *Crash*, alongside the relative weakness of the art-discourse in Britain. Even so, the outcome of these processes was not a given. People put their categories at risk each time they encounter a new film, and *Crash* was for many a particular surprise.

The variety of responses owes much to the way in which these generic classifications are brought into relation with the range of discourses which structure the way in which our audience conceptualise sex and sexual representations and the judgements they make about which practices are acceptable and which are 'beyond the bounds'. Beyond a generally shared view that sex and sexual representations should be consensual, intimate and emotional, and motivated by wider meanings than purely physical pleasure, there are wide variations in these moral and ideological judgements, especially where it comes to homosexuality and to the linking of sexual desire to death and injury.

In addition, there is another factor influencing the final judgement made about the film and that is the degree to which people are committed to boundary maintenance both in relation to their own and other people's sexual behaviour. This means that people making the same classifications can come to quite different judgements about how enjoyable the film is or how acceptable the film is for public exhibition. At one extreme the libertarians who relish boundary transgression refuse the process by which sexual acts or their representation are ordered into a hierarchy of acceptability, and at the other extreme there are people who approve of only a very narrow range of sexual practices and wish to police this as a social as well as a personal moral boundary. In between are a variety of liberal positions which evidence less certainty in how to reconcile their own emotional reactions and personal judgements with wider questions of legal or moral regulation. Similarly, the transgression of the boundaries of generic convention are unequivocally welcomed or condemned by some while for others it produces confusion and ambivalence. There are several directions one might go in making sense of this. The controversy over *Crash*, it might be argued, arose from its challenge to the boundaries upon which people construct their sexual subjectivities in ways which had not already been made conventional though genre. It might also – or maybe alternatively – be argued that it arose because of the persistence of the conviction that sexual practices are matters for political, as opposed to personal, decision and regulation.

5   The Shape of Positive Responses

In this chapter we examine in detail one transcript containing the very positive reponses to *Crash* of four women. Although there are some important differences among the four responses, we hope to show that a close analysis can bring into view a set of agreements. These agreements reveal a recognition among these respondents that there is an appropriate way to respond to what they see as a challenge set by the film. Within this it is possible to discern a set of conditions necessary for a positive response to *Crash*. This does not mean that all four give an unreservedly positive response, but that in the very ways in which some of them show occasional hesitations or reservations or criticisms, they disclose what would be necessary for a fully positive response. Indeed, what they do with their talk is in effect to produce an account of what unconditional enjoyment of the film would look like, even if they did not themselves always achieve this.

This is important since we can thus say something about the conditions under which *Crash* could play an important role in audiences' thinking, and thus through that the nature of its potential impact on audiences. The key here is our concept of a 'viewing strategy'. As we argued earlier, this concept enables us to explore in detail the ways in which different audiences prepare for their viewing of a film, how they experience the film in light of their preparations, and what they make of the experiences they undergo. Our audience tended to run to extremes in their responses, but the extremes of dislike for *Crash* were far more diverse and complicated. Positivity, on the other hand, is relatively circumscribed and undifferentiated.

The methodology used involves a structured analysis of the discursive organisation of respondents' talk: a close examination of the ways audiences talk about the film, and about the contexts in which they viewed it, in order to disclose not just the conclusions and judgements they arrive at, but – more importantly – the *moves* by means of which they arrive at those judgements. The analysis involves a search for *inherent categories*, *imputations*, *unstated but functioning assumptions*, *revealed criteria*, *operative premises* and *assumed purposes* which underpin and give shape to people's responses. We cannot of course know in advance how far any individual will reveal a coherent, unified response.

Nor can we know in advance how any individual will manage the relationship between acknowledging concepts and categories derived from the public sphere, and stating their personal orientations (acceptance/rejection, incorporation/distancing, and so on) towards them. For example, we did not know that the public controversies around *Crash* would play a substantial role in shaping the expectations of people towards the film – even among those who doubted or wholeheartedly rejected the reliability of the critics of *Crash* like the *Mail*. What we in fact found was that this happens through an uneasy adoption of the categories 'violence' and 'pornography' even by those who otherwise would want to question those categories and the implied judgements they carry. From this, though, it is possible to learn a lot about the *force* of these concepts, and the difficulties at this moment in history of orienting critically to them.

Stated formally, our goal was to disclose the structured processes though which audience members established for themselves the meaning of *Crash*. This covers several things. It includes all the ways in which the film was pre-structured for them by the controversy, but also by personal knowledge and experience (for example, by prior knowledge of this kind of film, or of Cronenberg's work, by their general views on film and cinema, and so on). It includes of course the experience of the film itself, and the relationship each individual builds with the film while watching it, and in reflecting on it afterwards. And it includes the fact of seeing *Crash* as part of our research project, and what significance that had for different people.

Our procedure, then, has been to approach each transcript with a schedule of questions, which aim to bring into view how people operate with implicit categories, assumptions, and other premises and criteria. The questions, adapted from our coding categories for the software programme NUD*IST, were as follows:

1   What prior orientations did people have which played a role in structuring their expectations and anticipations of *Crash*?
a)   What prior expectations (hopes, fears, anticipations) did people have? What did they know about the film, about Ballard, Cronenberg, *et cetera*? How did they understand and respond to the controversy?
b)   How did they understand and relate to our research project? Why did they want to participate? What consequences did participation have for their responses to the film?
c)   What were people's preferences and practices in relation to cinema, how did they categorise kinds of film, and how did they think about the proper/improper functions of film?

2   How did they respond to the film during and after seeing it, in terms of pleasure or displeasure, and in terms of subsequent evaluations?
a)   How did they respond to the cinematic organisation of the film (camerawork, sound, music, titles, editing and so on)?
b)   How did they respond to the narrative of the film: how was this understood?
c)   How did they respond to the characters in the film: how are they regarded, both individually and all together?
d)   What extra-diegetic concepts did they form, to help them manage and articulate their response to the film (concepts of the 'author/maker' of the film, concepts of the 'intended audience', *et cetera*)?

3   How in the light of all these did they understand the 'meaning' of *Crash*?

4   How were their ideas about all these articulated in the course of the interview, via their relations with us and with other interviewees?

Here, then, is the analysis of Interview 12. It is important when reading it to hold in mind our belief that a distinctive *set of patterns* is visible in their answers, patterns which permit the formulation of a model of what it means to respond positively to *Crash*. Our analysis aims to bring these patterns clearly into view. The interview took place on 14 March 1998 and was conducted by Jo Haynes. The total transcript comes to just over 12,000 words. From their prior questionnaires (before and after seeing *Crash*) we knew the following:

Nicola (27) is an administrator. Her reason for wanting to see *Crash* was 'interest in the censorship debate' – to which she adds that she is 'against censorship of any kind'. She knew about the controversy from friends and from the 'general debate'. There was no keyword on her questionnaire,[1] but at the interview she agreed with *fascinated*. She had not seen *Crash* before, and indeed does not see films often (both videos and cinema less than once a month). Her first reaction was that she thought 'the film would probably be out to shock'. However, the most striking thing in her actual experience of it was 'the way the characters were portrayed as deviants'. She found the sex scene between Vaughan and Catherine 'uncomfortable' since it reminded her of the violent way men often treat women – but she defended the film-maker's right to 'explore ideas and situations', even ones like this.

Lindsey (34), a pensions administrator, likes Cronenberg movies. This, along with 'obvious intrigue' as a result of the censorship debate, was her reason for wanting to see *Crash*. She fiercely opposes censorship, saying that 'I do not want to be dictated to as to what I can and cannot watch'. This is one reason why she declares herself keen to take part in the research, and thanked us for the opportunity. She had not seen *Crash* before, but goes to the cinema and sees videos between one and three times per month. Her keyword was *aroused*. She found the film 'very erotic' and 'strongly sexually exciting', and loved the 'twisted metal imagery'. In fact it was not as disturbing and dark as she had expected.

Kelly (33) is a secretary. Her reason for wanting to see *Crash* is that she has always found Cronenberg's films 'adventurous' and the subject matter 'often controversial, which makes them interesting'. She knew about the controversy from the *Guardian* and *Empire*. She also wanted to see how 'auto-eroticism affected me'. Her keyword was *thrilled*. She always reserves judgement on things until she can see them for herself. Even so, her post-screening questionnaire comments were that she was 'slightly influenced by the media attention, I expected the film to be sensationalist'. Kelly is a frequent cinema/video viewer (four to six times a month for each). Although she likes Cronenberg's movies, this one was not as she expected: 'the way the characters were brought out was unusual, with the minimum of dialogue'. She also comments on 'the sexual equality of the film – shown positively'. A 'great film'.

Mary (21) is a journalist. She wanted to see the film to know why there had been so much controversy. Did the film deserve it? Also to see if she would be shocked. 'From what I already know about the film, it will contain explicit and disturbing sex scenes of a dubious nature, and the film's theme is also suspect to me – but again I am eager to judge for myself'. As a journalist, she had access to a lot of information about the controversy, and indeed read a number of reviews. Her keyword is *provoked*. She was in fact shocked by it, in the sense that it showed people she had not thought could exist – although she does also say that in the course of her job as a journalist she has frequently arrived at crash scenes to find people photographing. Her judgement is strongly positive: 'I thought it was a ground-breaking, thought-provoking and fascinating piece of cinema' – but adds that she is not sure of her own feelings towards what it showed. Mary is a frequent cinema-goer and video viewer (four to six times a month for each).

None of them knew each other before meeting for the interview. All four had catego-rised themselves as Likers and Approvers.

In order to make the moves and the inherent logic of their positions as visible as possible, we have first presented their responses separately. This, we will see, is only a partial account since it misses out the ways in which, through the interview, they *produce* a response to the film collectively. A reason they can do this is because of their responses to the research project itself. The common element, initially, was that to take part in the project was to see something which the censors have tried to stop them seeing, and thus to take part in a debate about censorship. But this does not remain an isolated point – it becomes linked to a feeling that to take part in a debate about the film is worthwhile *per se*.

This is revealed, for instance, in Lindsey saying that 'it wasn't just a normal cinema visit, because of the research that was being done', which suggests that the research itself is part of a deliberative process, a gauge of representative reactions. Nicola, meanwhile, says that after watching *Crash* she 'talked about it immediately after with friends, but talked to friends and family about it and about the research that was being done and what I found was that it stimulated a lot of debate about censorship issues, so carried on from there, rather than specifically talking about the film, debating the censorship issue'. Mary told us that she talked about the film a lot after the viewing and 'everyone was very interested in why I'd seen it and what I was doing it for, they wanted to know what it was about and about the research'.

In each case it is as if it was *quite natural* to take part in the research, and quite natural that this should lead into the debate about censorship. Indeed there is a sense in which they are *grateful* that the research has allowed them both to see *Crash* and then to develop and articulate their views both about the film and about censorship. The four individual responses, then. Nicola professes a wide variety in her film tastes:

I like quite a wide variety. I don't particularly like action films, I think, sort of Hollywood action films, or I wouldn't particularly go and see a comedy in the cinema, I might watch it on video. Umm, I like Tarantino, and umm, I like things a bit sort of quirky, you know. If I watch a romance, you know, I might go and see *The English Patient* and that sort of thing I would go and see.

Her preferred cinemas are also diverse: 'the Watershed, the Showcase...' There are suggestions that she likes films that she can *debate* afterwards. At one point she says: 'I saw *Brazil* [1985] and Terry Gilliam did a talk afterwards, that was incredible, that was brilliant'. Clearly this could be for a host of reasons, but it also sits well with her simple liking for debating all kinds of issues around films.

She acknowledges video viewing as different from cinema ('Go to the cinema and you make a night out of it. Getting a video is part of a boring night in'), but the actual experience of the *film* may not be that different:

I do tend to watch a few videos. Umm, I, I, the thing I enjoy about watching films or, whether to go to the cinema or on video, is that umm, it gives you an insight into another way of life or another person's life, that you may not necessarily experience, so, especially British films like *Trainspotting* [1996] and *Shallow Grave* [1994], they, you really get into the characters, you can relate with some of the characters, and you can indulge in that life just for an hour or so and then come out of it.

So an important ideal for Nicola is that idea of 'insight into another way of life or another person's life'. Nicola both knew, and did not know, in advance about *Crash*:

I didn't know anything about the film basically, just that there was a lot of explicit sex in there. Umm, and that there was some controversy at the time it came out, and it involved car crashes basically. I hadn't watched anything previously by David Cronenberg, although I knew what it was about, and that's about all I knew.

Her only other comment indicating factors that would shape her prior expectations and preparations was the one that connected her with questions of censorship: 'I didn't see the film when it originally came out. I mean, I'm sort of interested in issues around censorship so I thought, get involved in the research.' She links the issue of censorship to her feelings about representative democracy, and feels affronted by the unrepresentativeness of those who make judgements on films:

Umm, a lot, you know, centres on people from BBFC or, umm, Broadcasting Standards whatever, they, umm, you know they're entitled to that opinion personally, but they're in a position where they're unelected, they're not representative of the community and they're judging what we can or cannot watch. I find that pretty patronising.

She senses that the controversy about *Crash* had some kind of political motive or 'agenda' behind it: 'I'm not really surprised that the controversy came out the way it did', indicating for her some kind of connection with a doubting, possibly broadly cynical feeling about the motives of editorial writers and those who follow such opinionating. And it affronts her because she feels *diminished* by this: 'It's insulting our intelligence'. It takes the obvious extreme cases to make her withdraw from this position, the standard fear-case in particular of paedophilia:

N I wouldn't particularly ban any film. Umm, no matter what subject content, unless it was illegal, you know, involving child pornography and things like that, where you know I would draw the line there.
M You mean you want to stop encouraging people to make them in that case though don't you, it's not that you don't want people to be seeing it, you don't want people to be doing it.
N Well I wouldn't want people to see it either particularly. But umm, any other film I'd never ban at all. Even if I wouldn't want to see it myself, I wouldn't want it banned.

It is interesting that she mildly resists the alternative response that Mary offers her, wanting to restate her own position – censorship, except in the *most* extreme cases, is patronising and insulting. She returns to this one more time, to emphasise the need for a more representative group to make comments on films. Agreeing with a comment of Mary that we should have a 'much broader selection of the community making judgements if there should be judgements at all', Nicola responds:

> Yeah I agree with that. I think, umm, the classification system, the people on that board are appointed by the Home Secretary, and they're not elected representatives of our community, and I think that would be much fairer.

There is of course an assumption here, that greater 'representation' would lead to more freedom. What is important is that in her mind that connection seems logical. In certain ways Nicola seems, of the four, the most ambivalent. Her tendency is to say things via a denied negative, as in:

> I think it was quite fascinating, the film. And, I didn't basically like the film that much, not because of the, nothing in it particularly shocked me and I wasn't offended by anything, but umm, it was just a bit hit/miss for me, wasn't any particular storyline and, I found the ending quite, quite, quite comical really [Laughs]. It was funny.

This is almost the only point at which she gives a direct judgement – and on its own it sounds quite negative. Yet her overall position was Liking and Approving the film. The puzzle becomes more explicable when we see how she responds to characters, and in particular to Vaughan. She discusses in particular the car-wash sex scene with Catherine, which bothered her quite a lot:

N I didn't particularly like Vaughan [Laughs]. Umm, I just felt that, you know, he is, there is a nasty side to him that I didn't like, I found that very [indistinct]. Umm, James Spader had quite, had an in your face character but I suppose that's a very good character and, umm I can't remember the woman ... Catherine, yes I felt she portrayed that she has quite a lot of emotional problems and, umm, that came across in her character. She was a very strong woman but umm, underneath that, you know, I don't think she was really that at all. So umm, those three characters, Vaughan I didn't particularly go for his character.

JH So did you not particularly like what he was doing, what he was pursuing in the film?

N Umm, I didn't like the way he tried to take control of the people, especially the women. Umm, especially the scene that I particularly didn't like with, umm, when he has sex with her in the back of the car?

JH In the car wash?

N Yeah where James Spader sat in front. Umm, and I know that that wasn't a rape scene and she did want rough sex but it just made me feel very uncomfortable, umm, with that violence in that scene, in that scene in particular.

This needs commentary at a number of levels. She *rationalises* her responses to characters other than Vaughan. With James and Catherine she either sees, or grants the probable existence of, deeper levels to the character. With James she feels a tension between his 'in your face' persona and what she senses must be there below that. With Catherine, she *feels* the disjunction between her surface strength and her emotional problems. Yet she cannot get past disliking Vaughan. The scene in the car wash worries her: she knows it is not rape, but it might as well be. Whatever the reasons for it – it could be as simple as sheer physical revulsion – it functioned to push her away more widely – but despite that, not to revise her overall judgement about the film. Yet the result is an *interruption* of her wider engagement with the film as a whole.

For Nicola, the overall meaning of the film starts from the fact that she 'didn't find it shocking'. The double negative here is important, both cognitively and affectively. First, it disproves the censors. Second, she passed a test. This then constitutes her formal statement of its 'meaning':

I thought it was a film that explored people's different sexual fantasies and sexual needs, you know, wider than just the main characters and, definitely shown through explicit sex scenes, whether it was to shock that was intended I'm not sure, but yeah I think the major theme is about sexual fantasies and fulfilling them.

The characters become in a sense 'representative' ('wider than just the main characters'), the film is about 'fantasies and fulfilling them', and it *may* have been intended to shock. Personally, if she had been watching it at home, on video, she would probably have fast-forwarded through the car-wash sex scene which she had found very 'uncomfortable'. This fits interestingly with, and adds to, the sense of the film as a *test* for her. This sense of a test recurs, but with a wider remit, a little later:

I don't think I could compare it with anything I'd seen before really. Umm, so it was ground-breaking that way, umm, and just this idea of filming, umm, of some people's fantasies, some sex in cars, and push the things to the edge, umm, in most mainstream films or smaller alternative films you don't really see that come through. Something that's quite normal, you know, some sort of sexual fantasy it seems sort of perversion or weird, you know it's portrayed in that way there. Whereas Cronenberg is saying, you know these, these are normal people, they do normal things, but this is what they do in their spare time basically you know, that's where the difference is. And, so it was portrayed in that way but I can't actually compare it to any other film I've seen before.

The ground-breaking nature of it *is* the significance of the film. That, plus the coupling of the normal/perverse. 'Normal', of course, just as much as 'perverse', implies a real-world referent or measure. The meaning of the film, therefore, for Nicola is as much its modality as its thematic organisation.

Our next respondent, Lindsey, likes a wide variety of films:

Yeah a pretty wide variety but, I suppose, things I would try to go and see at the cinema rather than wait until it's out on video would be, big, sci-fi. I like sci-fi. So, I think I benefit from watching it on a bigger screen. But umm, yeah something that makes you think as well.

She elaborates a moment later that she will 'probably give anything a try'. This does not by preference include 'American mainstream', although approximately the last ten things she saw were typical blockbusters. Yet she can 'particularly relate to British films, French films, they're the ones I enjoy the most'. What is crucial is her hesitation over how to describe the difference: 'Anything with a strong theme, you know, good interest ... I need a plot – not a plot, I need some depth there, something to hold my attention.' The indication is that this is something she has not had to put into words before, but she knows there is a difference and will recognise it when she encounters it. Yet she does acknowledge, with a laugh, that there is another side to her film watching: 'Mind you, I have a mindless job so if I come here, and there's a film and it's two hours and I've got to concentrate, then that's kind of an escapism for me.' It is therefore in part the sheer *difference* of being at the cinema that is important. The choice of cinema is less important, and can include the Showcase, the Watershed, even the old Bristol Arts Centre cinema.

Lindsey had a quite developed set of reasons for wanting to see *Crash*, and indeed a good deal of prior knowledge:

I hadn't seen it before, I hadn't read the book, but I really like David Cronenberg's films, I'd seen all the other ones, and so I specifically wanted to see it because of that but missed it, while it was on. And so, to be able to see it, get involved in the censorship side really sort of interests me as well. So, I mean I had a fair idea of the content just from reading reviews.

This meant that the film held relatively few surprises for her when she saw it.

You were prepared for a lot of it because so much had been written about it, there were so many because, umm, it was deemed to be so shocking, there was a lot of it, was this big censorship thing, yeah, a lot of the papers that were making such a fuss, sort of quite keen on the detail, what happened in it, and didn't seem to see a problem with that, so you knew a lot of the set pieces and a lot of the sex that was in it anyway.

Lindsey feels very strongly about questions of censorship: 'I don't like the thought of somebody else telling me what I should or shouldn't watch, I would prefer to make up my own mind'. This is the key element in her reactions. She speaks on the issue again when asked how she feels about other people holding opposite views. Here again, she connects with the question of *making up your own mind*:

> Oh I can fully respect somebody who goes to see the film and doesn't like it, because that beats the whole point of censorship, everyone is entitled to their opinion, and if somebody just doesn't like the film and decides for everyone, then yeah. But umm, I mean obviously it's a personal thing, why you see a film, why you don't. But umm, for somebody just to a blanket sort of 'nope', but not be able to reason why, what it, what elements were in it, whether it disturbed them, whether it's, as you said, people's sexual taboos and people find, people find watching sex uncomfortable. And particularly some quite odd sex.

Making up one's own mind therefore entails being willing to give reasons for one's reactions. It is not enough just to dislike, or to view it as 'weird': there must be *arguments*. And what is striking is how, for her, this links in fact to the particular character of *Crash* – it is a film about *willing participants*:

> I mean the whole, the whole point of it anyway, these people who are all doing this of their own free will, no one was going out and trying to involve people who wouldn't normally have stumbled across this little group of people, and they're all doing, you know, they've met through whatever circumstances and it was their little group and I think that was the major point of it, you know, that they chose to do this. It wasn't as if they were trying to involve, I mean, if if there had been that element to it, that they were trying to involve people who didn't want to be involved, then that that would have been, you know, totally different thing. But they weren't. Umm, so no, I, that to me was, was why it shouldn't have been deemed as shocking, because they all chose to do what they were.

This leads her to emphasise another distinction. Although she undoubtedly would not want to censor them, she opposes *Crash* to the standard Hollywood action movies, 'like Stallone-type things'. The difference with *Crash* is that its picture of things like sex is 'realistic'. So she works with several distinctions, and a kind of trust in ordinary people to see past the 'hype' the censors put on *Crash*:

> Well it's necessary, umm, the point you made because there are some things, obviously they shouldn't be being made in the first place, but the fact that they are, like snuff movies, somebody should be there to make sure that they are not going to be seen and rented out by 11-year-olds, which is, you know, a bit too common. But, umm, so I think there's a need for it. But sensibly, and ... I think there's a difference between censorship as in, something that is a, you know, say child pornography is the obvious example, snuff movies, or just deciding what people should and shouldn't watch. Because the person who is doing the censoring shouldn't bring their opinion into it, just because they find something shocking which is what this is about, the majority of people I don't think who

watched *Crash* did find it as shocking as they anticipated, because the censors had hyped it.

Again she notes the extreme case, but outside that it is a matter of choice. What is interesting here is that while she personally had read enough reviews, and gathered sufficient knowledge in advance to *overcome* the danger of expecting the film to be 'shocking', she still thinks that this was a danger for other people – the terms of reference set by the controversy had to be *fought against* in order to make space for the film.

Lindsey, from the start, declared how impressed she was, and through that revealed a many-layered response:

> Umm, the character, umm, I can't remember his name now the guy who stages the, the James Dean, I thought he was wonderful, I thought he was an amazing character. [...] And yeah that whole, that [James Dean crash] scene was probably I think one of the best in the film. This bizarre sort of re-staging it, you know. And the Jayne, and then wanted to go on and do the Jayne Mansfield one and his mate beats him to it [speaking through laughter]. No, I thought that was, and it really made me laugh a lot more than I was expecting. But yeah, I thought it was yeah, quite a sexy film.

The close combination here of 'amazing', 'best scene', 'made me laugh', and 'quite sexy' is striking. Interesting, then, that for her this did not constitute some hunt for deeper meanings, it was 'taking the film as it was'. Commenting on how her reactions differed from her boyfriend's, she says:

> I came to see it with my boyfriend at the time, and he didn't really like it. He thought it was, umm, well his opinion was very similar to mine, whereas the fact that it was soft porn, and, and, and he was expecting more, he was expecting it, I don't know what he was expecting, some sort of hidden message or, you know, come away feeling slightly disappointed by that and whereas I liked it for what it was. Yeah, so we argued [laughs] quite a lot about it.

For her, the implication is that the sex in the film was *integrated* and just part of the film, whereas for her boyfriend it became detached and semi-pornographic. So for her the film *was* the message. This couples with her repeated declaration of the power of the film: 'there aren't many films where you sit ... and feel riveted all the way through it', 'because as we said each scene was so right and interesting and had diverse elements in it', and (of characters and scenes) 'they were real, weren't they, they came across as quite believable'.

Yet this did not mean an uncritical acceptance of all characters/actors. At one point she details her differing relationships to the four central figures:

> L   What you were saying about the James Spader character, I thought he was brilliant, he was, the character was, you know, quite multi-level sort of believable as people. Umm, I didn't like Catherine very much, I'm not sure why, I think it was that sort of ... you didn't really feel there was anything to her other than,

umm, this sort of odd desires for strange sex, but whereas the others, you know, Vaughan yeah I liked him. When I say like him ... he amused me, I couldn't bring myself to say I liked the person but I just thought he was a very clever character. But I liked Holly Hunter.

JH *You did?*

L Yeah. She was good.

JH *Do you know what it was about her you liked?*

L Umm, I suppose like all the, she seemed the most normal out of all of them. She seemed like the most, you could have imagined, she's a doctor isn't she?

JH *Yes.*

L You could have imagined her perhaps, doing normal things where the others just seemed so off the wall, you couldn't really. Umm, but, but the fact that she had these odd desires and was obviously completely at ease with her sexuality, and knew what she wanted, went out and got it, that's a very strong woman.

Her affection for the Holly Hunter character arises *because of* her coupling of odd sexual desires with normality, which for Lindsey is what constitutes her as strong. This welcoming of strength links with her admiration for Catherine in the talk-dirty scene, which she calls 'brave':

L Yeah, the scene was quite a long sex scene with just the two of them, where she's telling him the things she'd like him to do and liked to imagine, I mean I thought I thought that scene was incredible, I thought that was quite a brave scene really.

JH *She was asking him to describe...*

L Yeah. And it was all her just ranting on, that was good.

The word 'brave' signals taking on a risky task, but one worth tackling. It pushed at a boundary, and Lindsey was thrilled by it. Indeed, when shown headlines, she reacts *very* strongly against those which called the film 'boring': 'How it could be described as boring is beyond me. Even somebody with the most extreme dislike of it ... it's still gripping, and there are still many elements of it ... I couldn't possibly describe it as boring'. It was for her a combination of erotic responses to seeing sex involving powerful women, and laughter at the brave breaking of taboos.

So, although she distinguishes her own from her boyfriend's reactions by seeing *his* as a search for, but failure to find, 'deeper meanings', in fact her account of her own reactions reveals just such a process – but it is *experienced* as natural. This is just what it is right to do with characters of this kind – to find them to be 'multi-level'.

Lindsey encountered the film simultaneously at several levels. It made her laugh, it aroused her, and she was kept on edge by its 'amazing' qualities. We have seen how she feels able to move from 'comments' made diegetically, to possible filmic comment. This implies a relationship in which the film is simultaneously taken *as film* (responded to via characters, narrative power, *et cetera*) and as *commentary on our world*. How does this relate to her repeated assertion that it was a 'very complete film'? The answer, we would argue, is that for Lindsey, the completeness of *Crash* is made up of several things: firstly its difference from mainstream film-making; secondly, its sheer eroticism; thirdly, its edge-of-seat challenge to her – a challenge which is vibrant enough to override even the flaws she experienced in the film; and through these, she gains a pleasure in seeing a strong woman.

Kelly indicates a liking for particular kinds of violent films: 'Not violence as in, umm, Stallone blowing away fifty people and then you don't really feel anything, but, I mean, a film that actually takes pain and structures it so you feel a bit more, like *Reservoir Dogs*' [1992]. A little later she repeats this, and adds 'Kung Fu films, I like those [laughs].' It seems reasonable to suggest that the laughter is partly in response to an expectation among the others there that this might be seen as a little strange, but also perhaps that she herself is amused/bemused at her own pleasure in these. For preference she will always choose a cinema like the Watershed, but because her boyfriend likes it she will go to the Showcase, although she hates it 'because they sit there with popcorn and make lots of noise'. The implication has to be that this disrupts the manner in which she would choose to attend to the films. This shows again a little later when she explains her general involvement in films:

> It's a source of entertainment where you can just sit, and just lose yourself for two hours. And then ... I prefer something a bit more thought-provoking, has a bit more content to it but I can do shallow if I just want to be entertained, just as much and you know it's disposable, you don't have to think about it again.

So although she has a range of kinds of pleasure from films, the most important are those where film and context viewing allow her to lose herself. And in that context cinema is important and preferable to video – it is a choice between taking the 15 minutes to get in the car and go to the cinema, and 'a slob-out in front of the telly'. Because of this commitment to cinema, it astonishes and annoys her that people pick on films as more dangerous than other media:

> It was interesting this, umm, there was lots of controversy, umm, specially about the wound. When the actual book came out I don't remember anyone saying 'Ballard writes amazing book', umm, which has just taken everything to the limit and, you know, you can write anything in a book, read Irvine Welsh, you know that you can write anything in a book, and it's just like [shrugs]. But as soon as someone actually puts it on celluloid. [...] Things tend to be described much more explicitly in a book.

Kelly, like Lindsey, knew Cronenberg's other work, but with a different perspective in several ways:

> I had no preconceptions because I never like to when I go and see a film. I'd heard about the controversy, umm, most of it from people who hadn't seen it apparently. Umm, I knew what the subject matter was, I also like David Cronenberg, I think he's a bit hit and miss, one film is good but the next film might be a bit bad or misguided, but, this one I thought was excellent.

Clearly a degree of self-guarding to preserve the directness of her encounter with films goes on – but this one left her in no doubt. Notice, also, the swift (and dismissive) positioning of those who criticised it. This does not of course undo a mental process of putting such knowledge aside as far as possible in order to have an untutored experience of the film. In fact, in some ways it could even make it easier – knowing that there is nothing there that can *disturb* you, you can enter into it *as if* it were unknown to you. Kelly was annoyed that film gets singled out as dangerous as opposed to, say, books. It particularly irked her that people who had not seen it should judge it, but further than this, she is concerned at the way films can get labelled as offending against some standard. She articulates this first when asked for her opinions on censorship:

> It's difficult because, umm, most films contain something illegal, when whether, you know, whether it's a person on drugs or swigging a bottle of whisky, umm, or someone being racist.

It bothers her that people may go round identifying the supposed viewpoint of a film, and condemning it on that basis. When she returns to this, she again emphasises that this poses problems: 'it's quite difficult because if you bring out a film and this one person could say that film glorifies sexism, but then the maker could argue, I highlighted this to show people that this was going on in this area ... I don't know if you then have to bring another little tag that says "you may think this glorifies sexism, racism or violence".' To argue this, of course, she has to be operating with a working distinction between *showing* something and *advocating* it – which is important. She also knows that she wants to hear the 'director's viewpoint'.

Kelly several times uses the expression 'a complete film', and uses it directly in association with her account of the characters:

> I think it was such a complete film because it had in there a great physical element, not just the sex and not just the, umm, the cars moving and the film's moving all the time, but the relationships as well, they're very human, they're very in your face. And I think they went into the characters quite deeply, even though the character wasn't there pouring their heart out. I think just the way the characters were projected to you, I mean, you go a lot further.

There is at work in this a very complex account of, and use of, the characters in the film, which could do with a lot of unpacking. First, everything combines, and this achievement of combination is what constitutes the 'completeness' of the film. Notice the shift between levels in the wording 'the cars moving and the film's moving all the time', eliding any difference between events and narration. Characters are 'deep' even when they aren't showing themselves as such, because they are not 'pouring their heart out'. And this is acknowledged, as a natural process, to be something *we* do: 'Just the way the characters were projected to you, I mean, you go a lot further'. The use of 'you' here marks a standing away from self to see self's reaction as a natural, and shared one. The interesting thing is that this judgement of completeness is repeated *despite* the film running counter to her normal filmic expectations:

> Everything was taken to the extreme and I found that quite disjointing in the film. But I did enjoy the film, and umm, you know, I think I expected it to be more of a beginning, a middle and an end, where it just wasn't, that wasn't there for me. But it was certainly fascinating.

Although *Crash* did not give her a normal narrative, it undoubtedly held the power to make her follow developments, as she shows in this next very complex passage:

> I think with Vaughan, Cronenberg tried to make him, make you not like him. But then if you sit back and look at it, he dragged people in, but then, not people that didn't want to be dragged in. So I disliked Vaughan to begin with because I thought these people are just being pulled into his little sexual fantasy nightmare. But, but obviously when it came down to it, they all wanted to be injured and strapped up and all of that. [Laughs] I liked Catherine actually, I thought she was extremely sensual, umm, I've seen her in something else actually where she was, umm, in a bondage relationship, umm, I didn't notice that she was shallow, particularly. Umm, but I got very sucked in with the film and I felt differently about Vaughan as I followed it along, you know.

The logic of this is that her relationship with narrative unfolding was created *via* her evolving sense of characters and their interrelationships. And this connects with her acute sense of the *believability* of what she saw and felt. This particularly related to her feelings about the sex in the film, which she calls 'really good, very realistic'. This passage also reveals the importance to her that everything was *consensual* – if she could be sure of that, then the risk-taking became all the more interesting and even exciting. In fact a general component of her relationship to all this was that it was *full of risk* for her. She described this in two separate places:

> No, there wasn't actually anything that made me go [sharp intake of breath to denote shock] because it started off quite strong and in your face and then it couldn't really get much, not worse that's not the right word, but much more shocking really. I mean once you've reached your, your shock level, and you're at that level, you stay at that level. Well I did anyway.

And again, responding to whether she would describe *Crash* as a violent film:

> I wouldn't say that was the main theme, but I think it did, did have elements of that, because I'm, I'm, you know, I was kind of on the edge of the seat, so I don't think [indistinct] like this, rather than relaxed. So, always had that edge, always thought someone's going to push it too far possibly. You know, they didn't, but I always thought that that was there.

In important ways she was feeling 'tested' by *Crash*, taken (willingly) to the edge of her normal range of pleasures and engagements. This is not the first time she has done or experienced this. It links with her prior filmic preferences, in a very revealing way:

> I mean I thought possibly this could be compared with, umm, Tarantino's *Reservoir Dogs*. Because umm, I thought, umm, the scenes where people were being, or where things started to get rough, he slowed things down a bit so you could actually feel the pain or, or, it was an odd pain, it was sort of erotic pain, but at that point I thought it seemed to slow down and you felt it rather than watched it. And I found that with *Reservoir Dogs*, especially when Tim Roth's

character was dying, you felt his pain because it wasn't like [swishing sound to signify speed], it, it, he was bleeding to death slowly. And I thought it was very much like that. [*JH: So it drew things out a lot more.*] Yeah even though I said it moved quite fast, it did, it flowed and it did move fast but, but at the same time, I think, it slowed your reactions down, when it came to things like pain, because you were really feeling this with her with him, and I found that with *Reservoir Dogs* as well.

In fact the film does not slow at this point – like all the rest, it operates within the scene in 'real time'. But it was *experienced* as slowing. The idea of 'erotic pain' as a paradoxical engagement seems to echo in her responses to *Crash*. This was something which held her and 'it was one of the most erotic films I've seen for a long time'.

For Kelly, then, *Crash* evoked a strongly positive response in her *by means and virtue of* its demands on her. It made her *want* to take mental risks, once she had assured herself that the sex she was seeing was consensual. It made her *want* to 'complete' the characters, even when they were not being presented as 'deep'. This amounts, for her, to a 'filmic ideal'. She is discussing representations of sex on screen, and signals a dislike for 'inequality' in this:

K   Historically it's quite often been very one-sided. A lot of directors seem to have lots of full-frontals of women, in the shower, and you don't often get a man walking around with no clothes on. We need to think about redressing the balance that way. That's what I felt about *Crash*, I thought the sexual relationship was very umm equal, you know. He was giving and she was giving and it wasn't all coming from one side, it was not focusing on the woman.
JH   *Right. Is this in terms of all the relationships that were going on or just between James and Catherine?*
K   I thought even people in the film who were who were being dominant, that they were doing it because that's what their partner wanted, I didn't get the feeling that anyone in that film was doing it, was having anything against their will.

However risky particular scenes and actions might have been, the film displayed full and equal consensuality, for Kelly. It has to be said that this is her construct – in fact, filmically, Cronenberg has continued the tradition of showing more of women's bodies than of men's, but that is not exactly what Kelly means or how she experienced it. What this allows is her judgement that this was such a 'very complete' film for her.[2]

The meaning of *Crash* for Kelly is therefore constituted slightly differently than for the others, in that she starts out with a preference for 'risky' films, the non-mainstream violent movies she seeks out. The edge-of-seat experience of *Crash* therefore was welcome to her, perhaps even a requirement for her full enjoyment. This meant that she found it very hard to name a 'meaning' when asked, just offering, after a lot of hesitation, the throwaway 'sex and cars'. Compare that with her final statement of her involvement as 'You even got deep into his character by watching how they had sex, what they enjoyed about sex, and how they went about getting it'. This indicates just how strongly the 'meaning' was for her a processual engagement with the film.

Mary's reactions are best described as *doubled*. We found evidence in her responses of a split reaction, which seem to reflect the double relation she found herself working with towards *Crash*: a personal relation – her response as a woman in the audience; and a professional relation – via her task as a journalist to write about the film (and we must note here that we also and separately interviewed her in that capacity). Mary calls herself 'open-minded' about films in general, but then says one or two things that mildly conflict with that:

> I like Cronenberg, I'm also interested in David Lynch. I go to anything that's a bit different umm, not your average run of the mill, I mean I don't mind going to see your average run of the mill, you know, if you're desperate for a bit of escapism that sometimes serves its purpose, but something that's a bit more thought provoking, a bit more intense and a bit more, you know, it's got a few more elements that you don't get in your average, America churning out feed-the-masses rubbish, something sort of a bit more different.

This notion of 'America churning out feed-the-masses rubbish' contrasted with 'something a bit different' bespeaks a loose but operative culture category. It is not fiercely held, and she will, as she says, indulge when 'you're desperate for a bit of escapism' (note, though, the slight denominalisation in the 'you' here). So, being open-minded does not preclude the use of judgmental categories. In concert with this ambivalence her attitude to cinemas is quite complex too:

> I'd go to the Showcase to see something big, something like *Titanic* or something like a big science-fiction film, I don't want to just see it, I want to see it as big as I can get it. So I might not come here [the Watershed] but I come here for a lot of things that don't go to the Showcase, or only stay there for a week and I miss them. Umm, small films, lots of British films, arts films, things in foreign movies world cinema that you might not get. […] I wouldn't come here to see something that I knew I was going to get at the Showcase as well, which is unlikely anyway, but. Yeah got different reasons really. I do like it here, I think it's a very nice cinema.

This indicates an awareness of, and willingness to go for different kinds of filmic experience – among which, importantly for her, are the films with a bit of 'difference'. It is therefore interesting that her description of why films are important to her veers between the one word 'escapism', offered as some kind of panacea, and a more elaborated account which marks out cinema as having capacities that other media just do not have:

> It's entertainment and it's influential and it makes you think, and I mean it's, it's a quick option to picking up a book a lot of the time, it's, it's, you know, you can do things in the cinema that you can't do in the theatre because of time, space, money, things that you can do much bigger better, science fiction is, you know, one example you can't stage a play but it can be really, it can be really just amazing to watch sometimes.

Cinema *per se* can be 'just amazing' and that is important to her. That is why video for her is always second best ('you've got all your world around you in the living room and I find it really difficult to have a clear vision. When I'm in the cinema I can't escape from it [the film], you know, it's in my face and there's nothing else I can do').

Mary says of *Crash* that she was 'quite prepared for it' – which has a slight sense of self-protection, not letting herself go into something she might not be able to handle comfortably:

> I hadn't seen it before either. I think I knew quite a lot about it, I'd read a lot of the reviews, umm, and read a lot of the controversy and the debate on censorship, I mean that was really interesting to me. And I've seen Cronenberg's work and it interested me. And I think I knew pretty much what it was gonna be, I mean, I'd read about, umm, the scene with the wound. I'd read about that in the papers and I knew a lot of the things like that that I was going to see, so I was quite prepared for it really.

The reference to the 'wound' strongly suggests a degree of what Annette Hill calls 'threshold management'.[3] Later on she returns to this, and acknowledges the potential hazards for herself in a film like this. Responding to whether there was anything particularly good in the film, she backtracked to her early answer:

> I agree with you, I don't think there was anything that I didn't like, or that I found too shocking, I think, like you said, once you started watching it you don't think that there can be anything more, but I knew things like the scene with the wound, I knew that was coming, I think I might have found that slightly, if I hadn't known that was going to be in the film, it might have it might have turned me off a little but because I might feel a little, you know [laughs].

But there is something in Mary that *wants* to take these risks. The controversy clearly made her more nervous about possible emotional traumas, nonetheless 'you know when somebody tells you, there's something shocking, you want to see it for yourself … Yeah, I wanna decide I wanna see it, I wanna know what everyone's talking about, I don't want people to decide for me.' This is therefore simultaneously a mode of cultural participation but also a political refusal, making the risks worth managing.

In one respect Mary experienced the film as very new, in relation to her measured and managed expectations. Late on in the interview, she was asked what *Crash* might be compared with:

> Very ground-breaking I think it led to many, new elements of cinema and it presented them in a in a very different way. I think it I was dissimilar to a lot of Cronenberg's former work, I think I was expecting something that would be a bit more reminiscent of [indistinct], which was good, to say this is a new project as opposed to I'm going to put my stamp all over it. Umm, I think there's a David Lynch film *Blue Velvet*, and it's, it's when Dennis Hopper was, very violent sex in that but, but, flashbacks but, in general the film no. No, not really I can't think of one film that I can say oh yeah, that's…

Mary had a personal problem, as a journalist, in being personally 'furious' when they pulled *Crash* from the cinemas in the town where she works, because of the death of

Diana, but having to write that up fairly neutrally: 'I had to be really tactful because everyone was so upset over Diana'. The local cinema manager had wanted to show it anyway, but lost her nerve and withdrew it after local councillors denounced it: 'Umm, I think they should have shown it in her memory'. She tries to work a distinction which in some way will mark her own position; responding to the question about people who hold opposite views, she argues:

> If the person, you know the person on the street thinks that, that's fine and if it's this reviewer, then that's fine again, but if it's not a review, if it's an editor of a newspaper then, well, that's not.

This allows her a distinction between genuine reviews and 'propaganda', which again insults people, suggesting 'we don't think you're up to it'. However, when she returns to this issue directly to address the topic of censorship, an important shift of identification takes place. Whereas above she was in a sense a *journalist* seeking to make space for legitimate reviews, now she becomes a member of the general film-going public:

> I mean, it should be questioned why they, you know, need to scaremonger people in the first place, what were they so frightened of themselves, what did they think it was gonna do to the average person if they saw it, what were they trying to protect us from?

There is a clear 'we/us' here made up of average people who are being patronised and insulted. She has then a well articulated position on what should be the function of a body like the BBFC, which she sets out like a position paper:

> I think what the censors need to be doing is not judging what we can and can't watch, but judging just enough to give us an idea of what we're going to watch and say, right OK, this is going to have this and it's going to have that. So what we need to do is introduce a new way of marking it, instead of just going from PG to 15, you need to be saying OK this is a 15 and it's got scenes of violence, and this is a 15 and it's got sex, and then you can let people judge for them-selves, by giving them a guide. I mean *Crash* could be an 18 but with some kind of claim or disclaimer, you know, something that people would understand, to separate it from another 18 like, I can't think of one, but one which would not be so violent or so sexually provocative, that might have somebody saying the f-word every five minutes. So you know what you're getting.

This has the feel of a position she has had the opportunity to rehearse, a thought-through stance which she brings to bear here. She isn't sure how this might be enacted, but she shares the sense that runs through this interview that perhaps a 'much broader selection of the community making judgements if there should be judgements at all' is the way to go. Mary related to the film through a sense of being forced to rethink things:

> Yeah I was trying to remember what it was. Yeah, it's kind of in touch with what you were saying, I mean it did really arouse and stimulate me in a lot of ways

but I felt as though I'd been forced to slightly, umm, because I felt myself being aroused in a way that I find slightly unnatural, it wasn't your average sex scene that you find attractive it was, it was so much to it than that. So I felt that, umm, it was forcing me think about things in a very, very different way and forcing me to question a lot of what I take for granted, but umm, that wasn't a bad thing. I mean I was very glad I'd seen it, and it stays, you know things were going on in my head for a long time after that really made me think.

This is a different, and rather more external, relation to the film than Kelly's. There is a judgement ('unnatural') but it is suspended because she wants to think about things she is seeing, and she welcomes that. When she speaks about characters, she has a real go at Catherine, and is obviously quite passionate in her judgement of her:

I didn't like Catherine, I'm not sure why. I thought she was a hard cold bitch and I didn't like her. She was so self... 'I want to get off on this, I'm going to'. But what I did like about her and James Spader relationship was it started off, she was in control, and she called the shots and it's her fantasy, and by the end of it it's switched completely so that umm James Spader was the one saying right this is what we're gonna do, and she's frightened, and I really liked that because it turned the tables on her. Because she, you know I think, at the beginning he was a little bit vulnerable, he was a little bit unsure, he wasn't quite as, as keyed up about the whole thing as she was, and he was following her lead a little bit. Umm and then it took him over and he got into the whole car thing where she was behind him, and it carried on like that, which I liked. Umm I did like his character, I thought there was a lot going on with him, he, he kind of showed us, umm, the human reaction to what was going on because he was a little bit wary of it at first and he was learning about it, whereas Vaughan was so experienced and you know he'd been into this for ages, and he was so much larger than life anyway, whereas Spader was more realistic and he was more how you would react to something you weren't too sure about, so you could see it from his eyes a lot. Catherine I just, I didn't find it nearly as believable, I didn't think anyone could be that shy really because that was all she cared about. By the end you started to see more of a depth to her because she was frightened and she wasn't quite in control any more. [...] I wasn't too sure about the Holly Hunter character. I'm not sure I understood her completely where she was coming from, didn't really seem too much of, umm, what was making her do what she was doing where she did the Spader thing. And she seemed to change quite quickly, umm, one minute you see her in the hospital, the next minute she's in the track when they're showing the James Dean thing, and I wasn't keeping up with her development, kind of how she progressed, whereas James Spader you saw every little bit, as he became more and more enticed with this whole thing.

Contained in this monologue are a whole series of things. First, her commitment to this aspect of the film ('I want to get off on this, I'm going to'). Second her mode of narrative engagement and how satisfying this was for her (seeing Catherine get her comeuppance – she starts out self-contained and then loses control to James, and indeed to

Vaughan). Third, her evident fascination with James – he is the most 'realistic', but meaning that she used him as a point of view ('how you would react to something you weren't too sure about so you could see it from his eyes a lot' – a really fascinating way to use a character she is pretty clearly attracted to). Seeing Catherine lose control enabled Mary to find a depth previously hidden from her (she starts out not 'believable' but 'by the end you started to see more depth to her because she was frightened'). With Holly Hunter, she was searching for, if you like, her operative principle ('I wasn't keeping up with her development'), which was the opposite of her experience of Spader.

'Realism' and 'believability' are not being used as literal terms here. It is partly internal logic (with Hunter, she was discontented at her periodic disappearance from the story-process), but more than that to do with *acceptability of narrative motivation*. Spader for her combines things that excite her: his vulnerability but willingness to learn from his experiences. Catherine had to be *forced* to experience, and thus became more interesting.

Her relations with the film were helped by her knowing in advance, as we noted earlier. It freed her risk-management process, and enabled her to see the film as invitingly 'fresh':

> It's just so fresh, it's such a different, fresh new film, I mean I've never seen anything quite as as, umm, what's the word, it's so unusual its, its theme, its plotline, what its *exploring*. I mean there are so many issues in it anyway, but he could have presented those issues with a different topping, umm, the whole sex in cars thing, I mean it was, I thought it was very ground-breaking, it was very different also what he was trying to say about it, umm, I've rarely seen a film which had a perverse sexual theme that they tried to say, right, we're going to make you think about this. They just write it off as somebody being weird, whereas Cronenberg was saying that these people, to them it's not weird it's, it's what they get off on.

To engage so strongly with something she several times calls 'unnatural' and 'perverse' involves a very interesting sense of self in relation to these. Mary thus manages a doubled relationship with the meaning of the film. There is the 'reviewer's version' of the meaning, in terms of cars, alienation, *et cetera* ('you know, car abuse is growing but the fact that we take it for granted that people have these accidents every day and it's normal'). But she actually marks the difference between that – we might even call it an 'official meaning' – and what really mattered to her: 'I thought, though, that was in the film and it was part of it, umm, I think what came across to me as what he was really trying to do was, show what you might take as perverse or an unusual sexual fantasy, or a group of people with this, this fantasy which is something that I've never actually thought about before'. So the meaning of the film to her as an individual, rather than as a reviewer, was in the questions she was forced to confront.

The interview as social interaction and meaning-making

Up to this point, we have been examining each person separately, in order to detect their individual viewing strategies and the moves on which each is built. In fact, in the actual interview, a great deal was produced out of their interactions with each other. In this section we consider some of the things that can be learnt from this. First, we consider how their interactions can throw light on something which is effectively missing from their responses; for interestingly none of the four have anything specific to say about cinematographic aspects: camerawork, presented images, sound, music et cetera. These seem to be taken for granted, as just part of the film. Nor do they particularly have things to say about maker's intentions or implied audience, our 'extra-diegetic constructs' in our schedule of questions.

There are odd moments where Cronenberg appears as a figure. For instance, as we have heard, Kelly says at one point: 'I think with Vaughan Cronenberg tried to make you not like him', but she immediately follows this with a discussion of Vaughan himself and how her relation to him changed. So it is as though Cronenberg establishes the *narrative premise* but thereafter the film has its own inherent logic. Or perhaps Cronenberg operates as the originary source of the imaginative impulse. That might be seen to operate in an (again) isolated comment from Kelly at the end of the discussion about good/best bits in the film: 'I get the feeling that Ballard [the writer] may have been reading Nancy Friday because there are so many different sexual scenarios in there'.

In another context, at moments where the film is judged by someone to have a problem, the 'author' enters. So, Nicola comments on the lesbian scene:

One thing I did find, I felt he tried to cram quite a lot into the film as regards the sex. At the very end of the film I felt we've had everything in here, all we need now is a lesbian scene. Umm, and it, at the very end of the film I felt well it's all we, you know, we've got, had everything in here all we need now is a lesbian scene. And bingo, Holly Hunter ... you know, so it was a little bit predictable in that way; it made me feel as if, why did he have to put everything in there...

The 'he' is clearly a vague reference to Cronenberg as motivating author, who has to be called to account for being 'predictable'. So the 'author' is called on at moments of dissatisfaction. But Kelly at this point offers a counter-interpretation which re-motivates this in narrative terms: 'But they wanted to experience everything there was, you got that impression' – on the back of which she makes that reference to Ballard borrowing from Friday. First, it shows that reservations about the film tend to be framed in terms of a *disappointment* at its not living up to an ideal which, here, Nicola is articulating. It should not be 'predictable', that is a failure of the contract, as it were. But for Kelly, that is recuperable – and indeed the need to refer to the author promptly disappears – by a demonstration that there *is* a narrative logic to showing the lesbian scene. Finally, though, what is also important is the *sheer fact of the exchange*. Between them, they are *producing the conditions of positivity*, and testing them as they go. This is the general tendency which we would argue inheres throughout the interview.

The 'generalised author' emerges at other points, to cover possible risks. Kelly, for instance, in discussing her edge of seat experience as we have seen, posits a 'they' who might – but never quite did – take her too far. Notice, though, the way an ideal balance is implied in this. When they come to think through whether there was a meaning to the film, they broach this topic area again. Lindsey opens this with the notion that there was an *intentional message* or 'comment' within the film. Importantly, she crosses directly from words spoken diegetically to a possible narrative message:

I was struck by the man's relationship with his car element. […] I used to work for a Ford dealership and, quite incredible really, women and their cars and men and their cars, and I was sort of struck by that element in it, it's just been taken that one bit further and actually involving them in sex. And also there were a couple of comments, umm, when they were stood out, when James Spader and his girlfriend were stood on their balcony, watching traffic, and they would comment on, was the traffic getting heavier? So I'm wondering if perhaps there was a very slight sort of comment on sort of enormous build up of traffic. Whether that was intentional or ... but it made me think of that, what was that called, is it gridlock?

Lindsey asks: if James and Catherine are commenting, does this make it a filmic comment? Mary responds to this, and makes the reference to Cronenberg explicit:

M I definitely picked up on that as well. You know, like I said at the beginning, so many people thought that is shocking, that's what he's trying to do. I thought that was one of the ideas that Cronenberg was underlying. Saying you know, don't we have a problem here?
L You could have taken the film completely on that grounds if you wanted to.
M Yeah, and not only umm, the fact that he's, you know, that car abuse is growing but the fact that we take it for granted that people have these accidents every day and it's normal. And wait a minute it's not normal, there are these incredible accidents and horrific injuries and it's, it's accepted, now that's just one of the things, you get in your car and drive to work you might end up in, you know, neck brace the next day, you know, and I thought that Cronenberg was also saying, it's become so commonplace for people to have these accidents and to be injured, umm, is this right, you know, what's going on? […] I thought, though, that was in the film and it was part of it, umm, I think what came across to me as what he was really trying to do was, show what you might take as perverse or an unusual sexual fantasy, or a group of people with this, this fantasy which is something that I've never actually thought of before. And so, it makes you really question how you, how you judge people and what you class as being, perverse or shocking, disgusting. And I think it that the car element of that in the sexual fantasy could have been anything, could have been sex with animals, sex with anything you would think right, yeah that's a bit strange. Umm, but it drew you in so you think about it, why why why you turned up like this, why you're shocked by it, what is shocking, think it made me question what I found shocking about other people's sexual desires.

Mary offers a 'reading' of the film – one which is posed as explaining 'your' (a generalised observed position) responses. As an overall framework for thinking about the film, it offers a measure against which any particular responses, therefore, can be tested. In terms of its content, what is particularly worth attention here is the move between attributed meaning, and her own thoughts, via the notion of 'it drew you in so you think about it'. But ultimately it was not the imputed narrative message about cars and 'incredible accidents and horrific injuries' that she wanted to think about. Rather, it was 'what I found shocking about other people's sexual desires'. This indicates an important separation between what a *cognitive process of attributing a 'meaning' to a film* and a *process of involvement in which questions are experienced as posed*. The fact that they do not coincide (at least here) is worthy of a good deal of thought.

Here, the theme of perverse sex and the invitation to think about it becomes crucial. Her relation to it is pretty complicated. What is good for Mary is that Cronenberg has issued no judgement on the behaviour, although it is clearly enough signalled as 'perverse'. This means that her own relationship to it has to be one in which she wants to be shown things that are adjudged perverse and to be able to make up her own mind. This is her test of *Crash*'s adequacy. Her judgement in the end is that 'Cronenberg handled it very well, it was very carefully done, it was slick, it was clean, it was a first-rate cast. I wouldn't fault it'. Cronenberg here gets plaudits as a kind of honorific closure.

If they have only a scatter of comments on the 'author', our interviewees say even less on implied or target audiences. The most there is came in response to the question about their views of people who hold opposite opinions, and then in relation to censorship. Lindsey, operating in concert with her principle that 'representativeness' would surely widen availability, imputes a response to a 'generalised other': 'the majority of people I don't think who watched *Crash* did find it as shocking as they anticipated because the censors had hyped it'. This imputation, casually made, is important because it accords with her rejection of the censors, and her belief that wider representation would acknowledge acceptance of 'difference'. In most other senses they experience *themselves* as the implied audience, and they signal this through a self-surveying use of 'you'. For instance, Lindsey responded to a comment from Mary we cited earlier about the talk-dirty scene:

> You were prepared for a lot of it because so much had been written about it, there were so many because, umm, it was deemed to be so shocking, there was a lot of it was, this big censorship thing yeah a lot of the papers that were making such a fuss, sort of quite keen on the detail, what happened in it, and didn't seem to see a problem with that, so you knew a lot of the set pieces and a lot of the sex that was in it anyway.

The 'you' abstracts from a personal to a generalised position. This tactic occurred often and indicates, we think, how far they see their own mode of response as just the natural one for the film. 'You' allows them to generate a common ground within which they can *test out a theory of their own responses*.

Beyond this, audiences are 'other' either in the sense of being refusers, people who will unacceptably judge without having seen the film, or who on personal and reasonable grounds judge that it is not for them. So, Kelly tells of one friend she hoped would accompany her: 'One of my friends had wanted to come with me to see it, who is very intelligent and thoughtful and I thought would have been a perfect sort of person to have taken part in this. But the subject matter put her off.' This is clearly acceptable to Kelly, although a pity. Nicola's response, though, grounds their acceptance in a way that establishes themselves as a group who have *achieved something*: 'It looks a bit deeper into people's taboos about sex.' They are effectively, and without blame, attributing to *others* as a limit and barrier, something which they themselves personally – and now together – experienced and managed and enjoyed.

The predominant feel of the entire interview is of people just really enjoying talking to each other about something in which they share a fascination. Of the four, perhaps Mary most finds the interview an opportunity to unfold a view that otherwise she might not have done, because of the tensions between her role as a journalist, and her responses as an individual woman. But collectively, they used the interview to create a shared space within which they articulated an ideal account of *Crash*, to which each then individually approximated.

Identifying discursive principles

What *moves*, then, can we see being made in this interview? By 'moves', as we've said, we mean the role played by categories, assumptions, imputations, criteria, premises and purposes which underpin and make sense of steps in people's accounts of their responses to the film. Clearly we are not aiming for an exhaustive list – if such could even be imagined. Our interest here is in those moves which are shared by our four respondents; and which are associated with the ways in which they arrive at *positive* judgements of *Crash*. Sometimes, of course, moves are revealed more explicitly by one or two of the four than by the others. We do not see this as a problem in principle. Only in a few places are there disagreements among the four – where such occur, we have noted them. And as we have shown, there are many ways in which the four are using the interview as a vehicle for developing an agreed account of the film. One person explicitly rehearsing a position means that it has become, in an important way, a common property of the group, unless another positively dissociates herself. And often, in fact, the explicit statement can be shown to be operating implicitly behind other moves made by the others.

We have identified seven major moves:

1. *Prior filmic categories*: this has two competing and indeed conflicting aspects. All four recognise the pull of the categorisations of *Crash* generated within the controversy: 'violent', 'obscene', 'pornographic', 'sensationalist'. Yet to recognise does not mean to approve. The first response of all four is to demand the chance to 'see for themselves'. The trouble is that this still grants something of the power of those categorisations. For to go to see *Crash* to check if it is 'violent' or 'sensationalist' is not like looking to see if there is water in the kettle. It importantly *prefigures* how they prepare to watch it: cautiously (since if it *were* as the critics said, it would be difficult to watch); yet defensively (because they do not trust those critics). This is therefore a *negative* consideration: conceptualisation of the film which they know is not their own, but which they cannot dismiss.

At the same time, they have their own *positive* categorisations which are relevant to preparing to watch *Crash*. All four variously distinguish 'mainstream' Hollywood films – which they do not object to, and will sometimes watch, especially for purposes of 'escapist entertainment'; and 'films that make you think' – a preferred category, which does not have the immediate force of a label, but into which generally they hope Cronenberg's film will fall. Nicola interestingly stretches this concept to seek a specific *kind* of thinking, about 'another way of life or another person's life, that you may not necessarily experience' – an explicit extension that we see as implicitly present in the others, as well.

How any individual will cope with these conflicting calls cannot be predicted. We suspect, though, that a deciding factor is not just the relative strength of each of the above, but something else. If an individual can not only distrust the *Mail*'s account of *Crash*, but can place their attack on the film within a broader (political) framework, they will be in a stronger position to turn aside the force of its categorisation. Rather than saying in effect 'The *Mail* has called *Crash* "obscene", I hope they are not right', they will be able to say something like 'The *Mail* has called *Crash* "obscene": they would, wouldn't they?' The attacks then become a positive *ground for believing differently*. In parallel with our remark, above, about how the press judgements prefigured actual responses, we note also how a remark of Kelly's shows the way such categories are always more than just cognitive. Read again her comment on her preferred kinds of film:

> It's a source of entertainment where you can just sit, and just lose yourself for two hours. And then … I prefer something a bit more thought-provoking, has a bit more content to it but I can do shallow if I just want to be entertained, just as much and you know it's disposable, you don't have to think about it again.

The telling phrase here is 'I can do shallow'. The implication that this is a *role* which she can take up, for specific purposes, is important. It is not a role that is central to her filmic and life preferences in the way that engaging with thinking films is – it is one that she can tactically adopt for those moments in her life when precisely all she wants is *not* to have a film further than the experience. The category 'entertainment' thus carries with it practical consequences.

2. *Reading the film as an integrated narrative*: when these four watch *Crash*, they do not see the sex scenes as something to be attended to just for themselves. They see them as essential for revealing the motivation of characters, and for rolling forward the narrative since that narrative is *about* the nature of these characters. This is possible, however, only because they are able and willing to see human sexuality as not only something important in its own right, but as something *symptomatic* of human reactions and potentials generally.

Lindsey brings this most to the surface when she compares her response to *Crash* to her boyfriend's. For him it stayed in the category 'soft porn', to be looked at for its own sake. For her, instead, it became a vehicle to characters' depths and potentials, and in particular (for her favourite character) a sign of strength in a woman 'completely at ease with her sexuality'. This does not stop the film being erotically charged. It means that the sex scenes are never *just* sex scenes. In line with Lindsey, we would call this move a 'search for completeness' – that is, an agreement that the film is worth investing in to the extent of trying to make a rounded sense of things. This then encompasses the sex scenes, and makes them amenable to understanding as part of the overall narrative.

3. *Cinematic/sexual ideals*: in various ways, the four of them make clear that *Crash* is valuable to them because they experienced it as meeting criteria they held *before* they watched it – most specifically, an ideal of 'equality in sexual relations'. Lindsey says this in a particularly revealing way. Her starting point, as we saw, was the recognition that that which precisely made *Crash* important to her, was what would have angered

critics – its dealing with 'some quite odd sex'. But its oddness was fully redeemed for her because people were doing it 'of their own free will'. This makes it for her, therefore, an exploration – a stepping into the unknown, to imagine *freed sexuality*.

Rare and ground-breaking because of it, *Crash* passed a test for them. And in doing this, it gave them the opportunity to experience and think about something they wanted. So, to have a cinematic ideal of this kind is not simply to get something you already know – it is more to *fill a known gap*, to discover an opportunity to step into a wished-for unknown. Hence for all of them the sense of *excitement* and *discovery* which they experienced with *Crash*. Hence the naming of *Crash* as 'ground-breaking'. Hence also the feeling that the film is 'brave', 'fresh', 'different' and a dozen other such words.

Here, we note also that this will to completeness further explains the almost total absence of independent interest in the cinematicness of *Crash*. It is only worth talking about camerawork, or editing, or lighting, or sound if these are responded to as a dimension separate from the film as a whole – as many of those hostile to the film in fact do. But for these women, the filmic qualities are first read as integrated into its overall nature, and only when all else fails – as in the occasional attributions to Cronenberg when they have small reservations – is the film discussed in terms of any of its components.

4. *Reading character depths*: there is a clear will in all four to find depth in characters, even when that depth is cinematically withheld. Kelly makes the most explicit statement of this: 'They went into the characters quite deeply, even though the character wasn't there pouring their heart out.' The other three clearly do what Kelly says: they search for motivations, seek out the logic of actions, generate rounded characters out of the clues and hints the film provides. This is their purposive relationship to the film. Having made the strategic decision that the film meets their general ideals, it is *worth* the imaginative investment to complete and round out the characters.

The signs of this process of 'reading for depth' are in the recurrent use of the idea of 'underneath'. Nicola, looking at Catherine, finds her presented as strong, but 'underneath' she does not think she is. Mary, also talking of Catherine, finds her hard to respond to while she is reading her as a 'hard, cold bitch'. But once she attains 'more of a depth', she becomes more interesting. Lindsey relates strongly to Holly Hunter's character because 'you could imagine her … doing normal things'. All four of them, then, *fill in* the characters. From fragmentary evidence, at best, they *complete* their relationships and motivations.

What is interesting is that this seems to them the *natural thing to do*, not an artificial construct. Lindsey, again, voiced this most clearly when contrasting herself with her boyfriend: she had 'liked it for what it was', as if the film was, for her, in some sense self-evident.

5. *Implicit modelling of society*: all four operate at various points with a model of our society which asserts that *variety* and *difference* are valuable. This shows in various ways. First, in their criticisms of the critics of the film, and of the British Board of Film Classification. Lindsey, for instance, imputes to the 'majority of people' that they didn't find *Crash* as shocking as the censors claimed, or even tried to create by 'hyping'. Her model of a general *tolerance*, if only people were not pressured by

things like 'hype' enables this move. It is interesting also that in an interview which does not contain much evidence of claims to membership of imagined communities, among the few occasions they do, it is to associate themselves with a general claim to greater intelligence than the critics allow: the 'our' in 'they are insulting our intelligence' bespeaks a community very like that which Mary associates with when she speaks of the 'average person' who really does not need the 'protection' they force upon us.

6. *Testing oneself*: an important strand running through the interviews is their *welcoming of the difficult demands that Crash makes on them*. This occurs in a number of ways, again. When Nicola defends the showing of the car-wash scene, even though it made her 'uncomfortable', she is skirting this kind of response. It is there also in Mary's recognition of her ambivalent response to the sex scenes: it was slightly unnatural in that it was 'forcing me to think about things in a very different way' and 'forcing me to question a lot of what I take for granted'. *Crash* was taking them to limits where they had to *watch their own reactions* as much as watch the film. This indeed constitutes the ground-breaking nature of the film for Mary, that the film deals in 'perverse sexual themes' and 'we're going to make you think about this'. Nicola too noted this address in *Crash* to the 'perverse' and, like Mary, she is aware that it operates by asking us to *question* the grounds for the distinction between the normal and the perverse, although she does not so directly address the question to herself.

Yet this is not the only way in which they experience *Crash* as testing themselves. Kelly went in to the screening of the film with the clear objective of watching her own reactions: to see 'how auto-eroticism affected me'. This is a sign of a broader self-watching which appears to constitute itself as part of the positive way of watching this film. The opposite of 'entertainment' and 'escapism', *Crash* is interesting to these four women *because* it makes them think, and because that thinking is of a kind that challenges assumptions, breaks boundaries, and explores the almost-unspeakable. This, in fact, is a higher-order, supervenient move, since it binds together several of the first-order moves, as indeed does the next.

7. *Filmic meaning as a process, rather than an 'object'*: in much recent film theorising, the 'meaning' of a film is something to be found by analysis of the text, and then weighed for its possible impact on audiences. It is a 'message', in effect, a set of themes and ideologies constituted within the film, and then delivered with more or less effect to the minds (conscious and unconscious) of the audience. This is not how *Crash* is experienced by these four women. Mary constitutes a test-case. As a journalist, she is well used to the way of talking about films which searches for their meaning, or message. Asked, she can do this with ease. But when pursuing her *personal* response to the film, the picture shifts: 'I think what came across to me as what he was really trying to do was show what you might take as perverse or an unusual sexual fantasy, or a group of people with this fantasy, which is something that I've never actually thought about before'. She arrives at *this* judgement through the *process of taking part in viewing the film*, rather than via an abstraction. The meaning of the film, in other words resides in her relationship with it and its characters.

Kelly describes a different version of the same thing when she says, *pace* her initial dislike of Vaughan, that 'I got very sucked in with the film and I felt different about Vaughan as I followed it along'. It was *through* this relationship and others that she experienced the film and felt its meaning to her. That meaning *was* its test of her, its taking her to the limits of her current beliefs. It is this which makes so interesting the 'realism' and 'believability' that they all attribute to the film. For it cannot be a literal realism, since all admit that they have not had such thoughts or experiences before. The believability therefore must lie in their conviction and investment in the *logic* of the film. It 'makes sense' to them, as they currently are. Its test of them is *right*, and the film in achieving this is thus 'complete'.

Being 'Positive' about Crash: a hypothesis

Among the reasons we chose to study this interview in detail, was because many of the complaints about *Crash* assumed that this film, if it appealed to anyone, would appeal to men – it was 'pornography', it was 'violent', and so on. To be able to observe the ways in which four women achieve positivity about the film tells us much; and this way of putting it is right: the four of them *want* to be positive, although two of them (Nicola and Mary) begin with reservations – and even to some extent retain them. Mary at the end still has some personal reactions she cannot rid herself of, but that no longer stops her acknowledging qualities in the film which, in an ideal world, she would delight in. The social process of talking about the film among themselves produces an account of what would be involved in a virtually unreservedly positive response.

With more or less comfort and confidence, all four see themselves as entering into the same relationship with *Crash*, a relationship which they agree is a challenging one. The challenge is to dare to cross a boundary, to consider what sexuality might be like if something different was tried. To do that, of course, they have to be ready to operate with the category 'sexuality'. Whether or not they have this word, its meaning is that sex is more than carnal relations between two people. 'Sexuality' conceives of sex as a source of potential for pleasures, for being a kind of person, for viewing yourself and others in perhaps new and different ways. It may even mark out something definitive about what a human being is, and can become. Because of this, for these four, *Crash* doesn't merely challenge their views of other people, it also challenges their view of themselves. The film operates as a mirror to self, provoking questions precisely by being awkward, disturbing, not easy to relate to. The characters are clearly *out there* in the film, but the act of making sense of their behaviour and motivation is always simultaneously an act of self-examination.

To enjoy *Crash*, then, there are a set of important conditions that a person has to be willing and able to fulfil. S/he must be:
• willing and able to engage with a non-generic film which withholds explicit explanation of the motivation of its main characters. Therefore, it requires of its audience instead that they supply that motivation *as part of the process of viewing*. For example, the sex scenes for Positive responses will be seen as *narratively necessary*, revealing much about the state and motives of the characters;
• willing and able to relate to the film in two simultaneous ways: *narratively* (having a 'way in' via caring about one or more of the particular characters, or being interested in the situation they are in); and *philosophically* (perceiving that the characters are involved in an exploration of an *idea*, pursuing it to its logical conclusion);
• willing and able to distinguish *showing* from *saying*: a minimal version of this is to refuse the step from 'it shows bizarre sex' to 'it is recommending bizarre sex'; a broader

version entails seeing the film as an investigation at the level of representation of an idea that is probably impossible at the literal level;

• willing and able to perceive that the characters are not *given to us* in depth, but that nonetheless they *have* a depth. Interpretative effort is put into seeing *behind* the faces shown on screen;

• willing and able to entertain the idea that knowing about these different, 'perverse' sexual desires, and acknowledging their human/philosophical interest and significance, is separable from sharing those desires;

• willing and able to perceive the sexual relations within the film as (minimally) *equal,* or (more broadly) as *empowering* to the main characters, including the women. For this to be necessary, a positive viewer has to have an operative category of 'sexuality' as something more than just sex as a set of activities – it must be conceived as a human potential;

• willing and able to manage a critical self-awareness of one's own responses to *Crash*. To Positive viewers, to call the film 'disturbing' was a mark of its achievement, for its very purpose for them was to test their boundaries of self-awareness.

The presence of those two terms 'willing' and 'able' is not accidental. In Chapter 8 we show that some of our audience could only meet one condition without the other. This leads to some striking *bargaining* between viewers and film, as they recognise the possibility of a fully positive response to *Crash* but either are not willing to meet its demands on them, or realise that they lack certain resources to do so.

We are not arguing in any manner that to fulfil them is morally virtuous, or a sign of superior achievement. But it is a *difference*, and to be able to identify what is required for positivity about *Crash* enables us to answer some other questions: What is the relationship between how the film, and its audience, was characterised by its critics, and how the film is understood and used by actual Positive audiences? What is the relationship between the revealed character of positive audiences' relations with the film, and the languages used by commentaries that sought to defend *Crash*, in this and other countries? What do these reveal about the state of filmic culture in Britain?

In the next chapter we compare this interview with four women with an equivalent one with four men – equally enthusiastic about *Crash*, but on grounds that are subtly different. The similarities and differences between them is a useful test of the model we have elaborated here.

6   Four Men's Positive Responses to *Crash*

Understanding positive responses to *Crash* is particularly important. Not because these responses are right, or superior, but for two reasons. First, they test the 'figure' of the audience which was widely propagated by the film's critics. Attacks on *Crash* repeatedly invoked a picture of a weak, corruptible viewer. This 'person', if not already damaged beyond rescue, might be tempted into harmful ways through becoming involved with the film. This is not new. The image of a vulnerable, even childlike audience has a long history, and is to be found in more than a hundred years of moral campaigns.[1] Our research shows that the critics were wildly and outrageously wrong. Second, it appears that there is anyway a distinctive relationship between positive and negative responses. We aim to show that those who disliked *Crash* were refusing something about it which its enthusiasts were able to 'name'. If this is right, the best way to learn about the Refusers may be via an understanding of the Enthusiasts. With this in mind, it becomes doubly important to underpin the hypothesis we offered at the end of the previous chapter. The interview we examine here was with four men, all of whom categorised themselves as Like/Approve. We will show that the enthusiasm displayed by our four women, whom we analysed in the last chapter, is very largely replicated by Michael, Mike, Philip and Tim whom we interviewed as one group [Interview 24].

Profiles

From their prior questionnaires we had learnt the following things: Trainee teacher Michael's motives for wanting to see the film were twofold: to compare it with Cronenberg's other movies, and to 'see what the fuss is all about'. An irregular cinema-goer (one to three times a month) but a more regular video viewer (four to six times a month), his keyword for his initial response was *hypnotised*. In the questionnaire he expanded on this to say that *Crash* 'explores the deepest, unspoken human desires', and adds that this is done in a 'non-judgemental' way, giving the film a 'matter-of-factness', adding:

> It was not as I expected. Newspapers gave me the impression that there was more to it in terms of being offensive to viewers/the disabled. Compared to other

so-called violent and/or sex films there was no good or bad, I guess, and that is where the controversy lies.

Mike, a computer software engineer, is a regular cinema-goer (four to six times a month) and a less regular video-viewer (one to three times a month). He wanted to see *Crash*, in his case for a second time, because: 'I was involved in a very serious road accident. In that "crash" my life partner died. I have become interested in the subject. I find the idea of sexual motives astounding. I also have some interest in media (film) studies.' Mike adds his personal conviction against censorship, that we should have the right to choose to see or not to see the film – a view he states in both question-naires. His keyword was *excited*, which he elaborated as follows: '*Crash* is shocking. It is both horrifying and exciting. Well worth seeing.' Several times in his answers he reiterates his 'personal connection' to the themes of the research: 'I was very affected by the debate the first time round. I just *had* to come if you would have me!' There is an interesting mix in him between the strictly personal (his crash, and loss), general leisure pursuits (the importance of cinema to him) and broadly political motives (a dislike and distrust of censorship).

Tim is only an occasional cinema-goer and even more rarely a video-viewer. A self-employed artist, which includes working in video, his work has included addressing issues of violence and sex in and through art and the media. He believes that *Crash* deals with these. In his post-film questionnaire, he wrote that he wanted to see the film 'to inform my work as an artist'. Tim is less aware of the nature of the controversy than the others, saying simply that he had 'heard a bit of "hype" but that is all'. Tim's keywords are *appreciated and related to it*, elaborating this with the notes: 'Good, bizarre sex + cars. Arousing. Fantasy – cars and their sexuality, power perverse.' He makes a point of saying that the film reminded him of 'hundreds' of other things, ranging from seeing people fascinated by their wounds, to fantasising with partners, and the general fascination people display towards crashes. He introduces a distinction which is important to him: answering our question if it was as he had expected, he says it was 'more graphic sexually than I had expected. But I did not dislike that, it was not sexy but it was arousing'. This qualified enjoyment is later explained in this way: 'I like the ideas dealt with in the film and I am very pleased I saw it. I'm not sure it is a good film, good script, *et cetera*'.

Philip, unemployed when we interviewed him, is an admirer of both Ballard and Cronenberg, although not a frequent cinema-goer or video-viewer. This had been his second viewing of *Crash* – and this second time had brought the advantage of seeing it 'without the aura of hype surrounding it'. His motivation for seeing the film was strongly connected with his feelings about censorship: 'My strong feelings refer more to the utterly ludicrous decision to ban the film – especially the rubbish spouted by *Daily Mail* do-gooders and politicians who *hadn't seen the film* [his emphasis] – this tended to mar the viewing because I kept expecting something really bad to happen to justify the fuss'. His keywords were *enjoyed/amused*. He expands on this by saying that 'I like weird films when well made', closely followed by the statement that 'It made me quite sure that I didn't want to have an accident!'

Several points arise from their prior accounts. Two of them talk of 'hype' around the film in a way which conflates publicity for the film with the controversy around it. This suggests that their general experience is that publicity regimes and press coverage become indistinguishable, and both contribute to a pressure of expectations around a film. It also seems that this pressure operates for these four irrespective of their knowledge of Cronenberg. If 'hype' has it that the film is violent, for example, this is hard to refuse, especially on a first viewing. Only Tim, who had least knowledge of either publicity or controversy, reversed this equation, finding the film more graphic than he had expected.

The interview was conducted by Ramaswami Harindranath. It was long, amounting to 18,400 transcribed words.

Prior Orientations

Orientations to film generally: Michael declares himself omnivorous:

> I think I watch almost anything except the Spice Girls movie. Umm, I like a wide range of movies in terms of, I can watch anything from a detective story to anything. Umm, I would like something preferably, umm … with a bit of, umm … a thriller with some violence. Like, like *Seven*, films like that I enjoy very much. I like love stories like anybody else. I like the sort of film noir type films. And I, I watch a lot a lot of films. I went to the films this week actually, once or twice, once. Saw *As Good As It Gets*.

His motives are partly because he is hoping to teach in the field of film, but as much to do with a combination of personal and political reasons. And that affects *how* films should be watched. So, special effects movies like *Titanic* must be seen at a cinema with a 'huge screen' – these are films to be experienced. But in other cases far more important is to go to form an opinion about it: 'Sometimes I go and see a film because it's had bad reviews, and I want to go and form my own opinion'. So, within his very wide range there exist a range of motives to see, and – correspondingly – a range of ways of attending to the films he sees.

Less overtly, Michael does reveal a significant category-preference. He came to our screening with a friend who 'very much likes films like *Wings of a Dove* [1997], you know, sort of arty-farty sort of films'. For Michael that was associated with a prediction that his friend wouldn't like *Crash* 'because I thought he was going to say, oh the violence, the, you know, the sexual thing, which were the bits that I found really interesting…' (to his surprise, his friend enjoyed *Crash* greatly). This kind of distinction indicates a preference for *challenging* films as against what he calls 'feel-good'.

Michael says two rather contrary things. Responding to the interviewer's question about what he knew before he came, he says: 'I'd really heard about it, well, I know about the book, J G Ballard's book so, umm, I was aware of it before it was a film. Umm yeah, I saw all the fuss in the papers about it, and so, I was, you know, I knew what I was coming to see'. This claim to knowing in advance is then somewhat at odds with a subsequent statement.

> And I think the reviews did not sort of live up to the film because, umm, I was expecting basically more violence, more sex, more everything, yeah? The way it was described I was like, thinking yes, you know, you're gonna walk out feeling extremely disturbed. And I just thought, you know, you know, what's the fuss

about? I mean I can see some points there about where there could be, you know, sort of controversy.

In fact the formal opposition between these – 'knowing in advance' and 'having been given a wrong sense of the film' – dissolves if we say that for Michael the important thing is that he had the information necessary to enable him to go in order to form his own opinion. With a film like *Crash*, the point is to go in order to form a judgement – and for that, it is important to be primed adequately.

Michael has an overarching political response to the question of censorship: who is doing it on behalf of whom?

> The controversy highlights a sort of nanny-type protecting, you know, anything that might offend or degrade or whatever, I'm thinking, if it doesn't offend me it, I think the problem is who are you talking for and who are you talking to, if you see what I mean. These people sitting in their little offices, with their little videos, you know with their videos, and telling me what's going to corrupt me, if you see what I mean.

There is a politics in here. To the question 'are there any films that should be banned', Michael's first response is the jokey one 'Margaret Thatcher's Life Story?' – a sense that those who live by the sword of censorship should die by it. He follows this with an outright condemnation of the BBFC:

> James Ferman should be shot. Anyway umm, I think the problem is umm, Britain sees themselves, you know, censorship is sort of BBFC as protecting all these people. But then the people don't have a voice, if you see what I mean. We can't say if we want to be protected or not, I don't have an option any more. It's like with pornography, you know, who are you to tell me, so basically I see that as being quite intrusive. Also because of the European umm laws, now you can move from the country, you can move all around in Europe or whatever you want, but you come into England, you're arrested. So I just, who are you protecting? Not me.

This categoric opposition between 'us', 'the people', and those with power spills over for him into issues of immigration controls by which he, as a black man, feels threatened. They are of a piece, for him.

Mike sees a lot of films, helped by the fact that he lives above a video shop. That, plus television, has become his predominant way of seeing films. But this is second best, for him, to seeing them in their proper environment: 'I don't do this thing of hiring videos for viewing because if I want to watch a film I go out and watch one'. This is important for his main motive for liking films and cinema.

> Television really is a different medium, I think. I'd like to go and see films, I really like to be to be taken away, taken to a different place for a film, and the problem with watching a film on the video is it's kind of like, oh just stop it here, you know, make a cup of tea or whatever. And it's, you're still in your own home environment. It's a tiny little screen, compared. I mean my favourite cinema in

Bristol is Cineworld. [...] That is, that is, not because of the environment of the cinema, because once you're in there and the film is on, the screen's big, the sound's good, the seat's comfortable, you're taken away.

He tells of seeing *Titanic* (1997) and staying for all the credits so that the cleaner had to wait. As they finally left she asked if they'd enjoyed it: 'We went yeah, yeah, it was a great film and they went "Ooh that's lovely because normally the men say it's too long"'. He thus marks himself off as a non-standard male viewer.

Viewing a film properly is important to Mike. Talking about the 'brilliant' *Trainspotting*, Mike recalled that after he'd seen it, he felt that the people who reviewed and raised a controversy over it 'had sort of left half-way through or before half-way'. This depends upon a belief that, if experienced, the *wholeness* of a film must surely communicate to viewers. This recurs when he says, later on, that 'I watch to the end, because otherwise I'm not qualified to comment and tell other people not to go and see it'.

Mike says little about his prior expectations of *Crash*, except that he 'expected it to be unpredictable'. This may be important in itself, in light of what he subsequently says about how he prepared to see the film first time round:

For me there's a lot in the film that's very personal, because I was involved in a serious road accident in which my partner died. And so when I first went to see the film, part of my reason for going to see the film was kind of a therapy. Like, this is something which somebody who's been through the experience that I've been through shouldn't do, but I'm gonna do it, to see how it affects me. Umm, and it actually didn't affect me as much as I thought it would.

To 'experience' the film, and to have the chance that it might prove therapeutic, he had to go relatively unprepared, to find out what it might offer.

Mike's main reaction to the controversy was the consciously perverse one, that if someone wanted to stop him from seeing *Crash* then that was a good enough reason to see it. There is a sense in here of his distrust of the people who would do this ('the whole controversy thing, hearing people saying those kind of things on the radio and reading what they were writing, that sort of thing made me determined that even if I was not allowed to see it I was gonna see it'). This is sufficiently strong that he feels the need to establish his differentiation from them, in advance of admitting to not liking something in *Crash*. Referring to his own reaction to the wound-sex scene, he prefaces stating his unease at the scene with a rejection of any notion of censoring it. It would offend against his rule of the *wholeness* of a film. As he himself said at the point where the others were asserting the necessity of seeing a film right through to the end, if you are to judge it: 'You also have to be allowed to watch all the bits in the middle.'

Philip is constrained by being unemployed, so cannot see all the films he would wish to, and often has to go at times when the seats are cheaper. He likes to watch 'a very wide range of films', everything from old Laurel and Hardy, and black and white films, to what he calls 'more left-field films'. He has a video player, and can watch films on that, but is very aware that this is second best. Not so much for the social aspect, though that is nice, but 'I prefer to go to the cinema to see a film, definitely'.

Philip's is a less articulated answer than any of the others. He repeats what he said in his questionnaires, that his primary expectations were not formed in relation to the *film*, but in relation to the issue of censorship. The curious thing is how even in opposition to censorship he readied himself to receive it in the very terms that the censorious posed to *Crash*.

> And also you know that, if you're going into something the first time and it's meant to be really shocking, and at the end of it, like you just said Michael yeah, it wasn't actually, I wasn't shocked, it wasn't so full of, you know, perverted sex and mayhem, so that when you go the second time you're not actually waiting for something, really bad things to happen.

Even for someone as opposed to censorship as Philip, the public assault on *Crash* still had the power to predetermine his expectations of what it might be like. Only at second viewing did he (partly) escape this predetermination.

Philip sees censorship as essentially an irrational process, based on exaggeration and fuss, and the foolishness if not villainy of the main critics who played with the idea that people might go out and 'copy' the film. Censorship is bad *tout court* except where (he follows Mike's lead in this) something stops being a 'film', and becomes a staged enactment. If it is a 'snuff movie', really happening and *known to be so*, that is different. The qualification is important, and is a sign of their will to limit even this condition – they cite the example of *Mad Max*, where a stunt rider was killed enacting a scene, but his part was still left in. That was right, however sad the death.

But Philip differs from Michael on classification, allowing that it is probably a 'good idea' – providing its purpose is that 'people should know that, yeah, there's lots of sex in it because you might just not want to see sex, so, perhaps you should know that'. This makes 'knowledge' a much more neutral thing than Michael would allow.

Tim watches a 'vast range' of films, within which he draws a distinction between 'tacky Hollywood films' on the one hand, and *Wings of a Dove* on the other. He does not in fact have much to say on this issue, except that films are becoming now more important to him because of his work as an artist. But this is said in passing, and not developed at all at this point. He does however later on reveal one facet of his attitude to films, which amounts to almost a sense of their and his 'deserts'. In the course of a discussion about why people who disliked *Crash* had not walked out, he interjected:

> I think I've once walked out of a film just because it was so bloody boring and I just couldn't be bothered but even if a film's really boring, I would generally sit through it because, you know, you paid your money and also to give it a chance and see if something happens.

The idea of 'giving it its chance' as well as not wasting your money signals a disinclination to give up at the first difficulty with a film. Tim expresses an unpopular view in the interview. While the others are in various ways criticising the censorship system, including attacking the film makers for compromising on their films for the sake of getting particular classifications, Tim asserts the issue of children:

> The important thing is to say that I do think, you know, that in people's formative years or whatever they shouldn't be watching some stuff. [Two voices ask why] Because I think it's unsuitable for young, young people. [...] Because I

think, because I think you need to go slowly, people need to slowly become aware of things, it's a gradual process. And if you introduce something to somebody, something, too much.

In the interview, Tim's comments led to an interesting exchange, revealing something of the way views get developed and redefined in such a context. Tim is aware that he has said something risky. Michael's response is to turn the issue of 'protection' in another direction, associating it with political/information censorship. The debate which follows is significant in focusing on a topic which is quite important to their whole approach to *Crash* – the issue of 'experience':

MI If children are aware of certain things, they know when they're being exploited and abused. So censorship means you have power of information that you're not giving people. By censoring information you're censoring my decision to decide, what is good or what is bad for me. [...] Because it means control of information and discourse. And that would mean that, withholding information I might need to make an informed decision. And if you, you know, you can't make an informed decision if you don't have all the facts. Children can't make an informed decision about sex because we don't tell them about it. England has got the, well, Britain has got the highest level of teenage pregnancy. I mean I used to teach in a school and sex education was absolutely laughable. And kids still think that they're doing something, they're gonna get pregnant. And I'm thinking...
T I agree with what you're saying but, like, we're saying this is a thinking person's film, you were saying earlier, whatever. And I think that when you see this film you're taking it on, you're understanding where it all fits in and you're placing it in...
MI A 12-year-old understands something at a particular level.
T At a particular level and I just don't know that...
MI It's like I did sociology when I was 16, and I didn't understand it till I was 22. If you see what I mean.
Mk It's the same as the issue that we were talking about earlier round death. If you, if you're protected from it and you're not exposed to it, then when it happens you're not able to deal with it. Whereas it you live in a country where it happens around you all the time, you just deal with it as matter of life, it's life.
MI It's like sexual abuse. By censoring information on sexual abuse, children don't know that they're being sexually abused you see what I mean, they think it's natural it's normal. It's like the film *Lolita*, I want to see it because I want to see how that particular type of, they say paedophilia I don't know, what the film is about, but I want to see how they deal with it. If you see what I mean. And by allowing people to, to watch this, you can make informed decisions, and say OK fine, this is what it's about, or this is an interpretation of what it's about.

For Michael and Mike, 'experience' is *per se* a good thing, since (a) if something is ahead of where you currently are, it will wash over, while (b) denial of 'experience' debars making informed decisions. What is clear is that Michael and Mike see the outcomes of a film differently than Tim, who remains cautious lest there be 'effects' rather than 'experience'. This seems to connect with their general approach to *Crash*, and what they wanted and got out of it.

Orientation to our research

All four were at ease with the general idea of taking part in the project, but two of them found it still imposed a strain on them. Michael was known to us anyway, and had taken part in the previous *Judge Dredd* research. Mike had personal reasons to want to take part, as we have seen, and his way of telling the story of his crash, and how he revisited the site of it, in the rebuilt car suggests that taking part in the research may well itself have been a component of the 'therapy' he sought in seeing the film, not once but twice. Tim however had found a problem in the screening, a problem set off by his intense awareness of being there for the sake of the project:

> I mean, because that was kind of weird as well. Coming into the cinema and knowing that everybody was, you know, it's not just going to see a film, you know, you come in here and you know that everybody is here because we are all, you know, doing the project. And that's partly why I wanted to do it as much as anything. I'm interested in the work, you know, in the whole idea of censorship.

The purpose of being there overrode the weirdness, and made it still worthwhile for Tim. Philip followed this with a comment on the problems of completing the questionnaire. His problem was having to do it straight after the screening. The process of coming to terms with a film, for him, was a lengthy one, and he had not had that opportunity: 'I always find that when you're, you know, couple of hours later in the pub with a friend or when you're home later on it's like they start going, Oh yeah, then there was that bit, and you start talking about the film, and, you know, when there's a distance from it. Straight after, I found it quite hard to think.' In fact all four agreed on the fact that making sense is a *process over time*, including for Mike that it changes and develops from first to second viewing. This made their responses to our questionnaire difficult for them.

Tim developed this. He hadn't been sure at first if it was a good film, though he was glad he had seen it: 'Now I see it's a good film but I, sort of when I left, I wasn't sure, I mean I knew I really liked it and it was really good to see'. Again this stresses a developmental account of making sense and judgements about the film. Tim turns his liking of the film into a basis for assessing its quality, but wasn't confident to do it at first.

How did they respond to the film during/after seeing?

... experiencing the film cinematically, narratively, and in relation to characters, and their own reactions to these:

The remarkable thing about these men's responses to cinematic features is their virtual absence from the discussion. Despite two of them claiming an affiliation with film/media studies, and despite all of them claiming enjoyment of a wide range of kinds of film, talk about features such as sound, camerawork, narrative organisation, editing, *et cetera* is just not there. This is not a failure, we would argue – it is because these cinematic techniques are for them wholly absorbed within the meaning-making potential of the film. This shows up where they do each have something to say, about the characters. What they each do, in slightly different ways, is to account for the characters in terms of symbolic potentials. Michael, responding to a debate started by Philip and Tim, posited his relation to the characters thus:

> I didn't see them as flawed, I just saw them as people exploring their desires and their sexualities. I mean, open relationships happen and, you know what I mean, I wasn't into that, but I know people who are in open relationships, number one, and it's sort of telling your partner what you do and then having, being turned on by it. And also the fluidity of their sexuality that, that in terms of, you know, man, woman or whatever, if you see what I mean. And that's been something weird not to do. Number one, you're in a monogamous relation-ship therefore you see it like that, and every single film we get, you know, if you're bad you're dead, if you're promiscuous you're dead, and I found these characters quite refreshing in terms of, you know [a cough conceals a couple of words], and we, you know, how many husbands could turn around and say to their wives, look by the way I fancy having it off with a bloke, I mean I think she'll probably hit him with a frying pan. I, I, so I found that quite refreshing.

The principle behind this interest is not, as Michael makes clear, himself doing or wanting to do these things. It is realising that this is a real human choice which some people make, and that the exploration of this in a film constitutes an investigation of the logic of these choices. Part of the relevance for him is precisely that it is *not* ordinary – that is what makes it 'refreshing'.

Michael has a productively troubled relationship with Catherine, in that he is made uneasy by the car-wash scene but in a way that forces him to *think beyond*:

> And I think the wife was quite interesting, I kept thinking, you know, she's being pushed too far, like the scene in the car. I don't think she was actually enjoying it, I just kept thinking she was being used. But then I think you sort of, you know, all those fantasies we have of sort of forcing somebody, or, you know...

From the platform of this observation he makes a general philosophical statement about how he feels the film gives him something important:

> I think we police ourselves too much and that's what I like about that film, they weren't policing themselves, I mean, we feel guilty for what we think, and you know, they did a really good social... you know, socialisation job in our heads, you think something and you think oh my god, I shouldn't feel that way, I shouldn't think that, if you see what I mean. It's like watching an Almodovar rape scene in that film, and you think, God, this rape is interesting. Not that, you know, and you feel guilty about it. And I felt that about the characters, they just did it because, because. There was no reason for doing, just because I, they felt like it. And that's what I found interesting.

This is much more complicated than the appeal of watching the forbidden – it is a piece of conscious anti-socialisation, a forceful reconsideration of what has been conditioned out of us. Indeed what enabled this to be particularly powerful for Michael was its 'matter of factness' – an expression he uses twice. In the second case he uses it explicitly to express something of importance for his sense of the narrative process of the film.

> Also the scene where the two men have sex, I think was quite interesting. You know, in terms of, nothing is static, therefore these two men just happen to be there, just happen to want to have sex and it was quite interesting that they just, you know, get on with it and, it was again, matter of fact.

The implications of this are that the sex between the two men is not prefigured, nor pre-motivated. Simply, come the situation, they decide to have sex. It is easy to see how, from other positions, this unprefigured, unexplained action would seem just like an inexplicable intrusion into the narrative. For Michael here, that would be the opposite of the truth – the very unremarkable facticity of the sex *is* its meaning. The characters are revealing precisely because they don't exhibit standard filmic motivational patterns.

Mike does not speak about any individual character but about the *idea* of such characters:

> These characters to me were concentrations of, I mean in a film you, you see those aspects of the characters that are portrayed, to tell the story, you don't see the entire character, I mean there's some character-building but you don't see the entire character, you see those aspects of that, that person, that fictional person. Umm, and these, these characters were kind of distilled, they were kind of concentrated, umm, bits of what's in all of us. And, and most people go around living perfectly quote normal lives, and have all these things in the back, I mean, like, you were talking about open relationships and things, umm, people do and, and they don't talk about it, with their work colleagues or people they meet on the street. They were in the company of people who felt the same way about it. I mean, I think he was, he was drawn into that, and, although he was doing a lot of other stuff, you know, his character was one that was open.

The striking thing here is the co-present acknowledgement that characters such as this are not fully developed, yet they are importantly 'open'. This is what enables them to have such a relationship with *our* lives. In a film, the limits posed by day-to-day life can be transcended; fictional characters can be set in situations and company that allow the development of those things which we ordinarily spend our lives denying. Philip states his relations to the central characters thus:

> I don't think I quite liked them. I didn't dislike them, umm, the main two characters, Ballard and his wife. But I didn't want to, I certainly didn't relate to them in the way it sounds where you want to be that person or something. Because they seem to have strange lives, I don't know if 'shallow' is the word or not but, you know, they're all very liberated, they're both quite happy to go and screw other people and come back and tell each other about it, have some more sex

while they talk about it, and then the whole crash thing happens but ... I didn't really relate to them and they were sort of, like, weird yuppies or something you know, I don't know where they were placed, it was not really me.

Tim connected with the central characters precisely because they had problems:

That was really nice that they were, I mean they were all really flawed, you know, completely. And you just don't, in other films you just don't get that, and that's why I liked them. [...] It's a funny thing, like you, I mean you say you found it disturbing or, particularly shocking, but I didn't find it.

The character that for him did this more than any other was Vaughan:

I think it's vitally important in your life or whatever, and that they did in the film is that you explore stuff. I think exploring is what life's all about. Whether that's going off somewhere or whether that's, you know, delving into the darker bits of you, or, and, and that's, and I wrote that I thought umm, the main fellow, not the one who had the accident, the big guy, Vaughan. Umm, I sort of said he was an artist. Umm, and he was exploring things, you know he was setting up, I thought he was being an artist, he was setting up these situations, and in my work as an artist I'm trying to explore things that I don't know about whether they're different worlds or different things.

This open-ended call to 'explore stuff', even 'delving into the darker bits of you' is for Tim a part of what it is to be fully human.

... what extra-diegetic constructs are formed:

Again, the remarkable thing is that, with a few small exceptions, none of them seem to operate at all either with a concept of the 'author' of the film, or with any concept of the 'intended audience' other than as themselves. Three of the four professed knowledge and liking for Cronenberg via his other films, but there is no will here to discuss *Crash* as the 'latest' in Cronenberg's *oeuvre*, or to discuss the relationship of book and film, although at least one of them mentions that he has read the book. It seems that the film is its own sufficient explanation.

There are some small exceptions to this, which arise at points of minor uncertainty. In the course of a debate about the homosexual sex scenes, which all four regarded as one of the few disappointing elements in the film, Mike interjects a possible explanation in terms of external pressures on the makers.

Mk Also the scene where the two men have sex I think was quite interesting. You know, in terms of, nothing is static, therefore these two men just happen to be there just happen to want to have sex and it was quite interesting that they just, you know get on with it and, it was again, matter of fact.

T Yeah, but I found that, I found that, I don't know whether this was partly, not censorship thing, I said both of the non-heterosexual sexual things were, both of them were far less graphic erotic, than anything.

Mk Because they couldn't be...

Ml The lesbian scene was much longer, I thought that was sort of voyeuristic in terms of male viewers, you know, look at these two women and that's sort of gay, but with the two men it was like [snaps his fingers].

Mk It could have been because, because he didn't want to make it a homo-erotic film. But I don't think it was, I think it was because, given that it's umm, going to cause a lot of controversy anyway, if they had shown the gay sex in that film as explicitly as they showed the straight sex...

Ml It would have been cut [Laughs].

This passing speculation takes Mike and Michael for a moment external to the film itself, to the 'he' who faced possible censorship if the lesbian scene had been as explicit as they felt was required. But having visited that possibility, their attention returns to what holds them: the film itself and its internal logic. This does recur a little more forcefully when Mike discusses his dislike of the wound-sex scene.

> We were kind of not given the idea that she is getting any stimulation from it, it's kind of like, it's as if to me that scene is not saying, umm, it's not saying what we've been talking about, that it's, that scars are erotic or that it's erotic to, to, that new healed skin or whatever. It's almost saying, it's almost saying to me, I think it was kind of trying to say to me, umm, he wanted to show a sexual act that he couldn't show. He wanted to show her, her clitoris being stimulated but he couldn't, so he showed her scar being stimulated.

It is again interesting that this occurs as a point of *dissatisfaction*. To Mike's unease, the film does not quite fulfil its own logic and requirements, so he turns for an explanation to a hypothesised maker. The film *should* have been operating on a principle of the women getting and seeking pleasure ('getting stimulation from it') but does not – or at least, Mike can't conceive of scars being stimulating. What is interesting is that Michael sees this implication behind Mike's assertion here, and queries it ('I think he was trying to show scars can be stimulating'), which, if true, would bring 'him' back in tune with the self-sufficiency of the film – to which again the discussion then returns.

How do the four feel about audiences who reacted differently? The interview contained an extensive discussion of their feelings about this. When the question was posed to them, Michael led the way by saying that it would have been interesting to have an opportunity to debate with such people, 'and I think it would be nice for them to try and persuade me and for me to try and persuade them'. To which Mike responds with a comment that normally you do get such opportunities, since you will often go with people who take a different approach. The two of them then discuss the difference between people who dislike the film having seen it, and those who judge without having seen the film – something which is anathema to them all.

But Tim then turns the conversation in another direction. Using the example of *Basic Instinct*, he turns objections to films into a positive sign:

> I remember having a chat with the tutor when I was at college when *Basic Instinct* had just come out, and it put, a lot of the lesbian community or whatever were outraged because it portrayed a lesbian as a, you know, a murderer.

Umm, and we were just sort of chatting and, you know, basically said, you know the day when someone who's gay can be portrayed as a murderer is a good thing, you know, not a bad thing you know, it means that there isn't a, you know, if you can't do that then there's something wrong.

MI There are two implications there. If you don't get a particular portrayal and then all of a sudden you get a negative portrayal it does have implications, with disability. You don't get many disabled people on screen, some people doing anything in society, and all of a sudden you have one where there, where there is that particular kind of disability if you see what I mean. It's like, it's like you don't portray black people now when you portray them they're criminals there is an implication there. And I can see the controversy around *Crash* in that particular way that that, you know, we don't, apart from Ironside in his wheelchair, I can't think of disabled people on television.

P Right, no, it's played down, isn't it?

MI Do you see what I mean? And then all of a sudden you get them but we get the sort of heightened.

T I didn't see any of those people when I watched that film as being disabled.

Mk People who are disabled are very sensitive about their disability, and, I, it tends to take me a little while to get in tune with what they're talking about.

P I don't think, I think we're talking about people who are, I think we're getting slightly maybe off the subject, we're talking about people who are disabled and people who are abled.

Tim's move is to make the opening up of possibilities on screen into a criterion of positivity, even if it generates some critical attacks. Michael concurs and reaches for the underlying criterion here: absence from the screen implies a lack of exploration of the possibilities for such people, but there are dangers attached to the first, or rare, exemplifications on screen. Disability then provides the test case in *Crash*, given the relative absence of disabled people in film and TV. But Tim resists the idea that the injured people shown in *Crash* are in fact disabled, in a full sense. But they begin to feel uneasy about speaking *about* and perhaps *for* the disabled – this is a sensitive subject, on which it is not easy to speak. Their solution is to stop the debate, by judging it to be 'getting off the subject'. When asked directly for whom they feel the film was made, a consensus quickly emerges. Tim first remarks that he simply doesn't know how women respond to *Crash* – he hasn't talked to any about it, and 'it's not actually something I've thought about at all'. Philip then offers an explanation whose implication is that likers of *Crash* have constituted themselves as a special group, a 'cult'.

P Thing is, you can't make things a cult thing, things have to become cult, don't they? The ones that tried to be made into ones failed miserably. But it's obviously got an immediate appeal to someone who likes J G Ballard, and if you like David Cronenberg. I wouldn't really say I was a big Cronenberg fan you know, but I do, having seen a few things I think that's OK you know, he's a good film-maker, not a bad film-maker.

Mk It's not made to be an entertainment film you know, it's made, made to be a thinking person's film, it's made to, it's for people who want to question want to think about things.

T   Which is much more valuable.

P   Absolutely.

The point of agreement hinges around the kind of mental engagement that they have with the film, supplemented a few moments later by Michael's proposition on who it is for:

MI For anyone who wants to go beyond the boundaries of classical Hollywood narrative.

Mk Yeah, feel good factor, the ones that can go and see, but they don't really raise any serious issues, and even if they do, they give you a horrible moral line on it, they're so...

T   And other films you said before, just thinking about it now, I guess *Naked*, it's Mike Leigh isn't it? I mean that was a film that I really liked and it's bizarre and disturbing, but also some of it, you think, well you know.

Here again, their argumentative journey takes them back to the difference with *Crash*, and the pleasures of being *challenged* by a film – but without tidy conclusions.

The only other point in the interview where they discuss other audiences is when (as we saw earlier) they broach the concept of 'harm'. This belongs to another universe of discourse for all except Tim who, as we saw before, wanted to insert a small cautionary note. Philip gives the majority view: 'they' (the censors) clearly do now know how films work. But Tim on this is less comfortable, as we saw earlier. Carefully circumscribed, he believes there are 'minor' effects – but follows this with an escape clause: 'I don't think the film-makers are responsible for anything ... any of the reactions that might happen after, I think that's the individuals.' This exemption clause both breaks the idea of any direct causative link between film and audience, and allows him back into the fold of the conversation.

At all other points than these, their discussion of 'audience' is one in which they themselves are strongly included. Since this is very much woven in with their conception of how meaning is made from the film, we deal with it under that.

... what meanings are made:

For Michael, Mike and Philip, and to a smaller extent Tim, the meaning of *Crash* is to be found within the process of their encounter with it. *Crash* does not have a 'message' of any kind – in fact, the opposite. To have a 'message' is to propose a moral stance, which this film positively, and in their eyes beneficially, refuses to do.

Michael, asked to sum up what the film meant to him, did it in 'Two words. Alternative lifestyles'. The confidence of this assertion is significant in itself, in that he does not see a need to say in what sense or to what it might be 'alternative'. But the meaning of the two words is complicated. Michael is fascinated by the possibility that people might find cars erotic, and crashes stimulating. The link becomes very clear when he purposefully re-uses his keyword in a discussion of his experience of cars:

MI I remember a time in my life when, when speed was quite an exciting thing. And I would, you know, not get turned on, but the whole aspect of driving a car very, very fast I found it quite erotic. So in that sense I was hypnotised. But I never wanted to [indistinct] thinking, oh, I want to crash at some point. It was just that sort of thinking oh, these are certain pleasures that I find interesting. In terms of, you know, deviant pleasures out there.

RH *So did you recognise those as deviant?*

MI Yeah. No, not deviant in, you know, 'deviant' in quotation marks. I just thought, alternative pleasures. Because I think if I get, if I can get turned on by driving a car really fast, and somebody, you know, somebody else can get turned on by crashing it. It's just this, you know, sort of danger element which I found quite exciting. You know.

We might call this examination of self by way of examining otherness. Two conditions aid this: first, something in you must resonate with that otherness, and, second, it needs a combination of the *intellectual* and the *sensory*, to be effective. 'Alternative pleasures', then, summarises his way of examining himself in relation to the film. This, he asserts, happens actually in the course of his watching:

It's like I was watching the film and I was, I kept thinking, you couldn't do that with an automatic car. Because the whole erotic aspect of it is changing gears, you know, you change from fourth to fifth or you know, and you speed up. And it's like when you're in the middle, when you're angling you sort of change gears, then the whole sort of sexual thing about being irritated, you know...

Michael is insistent on saying this in exactly the right way. On two occasions he corrects a formulation that is put forward, in order to mark his own sense of this process at work.

MI Because we're not able to deal with alternative lifestyles, I mean anything which is alternative is not acceptable.

P It was subversive ... I mean, I don't mind, I think it's great but I mean I think, you know, it sort of poked into those things that a lot of people don't want people to be poking into, you know.

MI I don't think it was subversive, I think it showed something subversive. Because for me, something subversive would be showing something that we wouldn't even think about, so that way it wasn't subversive, it showed something subversive.

This distinction between *being* and *showing* is important to Michael. It couples with his argument that what the film offers is a 'discourse' from whose position we can look at ourselves in a different light:

When somebody else is driving I always panic, I freak out when someone else is driving. And after seeing the film I kept thinking after I drove home, we were talking about it and my friend says, actually, you drive too fast, and you, you get very angry when you drive, because I get really irritated at people. And he kept saying, I said why didn't you tell me before? And he says, because there was never a context, and the film gave him the context to say look, you're driving too fast. So he, he, his reaction to the film, I think it gave him the guts to say, look, you're driving too fast. And it scares me. And the film gave him that ... discourse to say look, by the way, you are like them, you drive like that and it, it freaks me out.

The film opens a space, a context in which different kinds of talk about cars can take place. And Michael values exactly that in it, even as it scares him. But he goes further. For him, *Crash* is important because it embodies a certain *philosophical position* about sexuality. As we saw earlier, he is committed to what he calls a 'fluidity of sexuality' – that is, that people don't have necessarily fixed tendencies or permanent attractions. And he found it refreshing that the film showed people who admit this about themselves.

The unifying element in Michael's responses is that getting the meaning from *Crash* is a *processual* encounter. It is not so much a matter of what you have got by the end of the film, as of the experience as it is going along. He talks repeatedly about how he was forced to think about things while he was watching. A clear example occurs just after Mike has told his story of his crash and partner's death. Michael responds:

MI I think it's just the danger that, because when I kept, I kept thinking about it and I think, it's not the accident itself, it's the whole process in terms of danger, see what I mean like, the kink for me was, there needs to be this element of a line between sex, ultimate pleasure, and death. Pain and pleasure, if you see what I mean. And there was great pleasure and pain.

Mk It's the adrenaline rush, isn't it?

MI It's, yeah, the adrenaline rush plus ... If you think, you know, it's like I kept thinking, ejaculation and death, at the same time, sort of like, you know, that sort of connotation. You know, you come and you die.

What we see in Michael's part in this exchange is that the meaning of *Crash* is precisely in the relation he has with the film – its capacity to make him think alongside. It does this by making him relate to it simultaneously at sensual and intellectual levels, via the risk-taking it imagined.

Mike clearly has a very personal investment in the film, and it goes much deeper than simply his having lost a partner in a crash. It is also about his response to that crash and loss. Mike actively seeks to retell the experience, four times in different ways in the course of the interview. The two which most demonstrate how he is connecting this with his experience of *Crash* are, first, this:

The reaction of the main character in the film, after he had that first crash, when you were just saying about, oh there seems to be more traffic, and I can't think. I mean I had a serious road accident, I was the driver, somebody died in the road accident, somebody else nearly died in the accident, it wasn't in a one-ton vehicle, it was in a two and a half ton vehicle, and it, it, it rolled 150 metres down the road so it was, it was very serious. And, and after that it seemed like there were accidents everywhere, and you were focused on it. And I did, I have actually done exactly what he did, I can't explain why, but I've done exactly what he did in the film, it was commented on in the film, I bought exactly the same vehicle. And the one that I crashed wasn't actually mine, and it took me ten months to buy one, but I bought one that was the same and I drive it now. And I feel it saved my life, I mean that's one of the explanations I suppose.

The key to this, we would argue, is the conjunction between his doing exactly the same as the film, and the fact that he 'can't explain why'. He is aware inside himself of a need to think about his relation to cars, and *Crash*. Taking part in our research delivered an opportunity:

Mk I did actually go, go back. It's a very complicated story but it happened in Africa, umm, a fairly remote part of Africa, and I actually went back and they, the vehicle would have been a write-off in this country but it's, it's not like that over there. They rebuilt it, hundreds of Ugandans beat it back into, into roughly the same shape, and we actually went back, I went back with the other guy who survived the accident and we went back with an outside, third person. And, we drove down the same road, in the same vehicle, six months later, and completed the journey that we were stopped from completing by the accident. It is completion, yes, closing the circle you know. [...] The, umm, the night before because it was a long journey it was a ten day trip, the night before camping, the night before which was the last night, I'd done with my partner was, was very difficult. Because we camped in the same place, actually in the same spot.

RH *Did you do that deliberately?*

Mk Absolutely. We were both, we were both doing it deliberately. We didn't really talk about why we were doing it, or how, we talked about how we felt about it but...

Crash, then, could help him make sense of his experience. But he still insists on a distinction, one which quite closely parallels Michael's. Immediately following the passage we cited earlier, where Mike reports on his wish to see if *Crash* might actually be therapeutic, he added: 'But I still, I can't follow the premise that being involved in a road accident is erotic in any way at all.' This is important in itself, in what it reveals about Mike's management of the relations between his personal experience and his response to the film. But at least as important is that it in no way leads Mike to criticise or reject the film. To the contrary, almost in the same breath he says:

I think my immediate reaction immediately after seeing the film was that I was quite excited by it, stimulated by it, not in a, not in an erotic way but stimulated in a cerebral way.

His personal trauma required a degree of distance from the film, but this did not in itself constitute a difficulty – it meant that having identified (and rejected) the 'premise' that crashes might be erotic, he can proceed with the film. He was, and remained, 'excited' by *Crash*. This intellectual relationship to the film is shown in his repeated use of analytic expressions to define what he sees the film as doing: 'It does lay bare a lot of stuff that people, the kind of things that they want you know, there's lots of specific images that are shown in the film, the kind of thoughts that people have, fetish thoughts and that kind of thing, it lays them open'. The idea of 'fetish/ism' is used repeatedly by Mike, on one occasion to summarise specifically what the film would mean if he did not have a personal investment in it ('I think in general terms, if I didn't have that personal connection, it was about fetishism'), on another to generalise the purpose of *Crash* to be about that dark side of people in general ('it could have been about any other fetish and still raised a lot of the same points'). His final occasion of use makes clear that for him *Crash* was exciting precisely because it dealt with a fetish that he did not feel, but felt that he wanted to be able to imagine:

> But there was a point, I think for all of us, there seems to have been a point at which, at which for us the fetish was no longer erotic. But there was also, there was also a part of the film for which it, it was. So, it was kind of like taking the whole spectrum, it was like going from the why do you buy a red sports car, you know just, to the, to the bits that we all found, that isn't erotic, and it's really interesting to speculate that somebody else might find it erotic.

This combination of a revisiting of his personal traumas in a way which allows him to look inside himself, along with an intellectual stimulation to consider how fetishes work as aspects of a darker side of us all, is what made the process of watching *Crash* for Mike meaningful *because* exciting.

Philip is motivated intensely by his dislike of censorship, an anger at 'all that is small and petty-minded and middle, middle England'. Beyond this he is much less sure, but he clearly delights in the film because it is what 'middle England' will not stomach: 'It sort of poked into those things that a lot of people don't want people poking into'. There is an interesting imprecision about this statement. Philip had seen the film when it first came out, and then had been – despite his personal convictions on censorship – still overwhelmed by an expectation that it would be violent or pornographic. That had prevented him from getting at the meaning of the film. But even at second viewing he struggled to articulate his views, hence his difficulty with the questionnaire. When asked directly about his keyword ('enjoyed/amused'), he had to be reminded what he had said, and then thought hard about what it must have meant:

> They are my own words, right. Yeah I wasn't sure, no. Amused, yeah well, because I wasn't shocked by it, you know, because it wasn't, my time wasn't spent thinking, oh my gosh this is you know, it didn't bother me, so I found it, I found it an entertaining film. The stuff I was amused about, I was actually, I found that certain appeal, and I think I mentioned this, of those guys who set out to recreate the crashes, I thought that was, you know, it was like, a dozen people or twenty people watching on some little deserted bit of road somewhere, and the police turn up. I thought that was, you know, as an art form, I mean it's not something I'd want to go and see necessarily, but I found that, you know, a highly entertaining idea, of Ballard's initially, that there were these sort of people, and I remember thinking, this could only happen in America and then I'm thinking oh I don't know if that's true if this could happen in America. Umm, especially the Canadians but umm, so that sort of stuff amused me and I found that entertaining, the idea of these mad guys, you

know the state of their lives, or the state of society that you would form a little club, whereby you recreate, you know, you stand every chance of killing yourself in these crazy recreations.

The postulation that this 'could only happen in America' has a reductive effect. Unlike Michael and Mike, for whom what is shown is a philosophically interesting investigation into an unexplored human possibility, for Philip it is about 'mad guys' 'over there'. This distancing occurs in other ways, as well. Speaking of the James Dean reconstruction:

P   I enjoyed, as I said before, the recreation of the James Dean pile-up. Not necessarily the actual bang itself, but the way they were setting up, he had his microphone and it, it was very atmospheric and he really built the scene, yeah, he was an artist you know, his friends were just these, well they were kind of artisty, but they were just, you know, the people that, you know, the other guy does the driving and with the girlfriend and stuff, you know. Yeah, I liked that scene, I thought it was good the way, you know, there's thirty people like watching it or something.
Mk It was saying things about, about performance in general, wasn't it? About, about, well we're all voyeuristic, we go and watch shows.

Philip puts in a distancing here through his talk of the 'artisty' (or as earlier, 'weird yuppies') for they amount to oddities. We leave in Mike's response, though, which is clearly saying something more than Philip wants to say. It brings the issue home to *us* in a way that Philip would not, on his own. Explaining the sense in which he would now say that his views have developed and clarified, Philip says:

Has it developed, umm? I don't think it's as much as, yeah the minute you come out of the cinema, like I say, later on you can think about it. So yeah I thought about it more I think I enjoyed it, it was a good film, thought it was a, an interesting, you know, concept and it was a well made film and this is why it worked, he's a very good film-maker. I mean I don't know all his stuff, but I saw the *Naked Lunch*, I think it was the first thing I saw of his and I thought, oh right, that's interestingly done so, you know, he's a good film-maker and the guy, Ballard is a very good writer. Yeah.

By positing it through Cronenberg's qualities as a film-maker, again, it becomes a thing to be inspected, rather than something to be engaged with personally. So, significantly, the film has less impact and relevance for him than for Michael or Mike, precisely because he is that much more distanced. It is *just* a good film. Lacking the involvement, it has no impact beyond that. Tim makes some generalised statements about the meaning of *Crash*, built around the idea of 'exploring stuff'. Probably the most important element in this, though, is the way Tim embeds in here an account of the role of art, and then attributes that role to the *characters in the film*. *They* are artists, in that sense, and therefore embody the idea of living life to the full. This is the point and special role of art, and how indeed he sees himself as an artist: 'That's what I'm talking about: exploring and pushing things too far.'

What particularly struck Tim, and what became the heart of his considered judgement on the film, was its *graphicness*:

T   I thought it was the most graphic, explicit film I've ever seen. Or, just dirty, probably not necessarily graphic.
MI What do you mean by graphic?
T   Just really dirty.
RH *You're saying that with a smile.*
T   Oh it was great yeah. Umm, you know but umm, yeah the opening scene just straightaway, straight into that, and I mean that so many films have sort of sex scenes or whatever but none of it was anything like that.

The idea of 'dirty sex' is not at all a problem to him, indeed it is fascinating. But it is the sense in which it is dirty which is so important – it is because, unlike Hollywood cinema which would have *dramatised* the sex, here it was just 'cold'. He picks up and extends something Michael is saying on this:

MI I haven't changed my point of view that, there are pleasures there, that we might not want to think about, other pleasures that other people might have. And I think, in terms of the film it was quite interesting because I said to myself, I wonder if metal is erotic, if you see what I mean. And I thought umm, I think no, it's cold, so that was the end for me, in terms of the eroticism of metal. But...
T   But how does it matter that it is cold?
MI Sorry?
T   That's the whole thing, isn't it, that it is cold.

This is the meaning of 'dirty' for him, and it contains a paradox:

What I'd sort of with quite a bit of my work like to do is, that thing about amusing and disturbing at the same time, and I really like that, and the film did that a lot, and that, I think it's really nice to be amused and disturbed.

To be 'amusing and disturbing at the same time' is the quality he finds in the film, and it is what he seeks to create in his own artistic work. This, his being an artist who wants to create certain kinds of work, is clearly the personal link he makes with the film. Yet it has another significant aspect, this being the capacity of *Crash* to make 'hundreds and hundreds' of links with his own thoughts:

RH *Tim you'd said that you 'appreciated' the film. Could you expand on that? It sounds to me that you were you were being slightly careful or guarded in what you were saying.*
T   Well I don't know, was this one where you put an example word down, a few of them? And like I said, I, I didn't want to say it was a good film, umm ... I think, I think the strongest thing in the question that I remember mostly, was that for me, you said, does, did the film, umm, are there any things you recognise in yourselves in the film or, or, you know, not you know, in your life or

whatever. And I just put hundreds and hundreds and I think, that was the best thing about the film for me, it just brought all these things, you know, I just, yeah, yeah I know that or I recognise that, or yeah you know and these, whether they're dark things that, you know, don't approach much or, you know, I'm not supposed to. Umm, and so I think, that's why I said 'appreciate'.

The multiplicity of links to his own experience, including his thoughts about 'dark things', increases the worth of the film.

Tim's responses then are founded on his appreciation of paradox: the film is 'erotic because cold', the characters are 'good because flawed'.

Conclusions

This second interview confirms closely what was first demonstrated with the four women's responses. Individuals' reasons for responding are in each case different, and clearly much could be said about those differences. They are not what concern us here. All eight have much the same overall image of what it is that makes *Crash* significant, and pleasurable. The film called on them to play a certain, very complicated role. Being an audience for *Crash* is much more than watching and listening attentively. It involves a whole orientation to the film, a role which these four men and four women were pleased to play. This role cannot be captured by easy terms like 'identification'. What is involved is a complicated interplay between a number of separable elements: a set of interests and attitudes, particularly directed towards the variety of forms of human sexuality, in which *difference* is positively charged; an orientation to fiction, to story-telling which goes way beyond being clear about the difference between that and reality – marking that one of the functions of story-telling is to show things currently beyond our imaginings, to challenge our view of ourselves through strangeness; a willingness to work at a film and its characters where explanation is withheld, because the challenge their behaviour presents is seen to be worth the effort of understanding; and an interest in being made uncomfortable – that some things about ourselves, perhaps, can only be adequately grasped if daily comfort is temporarily shaken. There is no intrinsic virtue in either doing or not doing these things. Yet it may tell us a good deal about our culture, and our filmic culture, if we take a good look at these processes.

It does specifically give the lie to the moral simplisms of those who attacked *Crash*. Their account of the film depended on a 'figure' of the audience quite unlike anything we find in our enthusiasts. But it is not simply the *audience* who are different. An enthusiastic audience *has* to take up this kind of position, because of the nature of the film.

What we are offering is a model which seems to have the power to explain a great deal about the responses of our Positive viewers. The eight whose responses we have examined in detail in these two chapters are not being offered as typical, or average – as we have said, there are important individualising features within their responses. Our interest has been in delineating something we have discovered within their responses; a pattern which transcends them as individuals, produced by the challenge which they experienced the film as posing them. What we are doing, therefore, is to reach behind the individuality of their responses, to bring into view some common structuring elements. These take us beyond the differences between individuals, and allow us to construct the model of the conditions which have to be met for audiences to have a Positive response to *Crash*.

This leads us to the next test of the approach we have developed here. How far can our hypothesis make sense of what happened when people disliked *Crash*? Our proposition has been this: those who respond positively to *Crash* show a willingness and ability to meet the film on a terrain which we have been able to define with considerable precision – the seven conditions which we presented at the end of the previous chapter. To meet these conditions is to agree to play the role which *Crash* demands, and thus to be an enthusiast. Might it then be that inability or unwillingness to meet one or more of these conditions could turn someone into a negative respondent? In the next two chapters, we look in detail at examples of Negative and Unsettled responses, to see how far this idea holds up.

7   Refusing *Crash*

Who disliked and objected to *Crash*, and why? How do their responses relate to those of *Crash*'s enthusiasts? And how well does the model outlined in the last two chapters fit this other end of the spectrum?

There were many among our audience who disliked, even loathed, *Crash*. When we began the research, we had worried that it might be too easy to recruit defenders of the film, that people who would dislike it would stay away. We had even laid contingency plans to interview people who refused to come and see it. Our fears were quite unfounded. Among the 164 people who responded after our screening of *Crash*, as many ended up criticising, indeed rejecting, the film as liked and wanted to defend it. Thirty-seven classed themselves as *disliking/disapproving*, twenty-eight as *disliking/ neutral*, and five as *neutral/disapproving*. Although there was a degree of movement of opinion in the second and third categories, haters as much as lovers of *Crash* were definite in their views on the film. There is no doubting the passionate dismissals the film produced among many. Indeed, one of the many interesting things about *Crash* is how far, in Britain at least, it caused a rush to extremes, and extremes of judgemental kinds. It was very hard for anyone to say simply: not my cup of tea, thanks.

Asked to sum in one expression their first reactions to the film, these were (roughly grouped by meaning) the responses of the Refusers, as we henceforth collectively call them:

Dislike/Disapprove: *Disturbed*, *dismayed*, *distressed*, irritated, unsettled, annoyed, appalled. Bored, confused. Intrigued, interested, bored/funny, felt inconclusive, fascinated then bored.

Dislike/Neutral: *Bored*, irritated, exasperated, amazed, dumbfounded, disappointed. Puzzled, lost, detached, pointless, tedious, incredible, unbelievable. Uneasy, faintly uncomfortable, vaguely/sickly interested but not gripped, mildly perturbed, darkly amused.

Neutral/Disapprove: Fascinated and repulsed, absorbed, distanced, puzzled, bored.

NB: Words in italics were the most frequently given.

Several things are immediately striking about these lists. First, there is a strong presence of *moral concern*, that is, a coupling of dislike with distaste and a sense of worry about it. Second, and rather different, is a sense of waste – that the film *as film* claimed to do things at which it failed. Third (and to be dealt with in the next chapter) there is a strand of ambivalent responses, an unease which might or might not resolve itself over time. Although this is obvious in words such as 'puzzled', and 'inconclusive', the ambivalence is probably most importantly contained within the term 'disturbed' – which, as we saw, was also one of the most commonly used words among *Crash* enthusiasts for whom it meant, in effect, a welcome challenge.

In the previous chapters, we showed how our enthusiastic audiences changed and developed their views on *Crash*, even over quite short periods of time, with a tendency for these changes to resolve away ambivalences, or to come to terms with them. Often they did this by noting something about the film which they *could* have responded to, but declined to. Because of this, it was possible to construct ideal-types of the implicit positions around which people orient as they work out their personal positions on *Crash*. How might this work with Refusers? What kinds of ideal-type of refusal is it possible to identify?

We held six interviews with *Dislikers/Disapprovers*, three *Dislikers/Neutral*, and three with *Neutral/Disapprovers*, amounting to twenty individuals in all. These interviews again demonstrated that even placing *themselves* in categories squeezes the living complexity out of people's responses. The grounds of dislike and of disapproval were very varied, and perhaps more varied than the grounds of enthusiasm for the film. The interviews also showed that people's responses are not 'given' at the moment of completion of a film – many went away after seeing the film and thought about it, talked to others, and evolved in their judgements.[1] In one case, a married couple who came together to our screening deliberately refrained from (their normal practice of) talking to each other about it afterwards, in order not to contaminate their responses, and found themselves, in the course of talking to us, evolving *away* from each other.

For all the variety, though, the interviews support the sense, hinted at in the word-lists above, that there were two relatively distinct strands of criticism of *Crash*: a moral, and a filmic critique. At its most extreme, the moral critique of the film just couldn't see why anyone had bothered to make the film. It was 'pointless', or 'unnecessary'. Mary, a retired teacher, expressed this idea exactly: 'I thought what a waste of money. Why have they made this film? Did they want to shock people? Did they … in the pornography … did they want to go one better than everybody else? Attach it to a car. And I thought, well, how can you mix sex with car crashes?' [Interview 5]. Mary found so much of the film distasteful that a great number of her responses took the form of rhetorical questions. On the sex in the films, she kept asking: 'I thought oh why? Why? Why has the man done it? Why has the producer, why has he given that scene?' The way the questions were asked made it clear that no answer was going to satisfy her.

The distinction between a rejection of *Crash* on moral grounds and a dismissal on filmic grounds was well-caught in one interview with two retired men [Interview 6]. We use this as an opening case-study since it displays in microcosm many of the features we met elsewhere. Both men had disliked the film intensely, but they did not much agree on why. For Derek, who grounded his responses very strongly on religion (he greeted his interviewer with a sheaf of biblical quotations arguing that homosexuality is an 'abomination'), the film was 'quite unnecessary', and 'an unworthy film, unworthy, just that'. The meaning he gave this becomes clearer from the way he responded to a question specifically about the sex in the film. For him, this was simply not the issue: 'The film should never have been started but given that that group are going to make a film of that kind, then you know, one road crash is very like another, and one sexual act is very like another'. The problem with the film is in its very conception, which to him was 'appalling': 'I was appalled from the beginning right the way through. If you hadn't asked us not to walk out, I would have walked out.'

Derek's response to the film had two distinct levels to it. First, what produced an almost visceral disgust in him was, in particular, the way the film showed physical injuries. This he almost could not watch.

> As I said, we're a group of people here who encounter, err, disease and stress in old age all the time. I mean, it's well known here, we've had two people within the last nine months, we've had two strokes, we've had three severe injuries – that kind of thing – and we don't draw attention to these in any way. They're part of normal life for elderly people. And we try to help where we can ... err ... but ... you carry on. [...] But not because I'm at all squeamish ... not at all. I've served in three emergencies. I've served all over the world and I'm not squeamish. [...] The emphasis on the prosthesis of the injured woman was particularly offensive. In U3A [The University of the Third Age] ... there are many with ageing and who walk or manipulate with difficulty, and yet they live their lives with great dignity, and through beauty of spirit..

Derek's insistence that it is not personal squeamishness (he spent many years serving in military hospitals) must be accepted. It is a different kind of revulsion – one which transcends simple personal distaste. The word which catches it most directly is 'dignity'. Any kind of film which focused on deformities, or physical injuries, by definition will strip its characters of 'dignity'. He insistently used medical terms such as 'lesion' and 'prosthesis' to neutralise the idea of injuries and mechanical aids for disabilities. It is interesting that in fact Derek's strongest reaction was not to the wound-sex scene, but to the scene in which Rosanna Arquette makes play of her strapped leg to bewilder and embarrass the car salesman. It *drew attention* to her disability, made it a source of humour, with even an erotic strand as she displayed more and more of her legs to him.

With Derek even this was subsumed within a wider philosophy. He would not have been content with a judgement that some people might find it offensive. His critique of *Crash* as 'degrading' was simultaneously an *ideological* critique, not just for its breaking biblical rules, but for diminishing humanity as a whole. Throughout the interview he worked with an opposition between 'higher' and 'lower', 'human' and 'animal', and 'civilised' and 'uncivilised'. At one point he turned this against the research itself, accusing us of wasting money on a film that was simply not worth the research, and thereby giving encouragement to the bestial in us all:

> Now, your faculty is one of humanities, which by its very name implies a faculty above that of animals. If this film is typical, it should be called the faculty of animal behaviour, and relegated to a fellow department of zoologists. In no sense could this film be considered as an aspect of man in the image of God,

which I believe in. [...] In the Solomon Islands – because I was there for five years doing research in the Solomon Islands – toads can occasionally be seen attempting to mate with dead or dying members of the same species. But human beings are not toads, and you're part of a faculty of humanities.

At other times, it became clear that he was even setting his response within a frame not unlike older notions of a 'great chain of being', that chain in which human societies can be classed on a scale from the primitive to the higher. This allowed him to compliment 'primitive' (his term) peoples whom he felt would reject *Crash* because even in their primitive state they are more advanced than the film.

If Derek enunciates almost perfectly an ideal-type of moral refusal – with his personal slant of an add-on element of classificatory racism – it is worth noting that he shares one other element with a number of other people. Dismissing the film on *moral* grounds leaves space for complimenting it on individual qualities. In Derek's case – and he is not alone in this – the music was the striking element. Indeed he takes it so far as to comment, at one point, that in one of the sex scenes, which on moral grounds he dismisses as purely 'animal', the music *almost* lifts it to a 'higher plane'.

Derek's confident moral refusal of *Crash* posed a problem for the other interviewee, Graham, who had certainly disliked the film, but on quite other grounds. He had to make space for a different set of objections to the film. Almost at the start of the interview, after Derek had remarked that he had wanted to 'wash my mouth out' after watching *Crash*, Graham interjected a space-making comment:

> Can I just say that I wasn't put off by the amount of sex necessarily in ... the last film I think I saw before *Crash* was *Breaking the Waves* which had far more explicit sex in it than did *Crash*. Indeed the men got their clothes off as well as the ... err ... the women, which was noticeable in *Crash*. And ... but ... their ... the sex was part of the story and one could identify with the woman victim in *Breaking the Waves*, in a way which, err ... got one emotionally involved.

By contrast, he felt that *Crash* 'just seemed to be a group of actors and actresses who'd got together for their own mutual self-satisfaction'. The criteria at work here are vitally different from Derek's. Graham demands a *story* which satisfies him: 'something which tells one about the human condition, something which has representation of characters with their faults as well as their qualities, something to get your teeth into'. With *Crash* he found 'absolutely minimal storyline'. He further demands that there be an emotional point of entry into the story, so that it could 'convince' him – he repeated his feeling that the people playing the parts didn't convince him ('it just seemed to be actors and actresses dressing up as hospital patients and doing their thing, and it wasn't convincing for me').

For Graham, therefore, for lack of adequate storyline the film dissolved into just a 'succession of violence and sexual activities'. And for lack of adequate characterisation he just 'didn't feel the pain' they appeared to be undergoing. These are *filmic* requirements and criteria, as opposed to Derek's moral/ideological. His problem is not that such things should not even be thought, but that the way they were presented to him in the film was 'unreal', 'absurd'. They failed to establish themselves as genuine, adequate *fictions*, and he worked hard to record the difference between the two critiques:

It just didn't engage for the reasons I've given – no story, no character, just a succession of scenes ... scenes which were largely unrelated. The same-sex cuddles towards the end had no point to them at all ... they were just thrown in to make up the measure, it seemed [laughs]. So, I think that was my reaction. I wasn't appalled, I wasn't shocked. Err. I was just very surprised that intelligent professional people should have got together to make such a lousy film.

This then connects with his refusal of censorship as a response: 'I don't think censorship is the answer. And basically, for me, the film is simply bad as a film ... in cinema terms. It doesn't contain anything I would regard as being unfit for humans to see' (a comment which marks that he also had identified this criterion behind Derek's remarks). He reserves justified censorship only to situations where films might show real harm being done, parallel to the way news self-censors scenes too horrible to show.

Derek, without saying much about it, clearly believes that censorship is not 'strict enough'. There is an interesting complexity in this. A regular reader of the *Daily Mail*, from which he gleaned most of his prior picture of *Crash*, he nonetheless insisted on seeing the film for himself in order to find out if they were telling the truth about it – he was capable of a sardonic distrust of their ways of telling things. Yet his personal value system told him that the film had 'no merits'. Still, his argument slid towards the issue of 'children' in a way which suggests the adoption of a large part of the *Mail*'s rhetoric. Answering our question about his feelings about those who enjoyed the film, he said:

Well, I would question their moral judgement ... err, in other words, I ... I think they are in the sense of your advert depraved. The err ... umm ... and err ... and of course they ... the thing is that this type of violence, promiscuous violence really, unnecessary violence, is umm ... is err ... particularly directed now towards ever younger children ... And err ... certainly this appals me actually, that any child should see that film, and errr ... also that err ... well any violence towards children seems to me to be appalling, but to encourage children in violence in this way, to partake of it, to see it, is a perversion according to my beliefs ... I mean I ... I don't think the word is too strong, I think it is a perversion of human values.

The hesitations in this are interesting, especially from someone who, in most of the interview, held articulate views which he was clearly used to putting into words. It is as if he was aware that he was stepping awkwardly across a gap in his ideas. But what enables him to do it, in the end, is the wholesale adoption of a wide and inclusive concept of 'violence' – one which includes seeing violence, partaking in it, and being subject to it. Graham had also used the term 'violence', albeit more equivocally. When the interviewer queried in what sense each saw *Crash* as a 'violent' movie, Graham acknowledged that it did not really apply, that all acts in the film are consensual. Derek on the other hand immediately refocused on the wounds, in answering the query:

Let me take just two examples. One is the emphasis on the prosthesis, the artificial limb ... quite unnecessary. And OK, there's plenty of people with artificial limbs, they come to some of our lectures actually. We don't comment on it, nor are we ... we disturbed by it. They just get on with it. We get on with it, they get on with it. [...] But the other thing was this focusing on the lesion, err ... it was a very severe lesion which had only just healed, I should say. I know quite a bit about this, and err ... err ... this seemed to me again, quite unnecessary. Perhaps one shot to convey the severity of the injury, but that wasn't the purpose. The purpose was to draw attention to the prosthesis and to difficulty of getting into the car. [...] And the tearing of the seat and the embarrassment of the salesman, all of it.

Taken literally, these simply do not answer the question. They serve to remind just how upsetting Derek found the camera's attention on the wounds. Yet they only count as 'violence' if one adds in a whole metaphorically-driven theory of 'doing violence to people', as we saw in Chapter 4, which is of course exactly what the *Mail*'s account turns on.[2]

In Derek and Graham we can see the outlines of two ideal-typical refusals of *Crash*. One turns on refusing to see and judge it as a film, but instead as something between a document and a prophecy. The sheer existence of it, its ideas, and its showing of these activities is proof-positive of human decline and degradation. Only at the point where Derek has to say *how* it might affect actual people does he turn, for support, to the publicly available rhetoric of 'violence'. Graham on the other hand, while firmly declining any move to censorship, still goes far beyond saying simply that the film didn't involve him, personally. It is therefore much more than a refusal on grounds of taste. The film is a failure, and to be condemned, but as a film. The strength of Derek's moral/religious beliefs, coupled with Graham's resultant desire to mark his difference from Derek, led to these two positions appearing quite clearly. Other Refusers whom we interviewed were capable of mixing these two grounds in quite complicated ways.

As small samples, consider the degrees of tension between criteria embodied in the following:

'*Crash* was disgusting' + 'the music was in certain respects imaginative' – *Derek* [Interview 6]

'Boring and appalling' + 'nothing striking except the music and the makeup [i.e. the wounds]' – *Alan* [Interview 10]

'I thought it was pointless and tasteless' + 'The music was striking', 'strident and discordant and mirrored the theme of the film' – *Peter* [Interview 10]

'I hated it. It was very well-made – very stylish, very Cronenberg, very technology. But I hate sex and violence and find the whole thing too cold and very disturbing to watch. I hate porn as well – but it's an experience to watch.' – *Tejinder* [Interview 26]

'Do not watch it! You'll never drive a car again! It was disgusting, too much. It was so far from reality, I've never seen something worse than that. Yes, congratulations on the film. I'm shocked. Brilliant. But don't let that lead anywhere. Not in this case. No, I'm just disgusted. [...] This is the future? This film went so far

that I don't want to think about the idea at all. That can't be the aim, though?'
– *Ines* [Interview 3]

'One of the most boring films I have ever seen' + 'superbly filmed, the acting was very good', the soundtrack 'created a feeling of claustrophobia', some of the sexual positions were 'intriguing'; 'Yes, it was fascinating to a degree and it was also boring. I wanted it to end. Was I bored by the fascination? Now I have got this far in the questionnaire I think that was the point. The script was crap and it moved so slowly. But the fascination came from asking why.' – *Darren* [Interview 25]

Alan is in an almost identical position to Derek, and indeed his critique of *Crash* was every bit as morally-driven as was Derek's, although – from the evidence we had, at any rate – without the driving force of religion. Alan is as capable as Derek of holding a wholly separate view on some aspects of *Crash*'s filmic qualities. Peter takes one tentative step beyond this, in raising a question about the appropriateness of the film's *style* to its 'message' – but he will take it no further than that, and in the main Peter is as morally-critical of *Crash* as the previous two. But the remainder are dealing differently with the issue of the film's 'cold' style. For Tejinder, there is a clear personal refusal, because she simply finds *any* association of sex and violence too uncomfortable to watch. It has ceased, here, to be mainly a moral critique, rather, it is a matter of personal decision and preference.

Ines takes this doubling of responses even further. While still as hostile to *Crash* as the others, she acknowledges implicitly that there is a possible complex, clever and sophisticated meaning – and it is precisely *that* which she chooses to reject. So the film is 'brilliant' *and* 'disgusting'. Darren is led to quiz his own reaction of boredom, to the point of wondering if this indeed was what it was all about. But he declines to go any further than noticing the possibility of this – simply, the boredom was telling enough as an experience for him to want to go no further.

This doubling of responses is important. It suggests that three factors, at least, may be at work in shaping how people want to talk about a film like *Crash*. First is the experience of watching – what immediate responses does the film conjure out of people? The predominant aspect of this seems to be how willing and comfortable people are to watch its various kinds and levels of explicitness of sexual interaction on screen. The second concerns people's familiarity with slow-moving art-house cinema style, where the emphasis is away from narrative and explicitly-given motivation.[3] Third, is the moral dimension, as we have seen. But working through the relations between these happens over time and may involve talk with others – including, of course, the time and talk given to us, as part of the research.

As an example, consider two non-white interviewees who classified themselves as *Dislike/Disapprove*, although both in the interview insistently rejected censorship. The most repeated word they use for *Crash* is 'cold', as in the following from Jamila:

I don't think I was in the mood for watching a film at that time and that made a difference, I was just coming from work and wasn't really feeling in the mood to settle down sort of get into a film. And so, I suppose I was quite, you know, already went in with a bit of an attitude to it when I sat down. And it was just,

I mean, the characters were just ... dire, you know they were just, there was no development no depth to the characters and that, and I just couldn't feel for any of them, and I thought the scenes, the sex scenes were very unerotic, they didn't, they were very sort of cold. There's a very cold feel to the whole film I mean ... I can see what they're trying to create, they're trying to get that sort of emotion across, but I don't think it works, I mean from a film point of view and from what was being shown and being said as well really. I didn't, you know, the idea that sexuality is linked with this act of crashing cars, I can see the adrenalin buzz but I couldn't really see where the sexuality came into it. [Interview 17]

Jamila's major problem with the film was that she could feel nothing for the characters; she was unable to 'identify' with anyone. Patrick agreed wholeheartedly with this account of the film's emotional tone:

I could see why it was seen as a controversial film but I thought, as Jamila said, the whole idea about sex in crashes and the way things were portrayed in the film, the umm, the lifestyles of the characters, the constant umm, the continual sexual scenes related to crashes I, I just thought that didn't work very well and just, umm, certainly it was a bit of a farce. So it, I, I didn't think it achieved the aim that it, that it set out to achieve. And I probably used that word because it was closest to expressing the fact that I thought it was a ridiculous film. And I really, umm, did nothing for me. I mean I, I wouldn't go so far as to say I found some of the scenes hilarious as you said, I just sat there thinking that umm, yeah it was a cold film, if I just pick up on what you said. [...] Because there was no emotion in that film, there wasn't meant to be because cars, aren't emotional objects, and, people were getting off on what they do with cars and so, it's almost like the car's an extension of some sort of sexual entity and the whole thing was, you know, passionless. Which I suppose, in a sense it was meant to be.

Interestingly, in each case there is a half-acknowledgement that the 'coldness' may not be a *failing*, but something intended, even necessary. Given Jamila's admission that she was not really in the mood to see the film, that might have led to saying that this was just a case of not 'fitting in' to the film – in which case, there need be no judgement on the film's 'message', let alone on its audience. In fact, their talk led to them agreeing that the film was 'layered' (Patrick's expression) in that it had characters with a 'surface aesthetic' yet who were drawn towards Vaughan's scruffy ugliness. But both wanted to be able to give a judgement. The way they did it, therefore, was to collaborate in producing a judgement in the course of the interview. They talked up an account of it which defined it as an 'American', then a 'white' film, and thus produced a justification of their own dislike. Jamila began this by identifying the film as 'superficial America'. Between them, they set about unfolding and adding to this idea:

P   Arrogance.
J   Arrogance.
P   Arrogant characters. Wealthy, arrogant main characters.

J   In spite of their coldness and distance?

P   Possibly yeah. Very white, Anglo-Saxon arrogant characters.

J   They're sort of all, very hedonistic as well and umm, they sort of, you know just living for the sexual kick it seemed. I mean much more stylish in the scenes and they're quite open about their sexuality so, I suppose in some ways it was sort of, trying to, make a statement on modern relationships of couples and, in some respects that is also...

P   And also rampant consumerism. [...] And cars are really strong symbols of consumption. And so the number of cars that they seem to have sex in seem to mirror the fact that they're really rich, hedonistic people. Getting their rocks off in these different cars. Old and new. Collectors items and cars that you can discard quite easily. Does sort of feed in with the superficiality and the consumption.

J   And, and then also with that you know the power thing comes in you sort of, rich guy sort of, come in from that, you know, wealthy place and sort of go into the underworld for their kicks, you know, sex so it's kind of enormous slave-master relationship.

It is small wonder that, late on in the interview, they agreed that they would have trouble trusting someone who said that they had enjoyed *Crash*. This example shows the complex interweaving of discussions of the filmic qualities of *Crash* (which can even acknowledge its layered representations, its thematic consideration of the machinery of sex, and its deliberate 'coldness') with an assessment of its social and moral significance.

Understanding a refusal of *Crash* also requires us to consider the meaning of 'boredom'. Many people used this expression, and partly this simply expressed their dissatisfaction with a slow film. Yet there are signs as well that 'boredom' helped people manage what would otherwise have been upsetting. To class *Crash* as 'boring' put it at a distance where its unpleasantness could be set aside. This is how Linn made this move:

L   No, I was quite sure this ... the film was about sex and blood because it was forbidden and all films must have, must deal with something extreme to do with blood and sex, or ... it wasn't like a surprise but I kind of felt kind of do I have to confront with this actually? I'm sure that there is a deeper meaning, but the way the movie tried to generalise everything really, umm, pissed me off actually. Because I couldn't identify with this at all, not with these people, not with this world.

JH *Do you mean with the characters in the film?*

L   Yeah, and with the whole situation. I mean just this idea of the thrill of metal and crashes and sex. I can see it ... I can see [indistinct] how this linking, ... can be good in a way. And half the film I'd have to say that I was like, OK I can see this ... I don't like it ... I'm getting quite bored actually ... So you want it to sort of get somewhere but it doesn't, in my opinion. [Interview 3]

Boredom here becomes a *strategy* that allows Linn to hold *Crash* at a distance, and manage her discomfort at what it is confronting her with. She is disinclined to allow that the film could be asking her to take up a new position. Unwilling to follow it, instead, it is found 'boring'. 'Boredom' thus becomes a strategic reaction, as much as it is a disappointed lack of involvement. And that throws light back on something we have already examined in Chapter 4: the way some people measured *Crash* against the standard of 'pornography'. Peter, whom we quoted earlier, is a good example of this. He drew on his knowledge of pornography as a policeman:

> Why was I dismayed? Because it was just so pointless, I thought. Umm, it was neither fish nor fowl to me I mean if it was supposed to be pornographic, then ... why go to all the trouble of dressing pornography up with all the lots of sorts of ... the reason the pornography was going on because of road traffic accidents. I mean it was just glorifying road traffic accidents and I mean as a, as a police officer I've seen so many, I've seen fatal accidents, I've seen what they can do to people, and they can wreck other people's lives and not directly involving the actual accident and I just couldn't see any reason why anybody would want to make a film glorifying road accidents. *If* that's what they were trying to do, so what was it all about, was it merely pornography in which case it was very complicated, because we've all seen pornographic films and I guess in this job you see a lot of them, when I was on the vice squad. We used to have to view hundreds of them and decide whether they were, what category of pornography they came in. [...] Because this is a mainstream film so I mean there's only so far they can go with the pornography, isn't there? You only got the impression that a lot of sex is going on, whereas in pornographic movies are real sex. With everything in glorious technicolour ... I mean that's what pornography is. And you are invited as an observer to that, aren't you? Whereas this just seemed to be, how far do they carry it, how could they dress it up? I don't know, as I say, what the point of the film was. I'd be interested in speaking to the people who conceived it to find out what point were you trying to make, that would be an interesting conversation really.

His puzzlement about what kind of movie *Crash* was trying to be is at least partly allayed by seeing it as 'failed pornography'. But that failure does not make him *less* concerned about *Crash*. It makes it unpredictable, therefore in certain respects *more* dangerous. This need not be the case.

Another person, Maxine, also felt disabled by *Crash*, but being more comfortable with the idea of pornography merely wrote *Crash* off as a bit of a disappointment: 'I've seen some very good porn films – and this wasn't one of them!' [Interview 25] This led Maxine in quite another direction:

> The fact that people were getting off on, on accident victims and things like that, and I thought that bit, that was a very small part of the film, I thought the biggest part was basically it was just like a porn flick and that was it, and there was no, there was more I'm sorry but crap sex, I don't think there was any good sex at all, I've seen better pornographic films than that and it's a, it just, it became, I don't know, there was more of that in the film than anything, it had nothing to do with car crashes. I thought what is all this? Where did that come from? Because there wasn't that much of that in it at all.

It is a pity it was such 'crap sex' – she would have liked it to be better. But that fact leads her to turn her disappointment with the film into irritation with its critics. They are condemned for making such a fuss over almost nothing – it just was not worth it.

Understanding Refusal

In Chapter 5 we postulated seven conditions that audiences need to agree to, if they are to be enthusiastic participants in the world of the film *Crash*. To remind ourselves, the seven conditions were that viewers should be:

- willing and able to engage with a non-generic film which withholds explicit explanation of the motivation of its main characters;
- willing and able to relate to the film simultaneously *narratively*, and *philosophically*;
- willing and able to distinguish *showing* from *saying*;
- willing and able to perceive that the characters are not *given to us* in depth, but that nonetheless they *have* a depth;
- willing and able to entertain the idea that knowing about these 'perverse' sexual desires, and acknowledging their significance, is separable from sharing them;
- willing and able to perceive the sexual relations within the film as *equal*, or even *empowering* to the main characters, including the women;
- willing and able to manage a critical self-awareness of one's own responses to *Crash*.

What does this imply for the other side of the coin, *Crash*-refusal? The implication of that hypothesis is that people who reject this either will not or cannot agree to those conditions.

This is broadly right. Because disliking *Crash* is, for very many in our audience, not simply a matter of personal choices or tastes – or in other words, not the equivalent of not liking vinegar on chips, or brightly coloured clothes – because it is for most a matter of weighing the moral significance of the film, even if this was very hard to put into words, then to refuse *Crash* was to refuse an invitation it held out. But perhaps the notion of an invitation is misleading. For many viewers, *Crash* was simply bewildering. Whatever it was that it was saying, if indeed it was saying anything at all, was impossible to make sense of. It was unapproachable, and why would anyone want to try? This is the importance of that combination, in our seven conditions, of marking both 'willingness' and 'ability'.

For some, the very idea of being involved in the film was simply inconceivable. Even to consider such acts, and people interested in them, was beyond the pale. Even to show interest was to be besmirched. For others, it was much more the manner in which the film asked them to consider these. For example, hostile viewers often responded to the total 'lack of depth' in the characters. They just could not get past the still surface of them. How they put this into words, and what prior knowledge they called upon to measure the film against, varied enormously. For some, it was just bad acting. Those who knew previous work by Hunter, Spader, Unger and Arquette were less likely to make this move. For them it might be a function of the script, or of Cronenberg.

However they might frame their refusal, the difference between them and those who found the characters rich and complex *beneath* the surface stillness was in a willingness and ability to do a certain kind of interpretative cultural work. We come back in our last chapter to say a little more about what kind of interpretative work is involved here.

8 On Being Unsettled

This chapter is to some extent prefigured in our discussion of the 'doubled' responses to *Crash* cited in Chapter 7. For alongside those who objected to the very idea of *Crash* on moral grounds, an array of viewers displayed a mixture of dislike alongside an acknowledgement of powerful, even sometimes admirable qualities in the film. What newly concerns us here are those who, while in the end not willing to respond to it, recognised in *Crash* a distinctive summons; a role which they could play, but for some reason (often admitted to be very personal) would not respond to the call.

How should we think about situations where people say that they are uncertain, or ambivalent? When their responses to a film are unclear, even to themselves? What shall we call these responses, since they are almost certainly of several different kinds, at least? There is a large range of terms available, but all in some way presume the character of the response: 'hesitant', 'mixed', 'complex', 'indeterminate', 'ambivalent'. Yet although these are surely all too common responses, they have been little theorised and even less studied. Yet we do need a workable account of such responses, not just because they are common, but because of what they could tell us about the patterning of responses, generally. For now, we call this range of responses 'un-settled', not least for its obvious ambiguity between being disturbed, and being not-yet-settled.

Suppose, for instance, that un-settled responses are understood as not-yet-fully-formulated. In that case, explanation would need to emphasise the production of responses over time – an important step in itself, since many studies of audience responses essentially take snapshots, and do not try to pay attention to how views are formed and may develop or change. So it would be necessary to ask questions such as: is it, for instance, that responses move from the primarily sensory toward the cognitive, or are these two always present and interacting? We might need to examine whether different kinds of films or of audiences require longer or shorter time periods, or to consider what factors contribute to slow or fast settling of opinions.

Alternatively, un-settledness might be construed as resulting from lack of involvement – basically, that some people cannot be bothered to pursue the film any further. With this model, the distinction needing attention will be between commitment and involvement on the one hand, and lack of interest on the other: again important, since a good deal of research makes strong claims about the effects of 'becoming involved'. So, do different kinds of understandings of films go along with high or low degrees of involvement – for instance, do those with high involvement place greater emphasis on the narrative than others? Or do characters matter more to those who become involved (one possible implication of the idea of 'identification')?

Or suppose, again, that being unsettled meant that the viewer feels s/he cannot escape two incompatible responses. In this case, there may be two responses existing independently of the individual, each conceived to be clear and strong enough to have a 'pull'. Not only that, but they must feel incompatible with each other, that once adopted they take him or her in a particular direction. And the difference must matter.

These are by no means the only possibilities, and of course may not exclude each other. But they do show that unsettledness, as we have called it for now, is a significant problem, and not one easily understood. And part of the problem is that in labelling someone's responses as 'hesitant', or 'ambivalent', or 'contradictory', we are not only passing a judgement of some kind on them, we are also making claims about what a more sure, or unidirectional, or consistent response would look like. To date, to our knowledge, there have been three main approaches. The first and best known, derived from Frank Parkin and famously used by David Morley, proposes that such responses should be seen as 'negotiating' an escape-clause.[1] Morley was studying the ways different social groups responded to a popular news and current affairs programme, *Nationwide*. First, he and a colleague had conducted a semiotic analysis of *Nationwide*, and believed that they had identified a distinctive ideology at work in the programme, whose persuasive power he then wanted to explore. His model, of 'dominant', 'negotiated' and 'oppositional' responses, offered a predictive frame for examining how different groups made sense of the programme. The implication of identifying some responses as 'negotiated' was that those responding thus could feel two unequal demands on them: the force of the programme as a persuasive message, and something in their own lives which contradicted that. But they lacked (note the word) an alternative position of sufficient power to lead them to see through the programme's demands on them.[2]

A second approach is suggested, although not elaborated, by Janice Radway's classic study of romances and their readers.[3] Radway's account included identifying the dimensions of acceptable romance stories among her 'Smithton' group – her chapter 4 is given over to identifying their 'ideal' romance. They are ideal, she argues, because they are 'necessary to their daily routine' and 'help to fulfil deeply felt psychological needs' (pp. 58–9) for these women who have 'fairly rigid expectations' (p. 63). Although Radway hardly looks at unsettled responses, to be consistent with her general approach they would have to be seen as arising from a shortfall. A romance that does not quite meet the ideal requirements would be likely to produce a mixed reaction of part-pleasure, part-disappointment. This account has important implications. Clearly it only applies if readers have developed strong generic skills. But also it only operates if the audience are understood as in some sense hollow – with needs waiting to be met, a kind of psychological hunger which, if not met, would reveal a gap in them.

Both these approaches by implication look upon un-settledness as a kind of failing, or lack. The third approach starts elsewhere. It arose from the study which preceded this one, on the audiences for action-adventure movies in general, and *Judge Dredd* in particular. In their study of the patterning of audience responses, Barker and Brooks separated three dimensions: degree of involvement, management of possible disappointment, and singularity of response.[4] The first points up those who simply do not care enough to press a case – people who go to the cinema for a night out, not caring too much what they may see – as opposed to those who are richly engaged with the film. The second allowed for what they called a 'bargained' response to their film. This was marked by people feeling that their chances of gaining what they feel they deserve are very small. So they strike a compromise, consciously setting aside some of their hopes in order to get some pleasure from the film. The third dimension dealt with the difference between singular and mixed responses. Here, a new complexity arose. Audiences with low involvement in the film were more likely to mix responses: for example, mixing an interest in science fiction, with pleasure in Sylvester Stallone. They were able to switch their mode of response, and therefore their expectations of the film, without difficulty. Those with high involvement tended to produce a more consistent and unified response, to suit the way the film mattered to them.

These three approaches suggest very different ways of thinking about unsettled responses, but none of them fits too well what we found. In what follows we tackle what it meant to different people to be 'unsettled' about *Crash*.

The Nature of Uncertainty

Pretty clearly *Crash* was never going to be Easy Watching, that is, a cinematic equivalent of Easy Listening (although, as we shall see shortly, a few of our viewers made a brave stab at treating it in this way). In the main, *Crash* was seen by almost all viewers as a difficult film, one which pressed on people unrelentingly (whether for good or ill). The sign of this is the effective absence of anyone saying 'It was OK, alright, a reasonable night out'. This may seem an obvious thing to point out, but its consequences take it way beyond the obvious. We start, therefore, with the keywords offered to us by those – a smaller number than either Enthusiasts or Rejecters – who fell into our middle categories. Made up of Liking/Disapproval, Neutral/Neutral, and Disliking/Approval, they gave us this set:

Liking/Disapproval: Curious. Enthralled. Intrigued. Fascinated and nauseous. Discomforted. Enjoyed.

Neutral/Neutral: Interested. Tense. Unpassionate. Challenging yet boring. Thrilling. Bored. Disappointed. Interested/fascinated. Turned on. Pointless. Bored/shocked/ intrigued.

Disliking/Approval: Mixed mind. Bored. Fascination. Unimpressed. Passé. Nauseous. Interested. Surprised.

As one might expect for a group held in tension between enthusiasm and rejection, these responses are anything but tidy. At one end, one might think that the people who were 'thrilled', or 'turned on', were really positioning themselves among Enthusiasts. Actually, we will see that this is not right. At the other end, the 'nauseous' response looks difficult to distinguish from outright rejection. Not quite.

It is important to register that people who first positioned themselves in one of these three positions were quite likely to shift their ground. A revealing example of this: one ambivalent person, Vicki, told us that she had originally felt uncomfortable watching *Crash* because she felt it must be offensive to disabled people. But after the screening, she thought about this a good deal:

V   I think what you're saying about the car showrooms, the sort of sexuality of some body that is disabled, I found that quite a challenging sort of image because normally disabled people are sort of disabled and in a wheelchair and, I feel very sorry for them, that's it. I mean there's no sort of sexuality involved, so. So that was one point that I thought was quite challenging. And initially I remember thinking that I'd be quite offended if I'd been disabled and that's a point I've thought about in more detail and thought that maybe I wouldn't actually, maybe it's quite exciting.

JA   *What made you rethink that, just thinking about it for longer?*

V   Yeah yeah. Just my initial reaction was that I'd be offended but then yeah I just, it just stayed with me, that point, and I've thought it through a bit more, yeah. [Interview 19]

Holding aside changed minds, though, among these words one can detect different kinds of un-settledness. One group ('fascinated and nauseous', 'mixed mind', 'bored/ shocked/intrigued', 'challenging yet boring', and perhaps 'tense' and 'discomforted') register certain people's awareness of having two opposite responses. Another group ('surprised', 'disappointed', 'passé', and (we would argue) 'unimpressed') seem to signal that something more had been expected but failed to deliver. A third group register different degrees of engagement, but with perhaps a hint of reserving oneself ('enjoyed', 'fascinated', 'interested', 'intrigued'). To be sure what these might mean – and indeed what those surprise nominations 'enthralled' and 'nauseous' mean if they do not simply signal people mis-assigning themselves in our questionnaire – we have to turn to the fuller picture we gained from the interviews.

What seems to unite these responses, we suggest, is that these people seem to acknowledge in their responses their awareness of the filmicness of *Crash*. We saw that in various ways *Crash*-Rejecters wanted to summon up the figure of the film's makers, to call them to account, whereas enthusiasts hardly needed a figure of the 'author', since the film was sufficient unto itself. In effect for critics the makers were, Cronenberg was, even the actors were, on trial. How could they do this? What on earth did they think they were doing? Did they not realise how dangerous this all was? And so on. Always in the form of rhetorical questions, nothing except an apology could ever satisfy these critics. Not so here with these unsettled viewers. Within the responses, it is possible to discern three main kinds of concern with *Crash*'s filmicness.

1   The Discomforteds

On her post-film questionnaire, Della [Interview 9] reported herself as 'fascinated and nauseous' – surely a classic case of an ambivalent response. The grounds for this split in her are very interesting.

During the course of her interview, she told us several times that she found the sexual portrayals difficult. On the one hand, she told us more than once that she found the film arousing, but she felt distinctly uneasy about this very fact. On the first occasion, she said that the sex, whilst definitely turning her on, 'made me feel something dodgy ... it's not the sort of sex I'd go out and watch'. But she also marked the grounds for this – it definitely was not because of the wounds and scars. 'I mean the scars and that, that's not nauseous. Because I'm scarred and actually I thought that was quite good'. On the second occasion when she discussed the film's eroticism, in a more subtle way she again turned aside a possible explanation – the film's violence or 'goriness':

D I think the way it was done was very good. The way it was actually shot, and he was so eager to get all those shots, sort of got real close ups and everything. Yeah, I think it was really gory. And he was like, you were that person going round with the camera as well, and you were put in that position, and I thought that was very well done. So yeah. And also there's like that conflict. I felt quite a conflict in me, I was sort of thinking, oh yeah something like, oh god, you know that sort of thing. I couldn't, I couldn't watch these bits I felt sort of like bluh [sound of disgust] as well.

JH Did it make you feel uncomfortable that you had that conflict? You know, liking bits and...

D Yeah. Yeah I think so. I thought it had been done deliberately, I imagine by the film-maker. But I don't know what he was supposed to, what he was achieving by this, what he was trying to achieve by this. You know to make us feel disgusted at their voyeurism or to make us think oh yes we could do that as well.

JH What do you mean, we could do that?

D We could get into that. We have the mentality to get into that as well. You know. So it was like could be a little self-disgust in a way because like yes, I'm sitting watching this film and getting turned on by bits of it, other bits are disgusting me, but it's all part of the same spectrum really. Do you know?

Della turns aside the possible charge that *Crash* might be bad by being 'violent' by making this very quality into something to be praised. It is good because of the way it positions us in a way that makes us question ourselves; it makes us uncomfortable as voyeurs. In this way, Della is adopting a rather sophisticated version of the required distinction between showing and saying. It is not merely that they are different. It is that the manner of showing produces a question over what might be being said. But having praised just this quality, she re-introduces her own ambivalence (her awareness of feeling disgust). Yet again, she turns this on its head, with a recognition that maybe this was precisely the intended reaction ('I imagine by the film-maker'). This does not remove the disgust, since she cannot quite resolve the unease – was it designed to make us 'feel disgusted at their voyeurism' or 'make us think oh yes, I could do that as well'? Her gloss on this shows the source of her feelings. She feels its pull: 'We have the mentality to get into that as well'. Hence what she honestly professes to be a 'little self-disgust ... I am sitting watching this film and getting turned on by bits of it, other bits are disgusting me, but it's all part of the same spectrum really'.

We can see several processes at work here. Della will not allow herself easy get-outs, simple excuses – she is too honest about herself to do that. Instead, in exploring the uncomfortable reactions she had, she turns to a 'figure' of the film's makers, and repeatedly wondered if knowing their motivations might resolve her unease. Unlike many, Della turned mainly to the idea of the book's author, and whether the book might hold the key to the film. How did the book deal with these things? What made them turn the book into a film? What had got changed, for good or ill, in the transformation? If she could know the answers to these questions, maybe her own unease would be fully comprehensible. In the meantime she did have an explanation, one which might or might not be specific to her. In a tail-piece to the interview, when asked if there was anything extra she had wanted to say, Della added the following:

> Right, I think these sort of films, this film *Crash*, films with a lot of violence or sexual violence in, I think they create a ... I think I feel uncomfortable because it's projecting an energy that I don't feel happy with. And I don't like having that energy around me, and it makes me feel a bit unclean, as though I need to brush the energy away and get something better or more wholesome, you know, around me. Sort of, to compensate. So I don't want my head filled with images, I don't want to walk around with my head filled with images of violence, sexual violence. Just because it doesn't make me feel good. And I want to feel good in my life, I want to feel happy. And I want to see images that reflect that. I don't want, like, the Waltons twenty-four hours a day but ... know what I mean, I don't wanna have to ... I mean, if this is supposed to be bringing up some sort of philosophical point, what is it? You know, I don't think it was made clear and I'm not stupid. But I don't think it was a philosophical film, you know it did leave me with a lot of images in my head which I don't want to be there. And I think there's a lot of sort of sexual violence films, or films that involve child and horror, that's what it leaves with the viewer. You know, whether or not they believe it, whether or not they act on it, it leaves a bad energy.

The idea of negative 'energy' – something which saps her capacity to feel good – is hers, and she knows it. She wonders if other people might not experience it as well. If she had been able to identify a clear philosophical point of view in the film – for instance, in an expanded sense of characters' motivations – the problem might have gone away. At several points she felt the film was on the edge of doing this. And indeed this ambivalence is evidenced all through the interview. In the very context of discussing her dislike of films depicting rape, she suddenly referenced another film which deeply affected her, *Wait Until Dark* (1967), in which Audrey Hepburn plays a threatened blind woman. In recalling how intensely she had felt about this, she lost her way in the interview. For Della, it is evident, the line between movies that are just too compelling and those whose impact is simply unpleasant is endlessly blurred. Her personal choice is to avoid, where she can, that blurred discomforting area.

Della is one case, but she shares several things with others in this response-bracket: the self-awareness of split reactions, the search for a missing meaning in the film, and the figure of the author. These were overt in Della's case, while sometimes they were more embedded in others, and not always discoverable within single sentences.

The same principle is at work in another viewer, Fabian, who makes the same uneasy moves between considering the impact on himself and what the film might 'mean': 'I suppose I was wondering whether the film was trying to corrupt me or not. I suppose it, it was a mixture, it's trying to mix eroticism with crashes, and taking the two and trying to mix them up, which was a bit discomforting.' [Interview 21]

Fabian is in some ways a quite different case. A cinephile and former local councillor, his motivation to see the film was virtually as a pseudo-legislator: 'this was something that I could try and form a more detailed opinion of'. So, in answer to the question: would he ever want to see *Crash* again, he replied: 'I don't think I need to.' He had enough for his purposes, lest he should be called on to give an opinion on it. Yet that did not save him from emotional ambivalence and its consequences. In his further statement on this, he makes the explicit links to the 'figure' of the director:

> I mean if it's about corruption about how he was being corrupted then it could be quite a sort of a salutary warning, sort of. But I'm not too sure whether that's what the director had in mind or not. [...] I suppose the question I'd want to know is, I'd want to find out why the director took it on, and why he chose to do that film, what was he trying to get at. I think, I think you're making a film like that, you got to have some reason, I think the reason behind it's got to be important. [...] Umm, I think the question of why he did it was, was paramount in wanting to see it, you know, to try and find out what do you do, what he was playing at.

The 'director' here is not a dubious defence witness to be faced down with hostile questions. He is a source of potentially authoritative answers which, ideally, might change Fabian's own perceptions and judgements. At its best, it could be (in his words) 'showing without lecturing' (a clear version of our showing/saying distinction). Yet those very things which it showed were the source of his personal difficulties:

> The injuries or the scars and stuff like that which was quite, quite off-putting. But sometimes the sort of, sometimes the disturbing stuff was the stuff that was actually making a point about, where they turn up at that crash, and it turns out to be the reconstruction that this guy's done for real. The Jayne Mansfield crash with the dog and everything else like that. That was quite, that was quite a difficult thing to watch, it was actually making a point about how what they were doing was having an impact on other people's lives, and they weren't, they were so obsessed with it, they didn't care about the damage that, the chaos they caused around them. And, you saw the ordinary innocent people who had been hurt and all of that, and killed. And, they didn't really, all that they were bothered about was the mechanics of the crash, they weren't actually, they were, they'd almost switched off to the fact that there were ordinary people, lives are being affected by it all.

Fabian found it very hard to deal with watching a film which showed such a reduction to 'mechanics'. Hence his choice of ambivalent key expression: 'discomforted'.

2 The Defensives

The difference with the second group is that while they too believe that the film-maker has serious intentions – indeed, they may be more sure of this than the Discomforteds – they want nothing to do with it. All they want is the right to enjoy the film. We had a number of cases of this among our interviewees. Stephanie [Interview 19], like many others among Unsettleds, first states that she went expecting to be, but 'wasn't shocked'. She went with her boyfriend to our screening (although only she was subsequently interviewed), and this was important to her experience of *Crash*:

> We enjoyed it, you know, but we didn't have any expectations because we hadn't read the book, but umm we just enjoyed it for, like, entertainment value and just didn't take it seriously, fun sort of thing. Yeah, as I said umm, my boyfriend and I talked quite a bit about it, we talked about it in the car and back home and whatever. And umm, I think we both basically felt the same way. I think we were just quite open minded and, you know, it was just, like, modern film [laughs]. You know, and if you don't take it too seriously, it's just quite entertaining. And I spoke to a couple of my colleagues about it just because they knew I was going, umm and then sort of to people in the faculty, but I just explained to them basically that, I didn't find it at all upsetting or, you know it didn't sort of bother me in the least.

Stephanie and her boyfriend made a strategic decision. By insisting to themselves that the film was 'pure entertainment' they could factor out any disturbing parts and thereby find the film wildly funny, and pretty sexy. That meant an editing job. Those parts of the sexual encounters which ran beyond them were simply set aside: 'I think it's more in the beginning in the movie, rather than the end ... well, at the end it was more the two blokes, so obviously it got sidelined. The sexual aspects – nothing in specific just ... touch, or position or whatever – we thought, oh we'd do that [laughs]. [...] But then obviously they started off basic and then they developed and it became more extreme, so our identifying dropped off after a while.'

Watching in company with her sexual partner, and playing these mental games with it, was clearly crucial. It made their watching an intensely social affair, and multiplied the possibilities of laughter – as long as they restricted the film to being 'entertaining':

> So, it's just stupid things like that, I mean we enjoyed it, you know what I mean, it was a thrill. And I think part of it would have been because we were together. You know, umm, because there's someone else there that, you know, was sort of like on the same wavelength, umm, because we are partners and we know a lot about one another. And, and typical thing was, the showroom scene when we both went, I mean we were absolutely wetting ourselves and trying desperately to be quiet. [Laughs] Everyone else was just sat there. And I was thinking, why don't they think it's funny? [...] So umm, yeah, that's the way I was feeling because it was just entertaining and we were just going along with it. And umm, so there's bits of it that were funny and, which is probably quite sick in other people's perception, but we just took it as a movie that we'd gone to see for entertainment.

It was also an important constraint on her, however, that her employer, a serious, intent man, was in the audience. She told us that part of her will to suppress laughter was so as not to be heard guffawing over the sex! It is important to see that even as Stephanie was 'editing' the film to suit her own uses of it, she was very aware of how it could be taken.

Responding to a very different position taken by her co-interviewee, she declined to see the film as 'boring':

These people in this group, I saw that as part of their life and I was looking at it as though we won't get bored with that because they are doing the same thing, so it didn't seem the movie's boring, I saw what they were doing as not having any growth in it, no progression. [...] And, and so I didn't interpret it as the movie being boring, I thought what they were doing was repetitious. [...] You know, so I thought their lifestyle was being boring, not the movie.

The film was capable of being so enjoyable to her and her partner because they had performed a modality operation on it. Acknowledging its complications, but declining to deal with it at that level, it became a source of fun and arousal. She said: 'That's why I enjoyed it, because it was just ridiculous. For me it was so far away from reality ... if it was real, it would be sick ... and it would be scary, like I said, if it was going on here, I would have a problem with it.'

Strongly present in Stephanie's case (almost certainly aided by the presence of her partner), the same reaction was present more mildly in others. Lisa's [Interview 13] key expression was 'turned on': 'Well there was a lot of sex in it and I like watching that, umm, the fact of them getting sex from, the road crashes didn't involve me, I wasn't concerned about that, it was just there. [...] Yeah it wasn't what was, sort of, making them have sex, it was the fact that they were.' Lisa was strongly attracted to the idea of seeing sex on screen, indeed, when asked about her overall views on how sex should be handled in films, her answer was a very direct: 'I think there should be more of it'. However, with *Crash*, while she enjoyed the sex and found it arousing, the price was her distancing herself from why the characters were having it.

In fact, she and her co-interviewee Barry moved in the course of their interview. As they reviewed their reactions to *Crash*, they supported each other in becoming more enthusiastic about it, but both in the end re-mark a distance from the film, Barry by professing a preference for 'escapism' (film-going as purely a hobby, 'I like to be taken away from, you know, my reality'), Lisa by turning to a concept which featured largely in the responses of quite a few Ambivalent viewers: the idea of 'strange'. Picking up on a comment by Barry about the characters' fascination with each others' scars, she said:

I found that quite strange [...] It just seems like, I can't relate to it, I don't see what people could get out of it. Looking at people's scars and stuff, can't see how they can get turned on by that.

She was happy to be turned on by the film, but the price was a maintenance of her distance from the 'strangeness' of other people's desires.

3 The Disappointeds

A third kind of middle response comes from those whose responses are based on disappointment of some ideal expectations they had of *Crash*, its plot or characters, or of David Cronenberg. To some extent they are like the policemen we heard from in Chapter

7, who condemned *Crash* for being 'bad porn' but would not therefore consider that it might have been trying to be something else. But, as with the other Ambivalents, there is in these people a strong sense of the filmic: that *Crash* should have achieved something worthwhile, even important, but failed to do so.

A clear example of this arose with Stella and Stephen [Interview 23]. A first marker of the character of their responses was their tendency to talk in negatives marking failed achievements. For Stephen, for instance, *Crash* 'definitely hasn't given me food for thought ... I haven't talked about it at all ... I didn't find it shocking ... it didn't really do much for me'. The clear implication was that he might have liked it if it had done these things. What is striking in Stephen's case is that he has no trouble naming a list of qualities, achievements, in *Crash* that still do not add up to making the film a good one for him. Although 'some of the cinematography', the 'black and white imagery', and the 'moodiness' of the film were all good, and it obviously had a 'talented director', these were 'not enough to carry it off'. 'I think he was lucky that everyone made such a fuss of it ... I've seen far worse films, I've seen far more shocking films'. What was missing was a strong plot-line, and 'believability' (a term he shares with Stella and a number of others). For Stephen, it was 'unbelievable' that Holly Hunter's character should want to have sex with Spader's Ballard so soon after the death of her husband. Given that the film tells nothing of her motivation, it clearly cannot have been within his repertoire of conceivable responses for her to do that.[5]

Stella, his co-interviewee, used even more strongly a notion of the 'real world' as a measure of *Crash*. This particularly impacted on how she saw character motivations which she just could not accept. What is particularly interesting is that she might have been able to accept these if she had been able to cast them, not as jaded obsessions, but as youthful sexual experimentation. Then it would not have been a 'fetish thing', which she could not go with, but rather, if the actors had been younger, then 'they'd be experimenting, you know, when you're exploring sexuality'. That could have allowed her to see the film as centred on something which could be explored in its own right. As it was, the characters 'didn't have any personality; they didn't have anything else going on in their heads except this obsession'.

A different measure was proposed by Lawson [Interview 22], an elderly respondent who was very knowledgeable about Cronenberg's work, and indeed about other films dealing with sexual obsessions (he has a long comparison between *Crash* and Oshima's *Empire of the Senses* (1976)). His disappointment with *Crash* has to be considered closely to make sense. He does list a series of ways in which *Crash* is different and distinctive, including being 'very arty' and 'challenging'. Yet his overall judgement is that it lacks 'newness'. The failure was at the 'emotional level' where because the characters were found to be flat and unidimensional, the film 'didn't move me'. 'It was like a non-reflective surface, and it was all one way, not going to engage the audience at all'. Here again, a requirement for a certain kind of engagement runs up against the film's refusal to grant it. The result: disappointment.

Conclusion

In different but equally significant ways, each of these three orientations to *Crash* involves measuring a person's own responses against a perceived set of possibilities. Viewers are acknowledging a role that they could play, but for various reasons have chosen not to. In this way, these Un-settled responses closely fit our model of the seven conditions for a Positive Response, outlined in Chapter 5.

It is worth briefly returning to the issues with which we began this chapter: the question we raised about the general significance of 'unsettledness'. We would suggest the following for wider thought. First, it does seem to us that unsettled viewers are a sadly neglected, but probably proportionately very large, sector of media audiences. The close attention given to fans, as some kind of special audience, and often seen to have para-political virtues, is now being seen by many as a rather indulgent interest. We would suggest that there may be some methodological virtues in attending to the unsettled because, in the course of thinking out loud about their uncertainties or complications, they may disclose the wider orientations to their materials which they are aware are available, but which they are not personally willing or able to adopt. These wider orientations are among the things which audience researchers need to know more about. They are arguably one of the main ways in which 'interpretative repertoires' (as some theorists have called them) take concrete form.

The other point we would make, however, would be to argue against any tendency to a foreclosing theory which supposes to know in advance what is the general nature and purpose of unsettledness – a tendency which particularly lurks within that concept of the 'negotiated reading'. It may well be that unsettledness takes many different forms, and performs many kinds of functions for different viewers.

9   Sorting Through the Wreckage

What do we hope this book has achieved? Many of its conclusions are to be found along the way in its various chapters, in the detail of the materials our research gathered, and in the small and large patterns we have discovered and, hopefully, laid out clearly enough that they make sense to our readers. The function of this chapter is not to repeat what has been said. It is to point onwards to connections and implications, and to suggest how our findings mesh into other, wider debates.

Some of those debates are primarily political, some academic. We were provoked into this research by the political import of the claims about the dangers of a film, and a considerable proportion of what we will say here relates to the various factors and forces in collision in the *Crash* controversy. For example, our research has thrown into sharp relief the power which the *Daily Mail* in particular has been able to wield in recent years; yet it is not entirely clear where exactly this power derives from, or where it tries to take us. It has also become clear that a large part of the controversy has taken place through claims about a notional 'audience' – fictional figures whose qualities and weaknesses provide the explanatory keystones to claims and counter-claims. Where else might we find such figures at work, and what wider roles do they play? And our research has inevitably pushed into the limelight the question of censorship and its future. Yet although the *story* of censorship has often been told, the processes at work in it are as prone to (heroic and satanic) mythic figuring as are the claims about the audience.

Carrying out our research has involved drawing on, and now reflecting back onto, the academic research traditions and methods of investigation which guided our work. We have made important discoveries about the nature of *Crash*'s audience – but those discoveries do not sit easily with some main tendencies within audience research. Our findings about the special nature of the controversy in Britain raise questions about a 'national filmic culture' – but of a rather different kind than is generally talked about in much film studies. And our research could not have been carried on without the major developments that have taken place in some particular branches of qualitative methodology – although these are not as well known as they should be, and indeed there are worrying signs that just at the point where these kinds of research are most proving their worth, the sub-field of audience research appears to be in decline.

There is, however, a third dimension which we do not want to lose. This is the intersection of the above two domains. We are three academics coming from a media and cultural studies tradition, trying to do two jobs: to find out some important truths; and to make them relevant to public political debates. Media and cultural studies, of course, have been the targets of much vilification in recent years, as bogus and useless domains of pseudo-knowledge.[1] It is a sad and ironic fact that the major developments in investigating and understanding culture generated historically in Britain by our field are acknowledged world-wide by academics but are scorned and derided by many political, cultural and media spokespeople. This makes it hard to get a hearing, although many of us still try. Yet equally in recent years, perhaps partly as a result of this public dismissal, many academics in our field have retreated from public engagement, writing only for other academics and becoming more recondite in the issues examined and the problems tackled. What might have been achieved if the field had been more forthright and interventionist in the controversy? How differently might the *Crash* controversy then have proceeded?

Each of these broad areas has many subdivisions, and it is not possible, in one chapter, to delve into them all. Instead, we have chosen to pick up a few key ones in each case.

1. Crash and Politics

A Matter of 'Opinions'

On 11 November 1996, Julian Petley, a former journalist and now lecturer in Communications and Media Studies at Brunel University, wrote to the Press Complaints Commission (PCC) with a series of complaints about the campaign against *Crash* by Associated Newspapers (who own both the *Daily Mail* and the *Evening Standard*). The rules of the PCC are severely constraining. To be able to complain, Petley had to be able to demonstrate that the articles were seriously and prejudicially inaccurate. His complaint had to be posed in these terms, rather than as objections to the campaign they had mounted.[2] In a series of increasingly angry exchanges, Alexander Walker and Christopher Tookey argued the toss with Petley over a period of four months, until finally the PCC declared that there had been no breach of its Code of Practice, and that if there were inaccuracies they were small. The PCC further declared that newspapers were entitled to take opinionated stands – something which Petley had never sought to deny. The row then took another turn, when Petley, along with the BBC video reviewer Mark Kermode, wrote an account of the *Mail* and *Standard* campaign in *Sight and Sound*.[3] Responding to this, Walker more or less threatened legal action if Petley persisted in his claims (although he did nothing when Petley ignored his threats). The final act of this small battle was Petley's summary of the process, with his eyes focused this time primarily on the PCC's inadequacies, in the *British Journalism Review*.[4]

The story of this row is important in itself, since it throws light on the rules which govern the activities of the Press in a situation like this. The PCC's first and last resort was to the right of newspapers to express opinions, even if they do so strongly and using language which borders on the legal (for instance, one of Petley's complaints had been at the repeated used of the word 'pornographic' to describe *Crash*, when that has a specific legal meaning). Our research has shown that in numerous ways the border between news and opinion is completely specious. First, the *Mail* made its own opinions and the campaign which it mounted on the back of them, into news. It reported as 'facts' how others picked up and used its own language for describing *Crash*. The progress of its own campaign was featured as though this was some external event. And by dint of appearing on news pages, by dint of the force of the languages used to describe the film, the campaign against *Crash* had the force of turning their 'opinions' and 'judgements of taste' into proven facts. Not least among those was the invention and circulation of claims that watching *Crash* might induce various kinds of 'harm' in audiences.

An illustration: Petley complained that, while Alexander Walker criticised the film heavily, his original article was headlined by a sub-editor at the *Standard* – a fact which Walker himself stressed in one television debate on the topic, when he wanted to distance himself from the assertion that *Crash* was a 'movie beyond the bounds of depravity' – or in other words, something so extreme that it warrants special treatment. What Petley showed was that a series of subsequent articles in both the *Mail* and *Standard* repeated this phrase, and attributed it to Walker. Given the conditions under which it is possible to complain to the PCC, this had to be done on the basis that these newspapers were 'repeating an inaccuracy'. Their rules constrain complaints this closely. However, from our wider perspective, what is crucial is that this phrase singled out *Crash* even from the normal wherewithalls of the attacks on 'dangerous media'. Its repetition, mantra-like, had (along with other such claims) the force of establishing *Crash* as the equivalent of a dangerous dog. We have seen that it was sufficiently strong that many, even some Cronenberg fans, were effectively intimidated into not seeing the film – and among our audience were many who reported, even some months later, that they had approached the film with real nervousness because of what they had heard or read about it in the media.

The problem here is more specific than the broad critical claim that it is not possible to make the kind of distinction the PCC presumes between news and editorial, fact and opinion. We certainly subscribe to the general arguments made that all mediations involve representations, that is, they involve processes of selection and construction of a narrated account of events which inevitably privilege certain interpretations, but in this case we have observed something more specific. A campaign of this kind passes beyond the sphere of representations to become a tangible social force. In fact, it is interesting to ask how unfair it would be to compare the campaign against *Crash* with that in the 1930s Germany against 'degenerate art'.[5] There are clear differences – the 1930s campaign was mounted by a political party, and one in power, at that. Still, in the kinds of extravagant claim, in the extremity of the accusations and the millennial fears, and in the attempt to mobilise a movement against this film, the analogy is interesting. If nothing else, raising it makes a space to allow us to ask what were the real, as opposed to the claimed, motives of *Crash*'s opponents.

The Daily Mail

The key difference – but not one that could have been guaranteed – is that in the end the *Mail* lost. Having presented its account of *Crash* as an obvious truth, indeed having predicted that if this film were not stopped there could be dire consequences, the film was released and – like 99 per cent of films before – had its brief day at the box office and moved into history.

The *Daily Mail* has a long history, but its recent success is a phenomenon in its own right. Founded in 1896, the *Mail* from its outset celebrated imperialism, embodying this in an ideology of civilisation versus savagery. Always a right-wing newspaper, it is notorious among press historians for its celebratory response to the rise of fascism in Britain, most famously with its headline 'Hurrah for the blackshirts!'[6] More recently, from the late 1980s and clearly through its association with Thatcherite Conservatism, the prestige, influence and sales of the *Mail* have grown. As a marker, its sales have grown from 1.75 million in 1988 to over 2 million, with readership estimated at over 5 million, while many other newspapers suffered a decline. It has done this on the back of becoming ever more stridently the 'voice of middle England'. In the course of researching the background of this book, we have asked a number of researchers if there is yet a study of the recent history of the *Mail*. It has yet to be written.

It does need to be written. During the 1970s, Stuart Hall and others proposed an account of Thatcherism which they called 'authoritarian populism'.[7] Roughly, this proposed that a wholesale crisis of social and political legitimacy had emerged from the late 1960s. In response, the new style of Conservatism which Mrs Thatcher promulgated was an attempt to shift the ground of British politics wholesale, by creating a new 'commonsense'. In speaking directly to 'the people', the Conservatives were aiming to bypass and undermine the legitimacy of any organisation that could claim to mediate between State and individual/family. Hall *et al*'s thesis was subjected to many criticisms, and we are not trying to resurrect it here. But in important senses the *Daily Mail* could be seen to have come to believe their thesis. Its claim to speak on behalf of 'ordinary English people' seems to us different from the kind of claims made by other newspapers. Its serious and strongly campaigning style is distinctive and needs to be properly understood.

One point in particular is striking, and this is the *Mail*'s attempt to present itself as simply the voice of morality, rather than of a particular politics. We note the following paradox. Almost all the journalists whom we interviewed told us that they believed that the *Mail*'s campaign against *Crash* was politically motivated. Yet in the coverage of the controversy, and in the reviews of *Crash*, you would be hard put to it to find any discussion of this.[8] In that curious absence, the *Mail* won a large part of its argument, since the film was then discussed in and through *its* moral definitions.

Censorship

What is to be said about the BBFC, the institution at the heart of the controversy over *Crash*? Under intense pressure from the *Mail*, and from a range of moral and political entrepreneurs, in the end it stood firm and granted *Crash* an '18' certificate, uncut. It is unclear whether the BBFC was being 'clever' in timing the release of its decision to coincide with the announcement of the General Election but, that apart, it stood by its own sense of its principles. That in itself sets the *Crash* case apart from many previous instances where critics have railed against some of its decisions and rules. So, how do we make sense of this piece of its history? There are several good general histories of the BBFC, and they tell a story of social and political ideologies disguised as moral protectionism. Tom Dewe Mathews shows, for instance, the long operation of censors' rules to protect the Empire and refuse representations of colonial revolt, to avoid any suggestion of cross-racial sexual attraction, to downplay any representation of class conflict, and – perhaps most notoriously – to avoid offence to foreign powers such as Hitler's regime in the mid-1930s.[9]

The problem with this kind of history is not that it is false, but that it falls foul of several dangers. First, it tends to treat film-makers as virtuous souls producing art and argument, who are being stifled by outside moral and political forces. This leaves out of the reckoning the institutional interdependence of the BBFC with the film-makers and distributors. The BBFC has always derived its income from fees paid for its decisions on films. This produces, many have argued, a collusive will to protect the general interests of the film industry. Second, this approach leads too easily to a celebration of the present, a history of the BBFC as a gradual move away from the arbitrary and political towards sensible, balanced and research-informed judgements. Third, and perhaps most importantly, this history also over-focuses on the exceptional cases, the moments when conflicts have arisen or when the politics of the BBFC have intervened harshly. This kind of history-by-worse-case misses the dull proceduralism of much of the Board's work. Today, for instance, the great majority of its decisions are routinist and almost mechanical: helping distributors to fit films within the 'windows' of the various classifications. 'You want this action-adventure to be a '15' at the cinema? Then we are afraid you will have to trim five seconds off that scene, and please dub over these three expletives. For video, the criteria being a little stricter, you may have to alter another eight seconds' worth.'

Recent history has made understanding censorship processes even more complicated. The BBFC has grown enormously since it was given the task, after the 1984 Video Recordings Act, of overseeing video as well as film classification. That addition came, of course, on the back of the successful campaign, again led by the *Daily Mail*, against what became known as 'video nasties'.[10] Yet a series of other changes occurring alongside this have produced in recent years something of a personality crisis in the Board. Government and others have pressed for more transparency in its operations while at the same time trying to impose a tighter regime, initially through the Home Secretary's power to appoint a successor to the BBFC's retiring president, Lord Harlech. These changes rubbed awkwardly against the long paternalism of James Ferman's reign as its Director, which was coming to a close by the mid-1990s. Ferman himself was a strong cinephile, and encouraged decisions in favour of films which, judged on moral grounds alone, would have caused real problems. Perhaps his swansong was the Board's decision to allow Catherine Breillat's *Romance* (1997), with its clearly-seen male and female genitalia and its scenes of fellatio and sado-masochism, on the grounds that it was so clearly an 'art-house' film, would be subtitled, and therefore could be safely permitted.[11]

Recently, a number of other factors have come into play. The Board has become, via Ferman, increasingly enamoured of certain kinds of American socio-psychological research – one of whose recent moves has been to find that sex *per se* in films is 'harmless', while sex associated with violence is the real problem.[12] In his final years, Ferman has proselytised for this distinction, to the Board's subsequent embarrassment. One outcome of the government's attempt to tighten controls was the creation of an appeals system for video. The Video Appeals Committee, perhaps informed in part by Ferman's steer on sexual matters, ultimately proved more liberal than the Board itself, especially since its terms of reference required it to take account of the criterion of 'harm'. This has led to the 1999 conflict between Jack Straw, the Board and the Appeals Panel over a series of '18R' sex videos.

The demand for transparency, coupled with a rising awareness that there is not a simple 'public opinion' on what should be allowed on film and video, has led recently to the Board's 'Roadshow'. Members of the Board, along with experts from various domains, have toured the country to explain the work of the Board, and to sound out views on film issues, but with a new depth and complexity. Among other methods, the Board has used Citizens' Juries which hear debates on the issues, from which reports are drawn up to inform the future thinking of the Board. All this and more, and one thing in particular, has made it both more difficult but also more important to think about how to understand the institutional position and role of the BBFC. The additional element is the Board's awareness, stated repeatedly by Ferman in particular, that soon the very basis on which they make their decisions will be undermined forever by the arrival of digital convergence. The virtual impossibility of controlling digital distribution and copying made Ferman in his last years a strong advocate for the development of a version of media studies as an alternative system of protection for the young. If we can't stop 'em seeing the stuff, we can make sure they can see through it![13]

With all these new complexities, how does one get beyond mere description? A good place to begin, perhaps, is Annette Kuhn's important examination of the operations of the BBFC in its early years. Using case-studies of a series of films with the shared 'problem' of sexual morality, Kuhn mounts a powerful critique of what she identifies as the standard, commonsense account of censorship which she calls the 'prohibition/institutions' model.[14] Oversimplifying this, we can say that many public debates about censorship presume that censorship is a matter of finding a right balance between the freedom of the artist, and the safety of society, and of creating the right institutions through which this should be conducted. Kuhn's alternative approach centres on investigating the operation of socially-significant discourses within those institutions, within the film industry and within the films themselves. For example, she investigates the ways in which one film, *Married Love* (1923), became the epicentre of the controversies around birth control and the ideas of Marie Stopes. The film itself addresses these debates, explicitly through the title (which is taken from Stopes' most famous book) and through the figure of Maisie Burrows, a young woman forced on to the streets by her brutal father and her own refusal to accept a life of endless child-bearing. Kuhn is able to show that the controversy around the film cannot be understood without examining the debates at that time around the idea of 'propaganda films'. The problem with propaganda, it was claimed, was that 'ordinary viewers', and especially in the normal situation of cinema viewing, would not be able to deal with such a film at the appropriate level. It was therefore acceptable for it to be viewed in a special setting, as in a private club or when it was accompanied by a lecture. Kuhn quotes a BBFC memo:

> There are many scenes and subtitles which render this film in our opinion unsuitable for exhibition before ordinary audiences; while the title, taken in conjunction with the name of the book and the authoress referred to, suggests propaganda on a subject unsuitable for discussion in a Cinema Theatre.[15]

The key terms here ('ordinary audiences', 'unsuitable', 'propaganda', 'discussion in a Cinema Theatre') are not transparent: they mark the presence of wider debates which are going on in the film itself. Kuhn's argument is, then, that censorship is a *productive* process, producing the very ways of reading and responding to films which it claims to want to control. By describing and categorising films in this sort of way, censorship processes provide the means to understand them thus – both for and against. And of course it is central to her account that these discourses originate only in part from the institutions formally given the task of censorship.

We can learn much from Kuhn's account. Without question, the campaign over *Crash* produced the possibility of reading the film in the manner demanded by the *Mail*. It also produced the arena within which people could reject that reading. And as we have shown, those who wanted to defend the film became trapped in a discursive space outlined by the terms of the *Mail*'s attack. Yet we are in a position to do something which Kuhn could not. We have been able to access people's reports of their lived responses to the film. These show that for some people a distinction emerged between the responses they had expected to have, because of the terms and force of the controversy, and those which took over when they encountered the film itself. Often they struggle to find appropriate terms to express this experience. We would like to think that this book may help with this process. That, of course, raises a question about our relation to the responses which we brought to light, an issue to which we return in a moment.

2. Crash and Academia

This book is a contribution to several academic fields, but probably most importantly to the field of qualitative audience research. This field flourished after 1980, and for a time the tokens were promising for its future. There has been a tendency in the field to overstate the degree of newness, of doing things not previously attempted. Several critics have rightly pointed out that there are important precedents;[16] and most recently Andy Ruddock has given a useful, nuanced account of the history of American mass communications research which well displays how, at different moments, some of the questions and methods seen as defining contemporary audience research were already emergent.[17] There have also been inflated claims about the methods of research being used, especially with regard to the claim of being 'ethnographic'. Even so, it is clear that a significant change did take place in the last two decades, as a result of the confluence of a number of distinct influences.

The cultural studies movement, which generally spawned much of the new research, brought with it an interest in a range of new objects – forms of popular media and culture – which had often been ignored, if not dismissed, as too simple to be worthy of this kind of detailed attention. The challenge that everything from soap operas to game shows to blockbuster movies are complex symbolic formations, which relate to significant audience pleasures, knowledges and social positions, encouraged a new attention to their audiences, albeit swinging somewhat wildly between pessimistic ('these formations embody reactionary cultural representations or imaginings, and we are exploring their impacts') and optimistic ('the audiences are finding meaning in these minimal forms, therefore let us celebrate their semiotic productivity') poles. In a related mode, feminist interests in media and culture examined audience reactions in terms of proximity to versus distance from argued ideals of liberation. A few years after the emergence of this interest came the encounter with the systematic cultural sociology of Pierre Bourdieu. Bourdieu painted an influential picture of a hierarchically organised structure of tastes, within which individuals live out their assigned cultural position as if this were natural.[18] His work, along with a broader interest in the distinction between 'high' and 'low' culture, generated enthusiasm for examining forbidden pleasures, and for considering the consequences of the status that different forms of art and culture have gained. Bourdieu's name, if not his survey techniques of investigation, crops up in many a recent audience study as a resource for thinking.

What has happened in the last twenty years has been simultaneously exciting and depressing. The enthusiasm of the first years of this research programme passed, as results proved thinner than hoped, and as critics began to pick apart some of the more inflated claims. Also, many who tried out an audience study learned quickly how hard this is. Audience research is methodologically tricky, it is resource-greedy and time-expensive. A number of the better-known publications in the field are the outcome of doctoral researches, rarely pursued further by those who did them. For the number of researchers now active in the broad domain of cultural and media studies, the proportion pursuing audience researches is pitifully small – and shrinking. It is our distinct impression that there has been quite a widespread retreat from audience research in the last few years.[19] Yet at the same time it has become a hot topic to write *about*. Indeed at times it feels as if more people are writing critiques of audience research than are practising any part of it.

The critique has been heavily methodological. There have been (in some ways, just) complaints about the exaggerated claims for insight and unmediated access to people's responses.[20] There have been claims that studying audiences is not in essence different from studying 'texts' – after all, in both cases it is 'representations' which are studied.[21] And there has been a more generalised turn away from considering what used to be called the text/audience relationship into examining conditions of reception, and the practices and routines of everyday life. This third turn has been in some respects interesting and useful. Yet at the same time, it seems to us to have produced a strange mixture of an extreme descriptivism, with what feels at times like a cloud of theory achieving little.

Whatever the motives, there has undoubtedly been a decline in interest in examining the responses of audiences to particular films or other forms, or even to particular genres. This lack of interest sometimes turns into rejection. We met a small marker of this when we submitted our final report on this research to the Economic and Social Research Council. One anonymous referee, whilst making friendly comments about what we had achieved, nonetheless commented that perhaps this research signalled that the methodologies for doing this kind of research had reached their limit. And perhaps there was little point in further studies of this kind. All that could be achieved, had been. We very definitely do not agree.

With the issues we have faced, we have to say that *not* to address the film/audience relationship would be a sheer abrogation of responsibilities. The debate around *Crash* in Britain turned at significant points around figures of 'the audience', what the film might do to him or her, or what s/he might do with the film. If cultural studies says that it has nothing to contribute to such a debate, other than a response that such things are untestable because it is all a matter of discourses, then cultural studies departs the field that gave birth to it: the field of cultural intervention. We have demonstrated that it is possible to carry out worthwhile research in this area, and research which, if listened to, has enormous relevance to public debates and policy formation. No different than any other research (be it into gene-expressions, global warming, changes in family structures, or the psychology of mass murderers), any piece of audience research has to be aware of the limits of confidence its findings sustain, given the methods used and the scope of materials examined. We have tried to state our limits self-consciously. But with all the necessary caveats, we think this research has produced findings of considerable significance both for our academic field and beyond. Here we pinpoint three:

The question of the unsettled

A genuine surprise to us, as we were considering our findings, was the virtual absence of work which could help us make sense of what we came to call 'un-settled' viewers of *Crash*. Indeed the search simply for a name for such people proved to us how little consideration has been given to such people – who, as we have said, probably in most situations constitute a great majority of the audience. There are a number of more general points we want to make here about this area.

First, it is clear to us that this is not a singular group. People can have unsettled views for all kinds of reasons and in all kinds of ways. They can be still undecided – and indeed may always stay that way. With *Crash*, some of our viewers may never get past feeling an uncomfortable mixture of responses. But equally it is possible for people to be *decidedly* un-settled, to have come to a conclusion that the film *deserves and needs* doubled reactions. Some audiences identified opposite tendencies in the film, and were confident in this identification. The film was 'boring', but had good camerawork. This does not make the category 'boredom' transparent or obvious, but it does mean that we would be wrong to measure such people against some other ideal, to find them inadequate on some score.

Some viewers were confused about their reaction, a different kind of un-settledness. They were aware of finding certain aspects of the film sexually arousing, yet at the same time found that disquieting – they did not believe that a film of this kind *should* be capable of arousing them. Other viewers were confused in quite another sense, that they could not see why someone should have made a film of this kind – what is it *for*? what is its *point*? Some viewers, at the time we interviewed them, were simply still in process of sorting out their views on *Crash*; they had not yet settled.

As researchers, we believe that all these very different reactions are equally worthy of attention. They are not to be assessed for their adequacy or otherwise. Rather, they can usefully be investigated for their preconditions (what knowledges, emotional engagements or cultural engagements enable or disable certain reactions to the film?), for their patterning (how do people in each of these positions typically make use of socially available patterns of discourse?), and for their consequences (what uses do different people make of their responses, to link and provide impetus to other beliefs and attitudes?). But in the process of doing these things, we have to be careful not to impose on them a coherence, or a completeness, which isn't there.

We have said that we found very few resources to help with thinking directly about this.[22] However, we think it is worth pointing to a different area of media analysis, where a similar problem has surfaced. In the history of American mass communication research, a signal breakthrough in many respects came with the rise of the concept of agenda-setting, with its central slogan that 'the media do not tell us what to think, but what to think *about*'. In some forms, agenda-setting research was actually not much different from earlier attempts at 'magic bullet' accounts. Agenda-setters still used predominantly quantitative methods, assuming that there would be a necessary correlation between the *amount* of attention given to, say, a political topic, and the extent to which it became *salient* to readers and viewers. But in some hands, it became increasingly a qualitative tool, a ground for considering such matters as the *definition of the topic*, the role of *visual rhetorics* and the *according of status to primary definers*.[23] This work has parallels with ours in its wish to address text/audience relations, although little attempt was made at first to inquire into actual audience responses.

In the early 1990s, however, a debate occurred on the conceptual foundations of agenda-setting research, which was in part driven by the kinds of concerns which have motivated us. Alex Edelstein, in particular, investigates a series of ambiguities and unclarities in the idea of 'thinking about'. He points up the confusions in this concept. A public issue might have salience for an individual, or it might simply be that s/he acknowledges that it appears to have salience for the media. He questions whether frequency is a good measure of how important a topic is seen to be in the media, not least because frequency is not that good a predictor even of how people will rank their responses. He further demonstrates, both conceptually and by reference to empirical evidence, that it is not easy to separate, in the way supposed, thinking and thinking about. People's degree of acknowledgement of a problem is connected with their thinking about the possible steps might be taken to act upon it.[24] This is important and relevant in its own right, but has particular interest for us, since Edelstein finds himself using a series of variables in order to be able to account for the different ways in which people find issues relevant to themselves, and constitute them as 'problems'.[25] Edelstein's variables are not the same as ours, but his approach recognises, as we do, that people's involvements are always simultaneously cognitive and affective.

The significance of this is the recognition in another area concerned with the text/audience interface of a need to acknowledge that some people simply do not care enough to give 'salience' to particular media-defined issues, while others may experience conflicts in their attitudes towards them, and indeed may precisely respond *through* a querying of their reliability, *because* they come from a mass medium. The media's agenda may be identified as just that, the *media*'s agenda. And therefore a disinclination to agree to the media's schedule of issues, or even to become involved, may be a form of certainty. Our task, therefore, is to understand the different kinds of un-settledness we discovered, instead of measuring against some singularly perceived 'complete' response.

At the time of writing, we see this as a substantial gap in our thinking about audiences, and one which has been partly concealed by a built-in preference for certain 'ideal' responses seen to meet researchers' political agendas.

Conditions for a Positive Response

Another important aspect of our findings might seem to conflict with the above. This is our identification of those seven conditions for a Positive response to *Crash*. How may this aspect of our findings contribute to the field of qualitative audience research? What we say here has to be foreshortened, for reasons of space. Yet the risk may be worth it, if the resultant silhouettes still point up some useful contrasts. Our prime question here relates to the overall achievements of this tradition of research, and to what kinds of knowledge have resulted.

Some audience researches essentially work to show that there is a far greater variety and complexity of responses than is orthodoxly expected, or to show that particular groups have very different responses than are generally expected of them.[26] Such findings are useful in themselves, but can best be seen as posing, rather than answering, questions about how these responses come about. They are descriptive in a good sense of the word; and we have badly needed some reliable descriptions.[27]

However, a considerable proportion of qualitative audience research is more theoretically driven, especially by a will to look for 'influence', and a wish to identify those who may be particularly influenced by media texts. The problem is that such research depends on having working accounts of three areas. While such researches may focus on the audience, to do so in this manner they have to have at least a working account of what might be doing the influencing (the 'message', more or less), and a model of how this 'message' works persuasively on the audience. So, consider the strand of research which works within the encoding/decoding framework. Generally such work first researches media texts, in order to determine their embedded persuasive 'messages'.[28] From there the hunt begins for those (individuals or groups) who are most 'vulnerable' to them. We see a number of problems in this. How does such research mark the difference between audiences *agreeing* with the 'meaning' discovered by textual analysis, and *being persuaded* by it? What does such research have to say about those who do not display signs of agreement, other than that they do not appear to have been influenced? And, what happens if no one other than the analyst him/herself, or others opposed to it, identifies this as the 'meaning' or 'message'? These and other difficulties have plagued this approach, but it has lingered on, partly at least because of a lack of alternative models of text/audience relations.

Our position differs in several ways. First, we do not want to limit the notion of 'influence' or 'effect' to enforced agreement. Actually, in the ordinary sense of the term, among the most 'affected' by *Crash* were those who rejected it wholesale. They were disgusted, appalled, sickened, and so on. Alexander Walker was in this sense clearly 'influenced' by *Crash*, and those effects produced distinct behaviours – repeated hostile reviews and commentaries on the film (we have doubts as to whether Christopher Tookey was personally 'affected' to the same extent – there is a strong sense that the *Mail* opposed *Crash* for strategic political reasons, sensing campaigning opportunities). This alone points to some unstated problems in the encoding theory's picture of 'influence'. It seems to us that the model of the 'active audience' has disguised this, since that model is premised on a troublesome distinction: between those whose 'activity' is evidenced in distance and rejection of the perceived 'message', and those who, by showing signs of accepting the 'message', must have been less 'active', more 'passive', more 'influenced'. Thus, this approach depends upon distinguishing two different *modes* of relating to, and being touched by, the media.

This is important in a second way, in as much as, despite sometimes claiming 'ethnographic' status, qualitative audience research in the cultural studies tradition mostly consists of snapshots. Audiences are briefly interviewed, or observed. This is not wrong in itself, and a lot has been learned from such snapshots. But it does mean that at the moment of conducting the research, 'influence' has to be thought of as an already-laid-down textual residuum. We have argued for a more processual approach. People's responses evolve and take shape over time, and do not, except perhaps in particular cases, have a moment of completion. This suggests that a research snapshot has distinct limits; and if we combine this with our previous point about the wider possible meanings of 'influence', we can see where existing researches might have gone. David Morley, for instance, saw a group of shop stewards as being 'un-influenced' by *Nationwide* in that they could identify its ideological positions. But of course in real-life situations, to identify a source as inimical will sometimes lead to responses, or over time to challenges. This happened in the 1984/5 British miners' strike. Taking note of the media's ideological hostility to their action, groups of miners with their supporters set up alternative means of explaining their actions and seeking support. They acted out their hostility to mainstream news sources. This is not of course 'influence' in the sense in which it is normally conceived. But once take away the notion that 'influence' is of a different order from 'resistance', and such actions should be every bit as legitimately interesting to this kind of research.

To get at such consequences, of course, research has to be as naturalistic as possible. This is our third point. If we are to uncover the real dynamics of audiences, both devotees and hostiles, fashioning their responses over time, and incorporating those in significant fashion into the rest of their lives, then our choice of cases to study cannot be arbitrary. We have to concern itself with media materials which *audiences* have identified as important, positively or negatively, and our methods need to be able to pursue responses over indefinite periods of time. We did not wholly achieve the latter in this research. We had three moments of contact with our audiences (the questionnaires before and after the screening, and the interviews several weeks later) and we did directly inquire into how people felt their views had evolved. By the time we interviewed some, they told us that their memories were becoming hazy. However strong their immediate responses to the film, its image was clearly fading. 'Influence' is generally finite, although its span varies. We acknowledge the limitations of our research in this respect.

We have already touched on a fourth problem in this kind of research. In pursuing signs of 'influence', researchers have also to know, in advance, the media's 'message' which might invade the audience. This is tricky enough in relation to the news and other informational materials. Consider the complexities of the claims about news which the Glasgow Media Group put forward,[29] or the complex structures of meaning which John Corner *et al* identified in his nuclear documentaries.[30] Or consider how the identification of 'messages' in news coverage has been disputed, in for instance the controversy over television's coverage of the miners' strike.[31] If informational media are difficult enough, how much more complex is the case of fictions! Yet campaigns such as our present one against *Crash* are regularly awash with claims as to what the 'message to viewers' must be. The attribution of 'meanings' to fictional forms has become, in some cases, almost an industry – but with the peculiar tendency in the industry's productions that very often the 'meanings' discovered are not those experienced (enjoyed, absorbed) by the analyst, but are ones attributed as possible 'effects' on others.[32]

Our procedures in investigating *Crash* have taken us in a different direction. The 'meanings' or 'messages' of *Crash* are to be found within the strategies of interpretation and the consequential responses of different audiences. This may sound like a dissolution of the film 'text' into the array of different responses. That would be a serious misunderstanding of what we have done. Audiences, in producing their interpretations of *Crash*, have to have materials to work on. What they work on is the highly organised array that is the film. We reported a first small part of this in our examination of people's reactions to the first three scenes of *Crash*. Not everyone succeeds in producing a 'meaning' out of the film. Indeed, some people clearly decided early on in their viewing that they did not want to. The film was incomprehensible, as were the makers' intentions. Such viewers failed, or declined, or refused to see any point, meaning or message in the film – unless it was that they saw a perverse meaning being inflicted on others.

Yet others, those who arrived at a rich interpretative relationship with the film, found themselves challenged in ways that often surprised them. The risk had been worthwhile. The film was something which they were willing and able to submit to, for the period of its presence on screen. It was a form, a narrative, a symbolic presence with a power quite independent of them. Their interpretations of it struggled to be make sense of, to be adequate to, their experiences of the film. It is within the manner of their uses of the film, within the challenges which they experienced, that it is possible to discern the communicative invitation of *Crash*. It is not that *Crash*'s enthusiastic audiences are morally better, or aesthetically more clever, than the film's refusers. It is that the differences between them make the enthusiasts clearer sources for capturing the nature of the film's propositions than others. First, they engage more richly, and for longer periods, with the film. Second, they are less prone to adopt an external language (in this case, the *Mail*'s) to label their experiences.[33] A small, if risky, analogy: a researcher who wants to assess the body's reactions to a food will do well to study those who actually eat the substance, rather than those who spit it out, saying 'this is disgusting'. On this analogy, academic researchers begin to look like poison-tasters, searching the media for ideological toxins. Our own 'readings' of films are not secure grounds for evaluating audience responses.

Our criticisms are intended to go deep. At stake is a whole model of communication. Despite its ambitions of understanding the media within the total circuit of culture, in effect a great deal of qualitative audience research still works with an implicit linear model of communication. First there is a message, discovered and described by the analyst using specialist research techniques. Next, there is its mode and direction of influence. This tells researchers also where and how to look for 'signs of influence'. Only now does the research into audiences, the end-point of a process, begin. And when the research outcome is, as has mostly been the case, to admit that people show no such signs, the implication is that influence has 'failed' in this case.[34]

Our model of the Conditions for a Positive Response is the gateway to a different non-linear model. We do not deny that films affect people – but we want to stay much closer to the ordinary meanings of that word. People laugh, or cry, or care about characters, become enraged, or bored, or aroused. The conditions under which they do this, matter greatly. Not just the physical and social conditions of being in the cinema, or at home with video, or television, although these are important: being alert or tired, in congenial company or not, warm or cold, with clear vision or not, and so on. Yet every bit as important are the knowledges, expectations and orientations which people take with them into the act of watching. These constitute *states of readiness for novel experiences*. However, that is the point: to see a new film is to experience something novel. It is being seen for just that reason. It is to take a risk, for the sake of gaining a new experience. What if the outcome is negative? At its most minimal, the response could be of the following order: that was a bit disappointing, waste of time/money, a bit of a let-down. At a stronger level, it might become: that was terrible, upsetting, offensive, immoral. But what if the experience is felt to be positive?

To go to see a film, then, is to agree to play a role: the role of ready audience. At any point, of course, we can withdraw from that disagreement. But minimally, to count as an audience, we have to agree to try to make sense of what is going on, to follow cues and clues as to where events are moving, and to build up working pictures of characters and what they are trying to do. On its part, a film has to give us enough and of a kind that we are willing to work on. But of course 'enough' is anything but a given amount. According to their various states of readiness, different parts of our audience found, or did not find, adequate and agreeable materials in *Crash* to work with.

If, therefore, we have managed to elucidate the conditions necessary for a positive response to *Crash*, we believe we were making a substantial breakthrough. We suggest that what we have here is the outline (no more than that) of a distinct contemporary cultural orientation, of the kinds of symbolic resources which serve that orientation, and of the manner in which those resources are encountered and appropriated. To go further would need new kinds of research well beyond what we attempted here.[35]

3. Academics and the Crash Controversy

Media, film and cultural studies – during their recent history in Britain – have made a considerable noise of asserting the political nature of all forms of culture. Differently, but interrelated, each of these three overlapping fields has produced a stream of books, articles and courses whose central premise is that culture always involves power. More than that, in much of such writing, one will find claims that anyone researching cultural practices cannot free her/himself from these processes. Culture is political, film is political, and cultural research is political. Given the strength of this tradition, it is astonishing how silent most film academics were in the teeth of the *Mail*'s assault on *Crash*. Faced with real power-politics, as a field by and large we very badly fell short. There were one or two notable exceptions, individuals who spoke out courageously, but the overall silence is staggering.

Among those three fields, film studies has perhaps the strongest tradition of behaving strictly academically. With its roots in literary interests in film, film studies has never quite shed a sense of earnest scholarly enquiry. This, despite the fact that the *Screen* tradition – ascendant in Britain during the 1970s and still with great residual influences – taught that film was the medium *par excellence* which produced the gendered subjectivities required for 'patriarchal capitalist society'.

Other traditions, too, examined the role of film in the construction of national identities, and its use as a tool of propaganda. Film studies, nonetheless, has often stressed that it is a 'special case' of media/cultural enquiry. Partly, this is also a consequence of a long tradition in Britain of insulating academics from social and cultural life. While in America, by contrast, academics in the humanities and social sciences have never been shy about addressing public affairs, in Britain the image of the reclusive other-worldly don cohabits with its partial reality.

There were voices in defence of *Crash*, most notably Julian Petley and Mark Kermode. Their article in *Sight and Sound* was the most prominent public assault on the *Mail*'s case. They were among the people who spoke at several of the BFI's regional film centres which mounted screenings and debates. The debate at Chapter Arts, Cardiff, came shortly after an attempt by a subcommittee of their local council to bar the film from the city. A full Council meeting overturned the ban, taking the view that Chapter was a responsible venue whose judgement should be trusted. The debate brought together Mark Kermode with other specialist interests, including a representative of a Disability Awareness group. Nottingham's Broadway Cinema invited Christopher Tookey to debate *Crash* with, among others, Petley – Tookey declined, sending a fax which, read out, gave the audience rare moments of hilarity. Among the speakers defending the film was a man who had barely survived a motorbike crash. Tyneside's Regional Cinema, among others, also organised a debate on the film.

The notable absence in all this is the voice of film academics. The situation worsens when one considers what academics *did* say about *Crash*. In the journal *Screen*, a series of four articles appeared as part of the 'Debate' section, suggesting that perhaps they would at the least reference the terms of the controversy. In fact nothing of the sort. Addressing *Crash* almost entirely through the lens of different versions of psychoanalysis, the articles did not once refer to the public controversy, nor did the editors deem it worthy of comment.[36] Some small contact with the real world was eventually restored with a short article a year later by Annette Kuhn. Kuhn reconstructed the time-line of the controversy, and concluded from this that there was no evidence of a conspiracy by the BBFC to smuggle the film out.[37] It is still worth remarking that this article hardly transcends a descriptive retelling of the events. It takes no position on it all, nor does Kuhn draw on her own earlier re-theorisation of censorship. It is as if the complexities of the present defeat that account.

Still, at least she mentioned the campaign. For the rest, it is an unedifying spectacle of abstruse clerks fiddling with their concepts ignoring Nero striking matches to set fire to their house. Even more recently, an entire book on Cronenberg edited by one of the contributors to this debate, Michael Grant, manages to sidestep all the issues. The essay on *Crash*, by Parveen Adams, addresses the film through Lacanian spectacles.[38] It is as if, for British film academics, investigation of the politics of censorship has drained away into debates about psychic censorship.

This criticism of our own academic fields is not a claim that there was a 'line' which we would have expected every reasonable film or media academic to follow. Far from it. The three authors of this book are not in complete agreement on all the issues around classification, censorship and public policy on film. We do though share a view that the way the *Crash* controversy went was about as ignorant, as irrational, and as ill-motivated as it could have been. And that surely is the point at which those whose lives turn on intellectual enquiry, and on *some* kind of quest for knowledge, have to speak out. What do we expect archaeologists to do when mystics such as Erich von Daniken colonise public debates about the meaning of monoliths? What do we expect astronomers do when wild claims are made about the map of the stars? How do we expect social scientists to react when moralising politicians claim that there is only one kind of 'normal' family?

Research into film and film audiences needs to reach the public domains of debate. That can only happen on certain conditions. First, the questions asked have to be meaningful to more than academics. This is more than a call for clear writing (though some of own students might breathe a sigh of relief just at this...). It is a call for film academics to look at themselves, and ask in what ways what they are doing is relevant to public debates. Second, it will need concerted efforts at all kinds of level to get such research heard. There is a safety of sitting within education, and bemoaning the appalling level of debate about films. We will not always be able to choose the terrain of debate, or set its terms. Yet the failure to try to intervene is a scandal.

Because we cannot control when and where future arguments will arise, the research community needs to be ready to ask the difficult questions. Bearing in mind the present government's claim to be committed to the film industry and to expanding attention to film at all levels, we should be ready (organisationally, methodologically, conceptually) to take opportunities to conduct research that asks the questions about films that, often, those who make policy do not want to ask. That has always been a function of critical intellectuals. We wanted this research, and this book, to be a contribution to this task.

Methodological Appendix

We think it is important to tell readers who may be interested about how we conducted this research. This is, after all, in the end what differentiates research from commentary. In this Appendix, therefore, we tell the methodological story of our research. We set out the main concepts and methods through which it was organised and conducted, the main stages it went through, the important decisions we had to make at many points, and the key research implements we designed and used. We have tried to be honest in this section about the mistakes we made, and the problems we encountered and did not perhaps fully overcome. All real research, we believe, should admit its limits, and then say how confident the researchers feel they can be in their findings.[1] Everything in this Appendix, therefore, tells how and why we carried out our research, rather than what we learnt as a result.

Our research was made possible by a project grant from the Economic and Social Research Council (No. R000222194). The idea for the research came to fruition in July 1997 when we applied to the ESRC. We heard that this had been successful in September, and the research got underway at the turn of the year, with the appointment of our Research Assistant, Jo Haynes. Already, then, we knew we had to be content with dealing retrospectively with the controversy and its impacts. With the published journalistic materials, this did not greatly matter. It clearly had greater import for our investigation of audience responses, especially inasmuch as we wanted to explore the impact of the controversy on how people felt about *Crash*. Given (as we show in the main body of the book) that we found clear evidence of lasting impact on audiences (in the form of quite deep-running fears about what it might be like to watch *Crash*), this suggests strongly that at the height of the campaign against *Crash*, the power of the circulating claims would probably have been even greater.[2]

It matters where we were each coming from, since at the very least this shaped the questions we felt it was important to ask. All three of us involved in the ESRC application came to the project from a background in cultural and media studies, but with different research interests and orientations. Martin Barker had researched a number of past censorship campaigns, including the 1950s campaigns against 'horror comics' and the 1984/5 campaign against 'video nasties', and had become interested in particular in two aspects of them: the way such campaigns present themselves in overwhelmingly moral terms, when in fact research revealed other motives at work; and what it is about the attacked media that actually attracts those who are their normal audience. Most recently Barker had turned to audience research, to try to answer the second question. In 1995/6 he ran an ESRC-funded investigation into the meaning of action-adventure movies for their audiences, using the example of the comic-book based, Sylvester Stallone vehicle *Judge Dredd*.[3] This had particular relevance to the present project, in that the *Dredd* research supplied both our central method of analysis (the version of discourse analysis we have used to explore writing and talk around *Crash*) and some of our key concepts, which had emerged to prominence during the *Dredd* research. We set these out in a moment.

Jane Arthurs brought to the *Crash* project an interest in studying cinema as a cultural event, in which the evaluations made by journalists create a particular context for a film's reception. She has researched the controversies occasioned by two previous films, *A Question of Silence* (1982)[4] and *Thelma and Louise* (1991).[5] In both cases, the films were controversial because of their gender reversal of narrative roles; the women are the killers rather than the victims of violence. What they shared was a press response in which extreme hostility to and impassioned defences of the film spilled out from the specialist pages of newspapers and film periodicals into the wider arena of the news. The focus of debate was the women's violence and its cultural meaning and effects. From these studies Arthurs became interested in the discursive repertoires used to comprehend and evaluate films. In particular she is interested in the ways in which expectations about film genre, authorship, narrative and character interact with broader ideological discourses to create a reading and how this process is affected when the film is subject to widespread journalistic comment in advance of its distribution.

Ramaswami Harindranath's PhD research included a qualitative study comparing interpretations of television documentaries by audiences in India and the UK. Basing his argument on this case study he constructed in his thesis a conceptual framework linking audience interpretations and cultural contexts. He also co-edited a volume which brought together a range of approaches to the study of audiences, and set up a debate between the different orientations.[6] Harindranath brought to the present project his experience in collecting and analysing qualitative data concerning audience responses, and in dealing with questions of prior expectations in interpretations of film and television.

Any research needs from the outset a way of organising its materials, a way of sorting, categorising and comparing. Our proposal to the ESRC proposed a way of doing this which was derived from our first examination of the controversy. It had struck us that there seemed to be two cross-cutting dimensions. Along the first, people could declare their liking or disliking for *Crash*. In some sense, therefore, it was a dimension of taste, and could allow people to differ. The second concerned approval or disapproval, a dimension which did not so easily allow people to admit disagreements. Clearly it wasn't necessary that people would sit at one extreme or the other on either dimension. Therefore we constructed a Nine-Cell categorisation. This could allow us to do a number of things. First, it just gave us a means of grouping and classifying all our materials, whether they were reviews of the film, or our audiences' responses. Thereafter, it could help us examine the relations between criticism and defence of *Crash*: in what ways did they differ from each other, and how far did they take each others' terms into account, in formulating their views? It could help us explore the relationships between journalistic responses to the film, and subsequent audience responses – how similar would antagonisms to *Crash* among audiences be to those evinced in the press, for instance? And it could help us consider how unified each position is: are critics more or less united in their account than defenders for instance?[7] This Nine-Cell system stayed with us right through all stages of *gathering* materials. But we always had to remember that it was only a means of initial sorting, a groundwork from which we could move towards analysing our assembled materials. And indeed, in the end, our findings did move us away from what would have been a restrictive and over-rigid framework. But we believe that it was still an advantage to have had that grid for sorting materials in the first place.

The Nine-Cell Structure:

+ + = Liking + Approval	+ 0 = Liking + Neutral	+ – = Liking + Disapproval
0 + = Neutral+ Approval	0 0 = Neutral + Neutral	0 – = Neutral + Disapproval
– + =Disliking + Approval	– 0 =Disliking + Neutral	– – =Disliking + Disapproval

Key Concepts

The *Judge Dredd* project handed on to this one a central concept, and a number of dependent ones. Central was the concept of a 'viewing strategy'. This concept emerged in the course of the earlier research. Its principle is that audiences do not come unprepared to see a film – they have expectations (hopes, fears, prior experiences and knowledges, and involvements). Most importantly, these expectations shape *how* people will watch a film. The concept of a viewing strategy therefore required us to look for the links among all the following.

(1) What prior orientations did people have, when they came to see *Crash*? What did they know about the film (and the book, or Cronenberg, or the controversy, or *et cetera*) before they saw it? Why did they want to see it?
(2) Who did they feel they were watching with or on behalf of? The *Dredd* research had shown that when people go to the cinema, whether or not they are physically alone or in company, they always belong imaginatively to various groups: groups whose reasons for watching and ways of watching help form the orientation any individual pursues.
(3) How do they go about the process of watching? Which aspects of the film rise to prominence, which ones are ignored or forgotten? How do audiences manage the

steps across the 'cracks' in the film (for example, explaining the motivations of characters when these are not directly given; or, filling in gaps in the narrative when these are not made evident)?

(4) How do audiences move from experiencing the film, and going through processes of sense-making, to arriving at judgements on it? What processes after the film's end continue the work of meaning-making and judgement-formation? These questions can, of course, as well be asked of journalists and film policy-makers as of ordinary viewers.

Having this concept of a 'viewing strategy' does not predetermine at all what viewing strategies will be found (either how many, or of what kinds). Nor does it presume that all will be equally unified or purposeful. Indeed, the *Dredd* research brought into view some aspects of people's ways of watching which have not really been attended to in previous research. There were clear and important differences between people to whom it mattered greatly that the film should match their expectations, which were well-formed and carried emotional commitments, and those to whom seeing the film was a matter of a routine night out at the cinema. This was defined as a distinction between 'high' and 'low investment'. At one extreme, high investors claimed rights over the film, and felt cheated when it did not meet their demands. At the other extreme, low investors asked only that a film did a job of just being generally 'entertaining', and filling their time reasonably. In the middle were many who, aware that they were unlikely to get what they felt they deserved, made compromises in order to secure their pleasures.

But we could not adopt this concept mechanically since there were important differences between the two cases. *Judge Dredd* was a highly generic, star-driven movie, bidding for blockbuster status with, therefore, masses of extravagant publicity attending it. *Crash* was a determinedly non-generic film. It was therefore very important to be able to ask open-endedly with what kinds of expectations people approached *Crash*, and how these shaped the way they watched. Think, for a moment, of what might happen with the following combinations: a wish to 'find out for myself what the fuss is all about' (which could well be an expression of a wider concern about censorship and what 'they' are doing to stop 'us' watching), coupled with on the one hand a deep-seated concern about the ways sex is invading the public sphere (which constitutes, in our terms, one kind of 'imaginary company'), or on the other hand with a fascination with the forms and potentials of human sexual relations (another form of 'imaginary company'). The advantage of the concept of a 'viewing strategy', we believe, is that in principle it makes it possible to handle the kinds of complexity these could produce, and to give shape to the results.

The concept of a viewing strategy – a working definition:

The concept of a viewing strategy is designed to capture the ways in which the following elements of film viewing are interlinked: people's prior knowledge, and expectations, of a film; their ways of attending to circulating information, images, and issues around the film, both from publicity regimes and from other competing (for instance, fan, or sensationalist, or censorious) accounts; their choice of manner of seeing the film (what cinema; with whom; with what kinds of preparation); their ways of attending to the film (accentuating parts, ignoring others, producing a specific kind of narrative account, *et cetera*); their immediate responses (sensuous, emotional, cognitive, *et cetera*); and subsequent work on those responses to turn them into an account of meanings to self and the world. All these combine elements of the real, and the imaginary. So, a person may attend a cinema on his or her own. But s/he cannot shed a sense of who s/he is, what groups and communities of interest s/he belongs to, and to whom the film might speak. The concept of a viewing strategy is intended to draw attention both to the *differences* among people (in the kinds of orientation taken, the degrees of importance attached, and the extent of coherence with which it is approached, *et cetera*) and to the *commonalities* among people (adoption of socially-distributed and -maintained orientations, for instance). It further makes it possible to attend to the ways in which a person's orientation to a film may be interwoven with other facets of his or her life, interests, and beliefs.

The concept carries certain presumptions: first, however much a person may prepare for seeing a film, part of the point of seeing it is to experience something which could not be fully predicted. Part of any viewing strategy is to prepare for a desired novel experience, therefore a natural part of filmic experience is to find one's expectations disappointed, frustrated, upset, fulfilled, outstripped, or otherwise measured. A second presumption is that although the act of watching a film is finite and bounded, to understand the kinds of meaning and pleasure audiences may take from it requires attention to both the period of preparation for viewing, and to the processes through which audiences evaluate their experience of the film afterwards. In calling this a 'strategy', this approach invites exploration of the relations between the *reasons* for watching a film, the stance and orientation adopted while watching, and the steps taken afterwards to find shape and sense in the film, and in the responses it evoked. All these are, we argue, socially-shaped.

One consequence of this is that the 'meaning' of a film for any viewer is not something which is fixed or given at any point. Anyone's understanding of something like a film is produced over time. Post-cinema chat is not simply an ordinary extension or a bonus to the experience itself of a film, it is for many viewing strategies a necessary part, even a precondition of knowing the meaning of a film. With some kinds of film, it can even *be* the meaning, so that to go on one's own, for many people, is unacceptable. It is 'sad' (a term marking several kinds of social failure), it is pointless (why bother, if there isn't anyone to chat with afterwards?), or the film will simply mean less (how to get excited, if you're on your own?).

This means that people's perceptions and understanding of a film are likely to be subject to change – and among the things that could lead to change could well be participating in our research. When we asked people to think about the film, perhaps asking questions about the film and about their reactions to it in a way that they had not done before, we were not tapping into tidily arranged responses – or at least, not for most people. But that is not the same as saying that people were simply malleable, or that our research produced the responses it then claimed to analyse. Rather, in different ways, participating in our research was an impulse for people to think about their reactions, and perhaps to organise them more than they might otherwise have done. Many people, both friends and critics of *Crash*, welcomed that opportunity. But it did mean that we had to be alert to the ways in which audiences' talking to us and to each other in the course of our research was affecting the way they thought about the film.

Key Methods

Once our materials had been gathered, we had to have appropriate methods of analysis. Central to our research was a version of discourse analysis. We understand discourse analysis to be a set of procedures for analysing the social organisation of talk. 'Discourse' has become a central term in much recent thinking and research into culture, and there are a number of different accounts of its meaning, each tending to result in a different set of procedures for analysis.[8] A great deal of this has taken the form of theorising about the general character and functions of discourse. But our concern was with the most useful and reliable methods of analysis of discourse. In the research on *Dredd*, a detailed approach had been developed and tried out, which in turn drew on a number of already-published related exemplars, sometimes in quite other fields.[9] At back of this approach is the work of Valentin Volosinov who in the 1920s formulated an approach to language which stressed dialogue, and the ways in which speakers and listeners orient to each other. What the *Dredd* research did, and what we did subsequently with *Crash*, was to turn this towards the media and ask: suppose we think of a film as the 'speaker', and of its viewers as entering into dialogue with it. There are many steps from this general proposition to a working method of analysis, but this idea remained formative to us.

Methods of analysis don't just turn up at the end of data-collection, though. They control and drive how they are gathered. So, knowing that we would applying the discourse analytic techniques shaped the way we formulated our schedule of questions and how we organised our interviews.

Gathering Materials

Our research owes a significant debt of thanks to Mike Bor, then Principal Examiner at the British Board of Film Classification. Mike clipped national and local newspapers and magazines systematically for anything relating to issues of control and controversy around films, mainly for the benefit of others at the Board. Mike generously gave us access to his files on *Crash*, which immensely eased our problems of access to a vast range of materials. Through this, through our own gathering from the Press, and through materials supplied by others, we acquired a total of 400 *Crash*-related cuttings (covering news, reviews, interviews, editorials and the like) from the British Press. These were all read and sorted, and a body of prime articles selected in which an attitude towards *Crash* was being formulated, rather than merely relayed. Our aim was to find sufficient good examples to fill each position in the Nine-Cell structure, and of course to be able, as far as we could, to look inside each position to see how unified it was across a range of materials. Using the Internet and a web-based database and with further help from librarians at UWE, we gleaned a much smaller body of American reviews, which inevitably (because they have more reason to go on-line) over-represented large national and regional newspapers. A colleague visiting Paris helped us by gathering a range of French press responses to *Crash*. These were professionally translated for us.

We developed a set of ways of assigning all these to positions within our Nine-Cell structure. Different members of the research team presented preliminary analysis of each country's reviews to the rest of the team, drawing attention to the key markers

+ +	+ 0	+ −
British = 9	British = 4	British = 0
American = 6	American = 1	American = 0
French = 6	French = 0	French = 0
0 +	0 0	0 −
British = 6	British = 3	British = 2
American = 4	American = 5	American = 0
French = 2	French = 4	French = 1
− +	− 0	− −
British = 6	British = 5	British = 14
American = 4	American = 3	American = 1
French = 0	French = 2	French = 1

of (dis)liking and (dis)approval which warranted their Cell-allocations. The table above shows the proportions of materials we eventually worked from, by each Cell-position. At the same time, we were well aware that not all reporting was equal. The *Daily Mail* had self-consciously mounted a campaign, and it made sense therefore to select out all the *Mail*'s coverage and subject that to special analysis, to determine its terms of reference. What problems and dangers did the *Mail* claim to identify in *Crash*? For whom did the *Mail* claim to speak? What moral, or political, position underpinned its critique of *Crash*? If we could answer these questions, we would be able to ask in what ways the *Mail*'s terms of debate shaped the responses of the rest of the British journalism.

It was always part of our plan to interview some of the journalists who had written and taken a stance on *Crash*. We were interested not merely in what they had said about *Crash* but also about how they had come to that view. How did they perceive the wider controversy? How far had their published view been their own, how far that of their newspaper? How did writing about *Crash* fit into the everyday routines of their work? With our preliminary sort of major articles completed, we set about choosing a number of journalists. We chose according to a series of different criteria: positive vs negative; local vs national; and specialist vs generalist. In the end, we constructed a list of 14 journalists we wished to interview. Eleven gave generously of their time, and answered all our questions; even if one or two of them may have suspected that we would be hostile to their views on *Crash*, they nonetheless spoke freely and honestly and allowed us to tape-record their accounts. Three journalists refused to speak to us, despite repeated requests and explanations of the purposes of our research. We name them here, because it seems significant to us that they were the three who most wanted to call *Crash* to account. Having demanded that the film-makers take responsibility for the morality and possible impact of the film, Alexander Walker, Christopher Tookey, and Simon Jenkins declined to allow their views to be examined in a research process.

We here record our thanks to the following who allowed us to interview them:

Geoff Andrew (*Time Out*)
Anna Chen (*Socialist Review*)
Maria Croce (*Southern Daily Echo*)
Lesley Dick (*Sight and Sound*)
Tom Dewe Mathews (*Independent* journalist and author on film matters)
Bel Mooney (writer on *Crash* for the *Daily Mail*)
Suzanne Moore (*Independent*)
Mary O'Leary (*Weston and Somerset Mercury*)
Nigel Reynolds (*Daily Telegraph*)
Catherine von Ruhland (*Christian Herald*)
Dick Williamson (*Sunday Mercury* (Birmingham))

We also wish to thank two others involved in different ways in the *Crash* story, who also gave generously of their time:

Chris Auty (Co-Executive Producer of *Crash*)
James Ferman (Director of the British Board of Film Classification)

We have not written directly about this part of our research in this book. Our plan is to present this in a separate article.

The Bristol Screening

Crash had been shown in Bristol, at one screen in the Showcase multiplex, albeit for a short time (for whatever reason, it was not a box-office success). We had always planned a special screening, and had a preliminary arrangement with the Watershed Media Centre to hire their main screen for an evening performance. With a capacity approaching 200, our task was to recruit an audience. There was no notion of seeking a sample or 'representative' audience – representative of what? Our aim was to include among our audience a range across all the following variables:

• Age (with the limit that *Crash* was classified '18')
• Gender
• Ethnic background
• Reason for wanting to see the film
• First-time/second-time viewers
• People with specialist interest in (a) cars/car crashes, (b) disabilities, (c) films, (d) crime and its control.

We recruited our audience using a mix of methods. Four local newspapers carried reports on our research, including an invitation to people who would like to take part. Posters were put up in a variety of places (including community centres, libraries, and other public places). Many local groups were contacted, usually after an introductory letter. Snowballing (i.e. using networks of friends and associates) was used, including our own friends, relatives, colleagues, and even football-terrace contacts! We worried from the beginning that we might tend to recruit primarily those who would want to defend the film, and had in mind some fall-back plans to interview people who would refuse to see the film. As our figures showed, our fears were groundless – our audience split almost equally between Positives and Negatives.

Every person agreeing or asking to come to our screening was asked to complete a short questionnaire in advance. This gave us: name, address and telephone; sex; age; current occupation; where they heard about the research; why they wanted to see the film; whether they already had strong opinions about the film (and what they were); how much they had heard about the controversy, and where from. All this was entered into a database, to which was added the second post-film questionnaire.

167 people eventually attended our screening. Martin Barker spoke briefly before the film. He emphasised two points: first, that we wanted to hear all points of view on the film – we were equally interested in positive, neutral or negative responses (and therefore, he specially asked that people who disliked the film not to leave before the end, if at all possible – although we did have a fall-back plan to catch early leavers and record their views quickly before they fled!). Second, he explained that a questionnaire would be given out at the end, and people would be asked to complete it before they left; and that after we had had time to look at these, we would be making contact with some people, and would be asking them to let us talk to them in small groups. The film rolled. Two people walked out immediately the film ended, refusing to take any further part. 165 completed the questionnaire, which was given to them as the final credits were still rolling, as we wanted to garner their immediate, unreflective responses. The post-film questionnaire had four pages. Page one asked (with spaces for quite lengthy answers):

> Tell us your first reactions to the film – suppose you were telling a friend what you thought of it.
> What seemed to you the most striking or memorable aspects of the film?
> Are there other things (such as other films, events, personal experiences, or whatever) that you found yourself relating it to as you watched the film?

Then, crucially, we asked people to classify themselves along our two dimensions: first, asking 'how you felt about it as a film'. The wording of this had cost us much energy and argument. Many wordings seemed to raise problems. For example, asking if they 'liked' or 'enjoyed' the film seemed to presume a particular *kind* of pleasure or involvement, which might exclude some people. In order to get round this, we asked them to circle one choice Very Positive, Mildly Positive, Neutral, Mildly Negative and Very Negative; this was accompanied by a box in which people were asked to choose that word or expression which came closest to summarising the nature of their reactions. This proved an invaluable procedure, and gave us eventually a portrait of the range of semantic responses which gave us significant clues to the overall pattern of responses to *Crash*. Subsequently, we simplified their responses for purposes of the next stage to, simply, Positive, Neutral, and Negative. But we felt it important that people should feel that they did not have to have an extreme response.

Having given so much thought and attention to this first question, we should have known to be as careful with the second. Put it down to momentary exhaustion – whatever the reason, we got it badly wrong. Our question for the second dimension read:

Now, thinking about the public controversy over the film, please indicate to what extent you now *approve* or *disapprove* of it.

The fatal ambiguity in this only hit us when one of the last members of the audience, completing his form after most had left, asked us whether we meant approval of the *film* or of the *controversy*. Around such mistakes is research built. It meant that shortly after the screening we had to write to every single person who had completed the questionnaire, asking for a clarification. One person, our third loss, never replied, despite repeated attempts on our part,[10] leaving us with 164 participants overall.[11] In one respect we managed to turn this error into an advantage. The week's gap between the questionnaire and its corrective supplement meant that a small number of people had already changed their minds! This was something we could explore further in our focus group interviews – what exactly goes on when people shift their opinions over time?

The remainder of the questionnaire, first, gave space for people to expand on the reasons for their initial answers. We asked those who had seen *Crash* before to compare their experiences between the two viewings; and those who were seeing it for the first time how it compared with their expectations. We asked what were the *most important issues that needed discussing* about *Crash*. We asked people to tell us (from multiple choice boxes) how often they went to the cinema, and how often they watched videos, per month. Finally, we asked them to say (again) what had made them want to come to our screening.

All the questionnaires were databased, after a process of developing category-headings under which the different qualitative responses could be recorded (for instance, we categorised Striking and Memorable Moments under 13 headings). Not all questions proved equally valuable. Very little emerged, for instance, from the answers to our question concerning other things which people found themselves relating to *Crash*. A random scatter of other things, from the book of *Crash* to the death of Princess Diana, proved unrevealing (although it might be argued that the very randomness of this is perhaps the most revealing thing – it seems that *Crash* does not have any ready comparisons).

A complex tabling of striking/memorable moments and of issues raised, which included the evaluative accent (Positive/Neutral/Negative) which people attached to these, drew out some interesting items for consideration. Centrally, we learned that there were only small differences in *what* people found memorable; the differences were in how they *evaluated* these. But the evaluations were complicated. While the Negatives were almost uniformly hostile to the kinds of characters in the film, the Positives were mixed – suggesting that positivity does not have to mean simple *liking*. More detailed comparison of the most frequently mentioned items showed that for the Negatives these were (absence of effective) storyline, and their (hostile) responses to characters; while for Positives they were general aesthetic appreciation of the film, along with a positive recognition of its themes linking cars, bodies and sex. The quantitative information on cinema and video-viewing habits supported the general notion that those with greater cinematic 'literacy' were generally more likely to be favourable to *Crash* – but the association was not very strong.

Combining Cell Positions into three bands reveals gender and age differences among Positives, Neutrals and Negatives. Men were divided 49/11/40 per cent, while women were divided 21/27/52 per cent. Some interesting differences emerged from the statistical analysis of Remembered Elements, which are best gleaned by comparing the most-remembered elements from Positives vs Negatives. These were:

POSITIVES	NEGATIVES
Camerawork and soundtrack	Absence of storyline
Connections made between cars, bodies and sex	General characterisation
	Connections made between cars, bodies and sex
Acting	
The storyline	General feeling of the film
General characterisation	Injuries, scars and wounds
Relations to the book	Sex and nudity

When these were unpacked into their more specific comments, some interesting things emerged. For instance, the Positives' most frequently mentioned aspects were *Crash*'s filmic qualities, the camerawork and soundtrack. Yet when it came to focus groups, they were less likely to mention these than the Negatives. This seems to have been because they enjoyed these *as part of the overall package* that was the film. For the Negatives, where they mentioned them, they were the *exception to the rule*, residual qualities they would not deny, but which did not compensate for the general badness of the film. Equally, where the Positives frequently mentioned Acting, this took on a complex meaning in the interviews, where it was frequently the *ability to present an impenetrable surface* which provoked praise. The same attribute, to the Negatives, was taken to be *absence of any depth to characters*, and therefore condemned.

Most productive of all were two things: first, people's self-placement along our two dimensions. This enabled us to organise our interview groups. People placed them-selves on our dimensions in the following fashion:

+ + 51	+ 0 5	+ – 6
0 + 10	0 0 13	0 – 6
– + 8	– 0 28	– – 37

Second the box in which people gave expression (their 'keywords') to their first and main reaction to the film. Over time, and cross-checked with other aspects of their responses, this developed into the chart overleaf which seems to us to capture, with both accuracy and explanatory power, the broad patterning of our audience's reactions to *Crash*. Those keywords also provided us with a pivotal introduction in the interviews,

Patterning of Semantic Responses

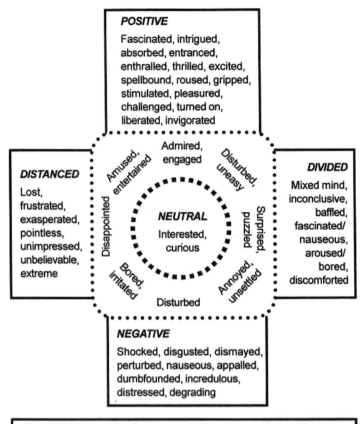

POSITIVE
Fascinated, intrigued, absorbed, entranced, enthralled, thrilled, excited, spellbound, roused, gripped, stimulated, pleasured, challenged, turned on, liberated, invigorated

DISTANCED
Lost, frustrated, exasperated, pointless, unimpressed, unbelievable, extreme

Admired, engaged

Amused, entertained

Disappointed

NEUTRAL
Interested, curious

Disturbed, uneasy

Surprised, puzzled

Bored, irritated

Annoyed, unsettled

Disturbed

DIVIDED
Mixed mind, inconclusive, baffled, fascinated/ nauseous, aroused/ bored, discomforted

NEGATIVE
Shocked, disgusted, dismayed, perturbed, nauseous, appalled, dumbfounded, incredulous, distressed, degrading

Note: these terms and their allocations are derived from respondents' post-screening questionnaires checked, wherever possible, against information from interviews.

where we asked people to explain why they had chosen their expressions and what they intended by it. But as with the corrective supplement, it must be noted that a number of people had trouble remembering, and had to go through an active process of recall and self-explanation: a process which is very much a sign that views on the film were not entirely stable, and indeed evolved over time.

Knowing the distribution of audiences by Cell-Position, we were able to select people for interview. Again, we went for range. We debated among ourselves whether groups should be single-sex, and indeed whether they should have a same-sex interviewer. Having completed four trial interviews with readily available student groups, and discussed the issue with them, we decided against this. It would in any case have been very difficult to work with single-sex groups, given that in two cases we wanted to interview husbands and wives. Our decision seems confirmed by the fact that noone raised the topic in their final feedback questionnaires which all interviewees completed (whereas several questioned our decision to interview Positives, Neutrals and Negatives separately). Ultimately we interviewed 63 people. Our original ambition had been to conduct interviews in similar-sized groups, but some people proved difficult to locate and arrange dates. Fearing that the film was receding in people's memories, we compromised on group sizes in order to ensure that all people selected were interviewed as soon as possible. Also in some of the Cell groups, the numbers were quite small, making the idea of separating the sexes even more tricky. The eventual distribution was as follows:

+ + 18 (5.3^{12} gps)	+ 0 5 (3.3 gps)	+ – 3 (3 gps)
0 + 6 (3 gps)	0 0 8 (2.3 gps)	0 – 4 (3 gps)
– + 4 (2 gps)	– 0 6 (3gps)	– – 12 (6 gps)

This meant that 10 people were interviewed individually, 15 in pairs, 5 in groups of three, 2 in groups of four (= 63). It is possible to wonder at the differences this might have introduced, but we have not identified any variations resulting from this necessary decision.

Over time, and after piloting them in four interviews, we arrived at an agreed schedule of questions:

About seeing Crash:
What did you know about *Crash* before you saw it (via the novel, or Cronenberg, or previews, *et cetera*)? Was it as you had imagined it would be? After the screening, did you think much about the film, and/or talk to other people much about it?

For each person, separately:
In your questionnaire, your summing-up expression for the film was .... Can you tell us more about this reaction? Have you changed your mind about the film, since you completed our questionnaire? How did you feel about the main characters in the film? Were there parts of it that you particularly liked? Are there any scenes which you wish had been cut? What prompted you to want to see *Crash*? Had you seen it before? Would you watch it again? Why? Would you have wanted to see *Crash* anyway?

General viewing processes/practices/routines:
What kinds of films do you normally watch and enjoy? Where – at the cinema, on video, on TV? What cinema would you normally go to, if at all? What did you feel about

watching it at the Watershed? Are films important to you? Can you say why, or why not?

General responses to Crash:
What did you think the film was about, centrally? Can you say in a sentence what you think it was about? What other films would you compare it with? What do you remember about the controversy?

Here are some of the things which various reviewers and critics said about the film (newspaper quotations laid out on a photocopied sheet):[13]

> 'Sex 'n' wrecks' ... 'A movie beyond the bounds of depravity' ... 'Not because it's obscene, but because it is boring, ludicrous and pretentious' ... 'Left this viewer cold' ... 'Disturbingly steely, often darkly funny' ... 'A philosophical cinema, based on a subversive imagination' ...

What do you think about these judgements of the film? Who did you think the film was aimed at, in the end? Did that include you? What are your thoughts about people who hold different views than you about the film? Can you understand their reactions to it? What do you think now about the controversy, having seen the film?

Connections with wider feelings about films, censorship, et cetera:
Why do you think there was such an outcry over this particular film? Can you think of any other films that you personally would like to see 'banned'? Do you think it should be released on video, or shown on TV? Do you have any general views about how much sex there is/should be in films? Or about in what ways it should be shown? What are your personal views on film censorship? What do you think about the current ways of dealing with this in this country? Anything we've missed out, that you would want to comment on?

At the end of the interview, every person was given a short final questionnaire in which they had the opportunity to say, first, whether they had been able to say all the things they had wanted to, and second, whether they had found themselves changing their views, or how they expressed them, in the course of the interview. Only one person stated that they had felt in some way constrained by the interview process. Most expressed varying degrees of enthusiasm (and sometimes gratitude) for having been able to take part and express their views. But quite a number did say that their views had developed in and through having to discuss them with us and others.

Enter NUD*IST

Once transcribed, all transcripts were analysed in several, eventually interlocking ways. Each transcript was given a first examination by one member of the research team, who presented his/her account of it to the rest of the group. From these individual examinations, a set of topics for further discussion emerged, and a series of themes were identified. At the start, these only worked at the level of individuals' viewing strategies. At this stage, we made no serious attempt to produce any broader generalisations or models.

At the same time all the transcripts were loaded into the qualitative analysis software NUD*IST (acronym for Non-Numerical Unstructured Data * Indexing, Searching, and Theorising). NUD*IST allows researchers to code their materials in as many ways as they choose, and then to generate links across codes, or (parent/child) hierarchies of codes. As a team, we began to formulate a set of codes derived from the issues we were identifying through our individual analyses. The codes were intended to capture different kinds and topics of talk. With a first draft of these to hand, a sample set of transcripts were coded, to see how well they captured them. A series of small problems surfaced (for example, overlap between codes, and a need for additional ones to capture missed elements). Once ambiguities and gaps had been removed, and clear definitions of each heading had been agreed, the full set of transcripts was divided among members of the team, and all were coded. A check was later run, to determine if there might have been any inconsistencies in the way we each coded. It did in fact throw up a problem – one of us seemed to have been more parsimonious in coding, marking up smaller segments of their transcripts than the others. A blind check was run, in which the other three researchers each recoded two of these transcripts, and the results were then compared. In fact the recoding showed minimal differences, which suggested that chance distribution of transcripts had led to one person having had transcripts with lower proportions of key kinds of talk.

These were the agreed codings. We hope it is clear how they relate both to the overall concept of a viewing strategy, and to our question schedule:

NUD*IST CODING CATEGORIES, to capture talk about or revealing:
1. Prior Orientation: towards *Crash*; including the controversy; Cronenberg; Ballard. This should cover knowledge of any of the above, expectations of the film and motivations set up by these for seeing the film.
2. Accounts (imputed or reported) of the making/makers of *Crash*: talk about motivations of those responsible for the existence and nature of the film.
3. Talk about Intended/Implied Audience(s): who it was directed at, including opinions about those with opposite reactions.
4. Emotional expressions/responses: the emphasis here is on responses which are centred on feelings as opposed to talk grounded in articulated frameworks, which come in …
5. Ideological/moral frameworks: explicit evaluative talk about the film which evidences frameworks of beliefs (political, moral, religious, ideological) external to the film which shape evaluations of it.
6. Censorship talk: talk about the general idea of censorship, on its practice in the UK and on the application of this to *Crash*; also talk about censorship of cinema vs video, or books *et cetera*.
7. Orientation to films generally: covering film tastes and avoidances, cinema preferences, how people prefer to see films (e.g. alone or in groups), comparisons with video, or books or other such.
8. Post-filmic consequences: whether actual or imputed, what has happened or might happen (behaviourally, emotionally and mentally) as a result of watching the movie, to self or to others.
9. Narrativisation: narrative talk, recounting the structuring and process (or lack of these) of the film.

10. Occasion of viewing: everything to do with what went on *as* people watched the film: including discussions of the cinema, the rest of the audience, the effects of being researched, *et cetera*.
11. Cinematic codes: how meaning is produced for viewers through lighting, editing, camerawork, music, aesthetics, acting, setting *et cetera*.
12. The meaning of the film: attempts to summarise meaning and overall purpose/intent of the film, plus accounts of particular scenes which are talked of as typifying/revealing the nature of the whole film.
13. Character talk: all talk about particular characters, or relations between them
14. Modality talk: all talk assuming or exploring relations between the film or the filmic world, and the world beyond the film; also all talk assuming or exploring how the interviewee (or 'audiences' more widely) can or cannot relate to the film/filmic world.
15. Sex talk: about sex and eroticism in relation to film generally, and *Crash* specifically.

We also had a 'wild card' coding category, as an aid to recall, whose number just seemed appropriate...

42. Key passages: to note all the elements in transcripts that seemed to us particularly revealing or significant, including all those which seem to reveal people's strategies for reading and making sense of the film, how they draw on their own personal and cultural resources for this, and how their views have unfolded from prior orientations to talking to us.

NUD*IST spooled out its results, and gave us our second set of quantitative measures. This now allowed us to begin to test the usefulness of our original Nine-Cell categorisation, since we could now compare the amount of different kinds of talk according to Cell Position. For instance, were those who were Positive about the film more or less likely to address questions of the sexual content of the film? In what way might those were neutral or ambivalent about the film be different from those with strong opinions either way?

NUD*IST would not distinguish individuals within interviews, therefore could only tell us what proportion of each transcribed interview involved talk of particular kinds. It did however perform the labour-saving task of assembling from all transcripts all talk that had been given the same code – a priceless benefit, when we wanted to compare closely. All bar one of our focus groups (a trial one) had been organised by Cell Position, so the potential was there to compare proportions of talk by Cell. To draw out the maximum possible significance of NUD*IST's results, the results were processed in two ways – and findings only seriously investigated where they demonstrated a marked difference along both axes.

(1) NUD*IST allowed us to calculate the *average* amount of each kind of talk by Cell-Position. So, for instance, we could discover which attitude-groups talked most or least about censorship, or about the characters. We could also look to see if there were distinctive patterns across the range of attitudes to *Crash*. For instance, were there any kinds of talk that showed a steady increase or decline as Positivity declined? This then was our first set of NUD*IST quantifications.

(2) But because the numbers of interview groups were relatively small, we could not place much weight on this calculation. We therefore re-examined the same materials from another angle. Listing the top eight and the bottom eight transcripts (which amounts to almost 50 per cent of the whole set) for each coded kind of talk gave a second measure. By measuring the proportions of positivity vs negativity, and separating the two dimensions of liking/disliking and approving/disapproving, we had a second way of checking what associations there might be between tendency to use certain kinds of talk, and attitudes to the film.

Several dimensions did in fact reveal a consistent direction and differentiation along both measures. Some are not difficult to understand. For instance, there was a strong tendency for those with positive orientations to *Crash* to engage in talk about their prior orientation to the film. This was more true of those who *liked* the film than of those who *approved* of it. We believe this arises mainly from the discrepancy the nervousness induced in many viewers by the *Mail*'s campaign, and their realisation that they enjoyed the film. Those most strongly registering approval were more suspicious, we suspect, of the *Mail*, therefore less fearful in advance of the film. There was a smaller, but still noticeable tendency for Negatives, and especially Disapprovers, to want to talk about intended/implied audiences – which fits well with our perception that those who disapprove a film such as *Crash* will tend to work with a 'figure' of some other audience who might be affected/harmed by it. Other tendencies were less obvious. For instance, while it was not surprising that our figures showed a generally high readiness to talk about censorship (given that we asked people about this, and given also the controversy), it is still striking that the Positives (both Like and Approve) were considerably more keen to speak their minds on censorship than the Negatives. This fits well with the view we formed from our qualitative analysis that few of even the most ardent critics of the film wanted to argue that *Crash* should be censored.

A more puzzling finding was that Likers and Approvers were much more likely to want to talk about characters; while in the opposite direction it was especially the Disapprovers who avoided such talk. These tendencies are sufficiently strong to provoke some speculation. Might it be that the Disapprovers tended to be so strongly hostile to the film *per se* that they declined to discuss the characters as such, since to do so would be to allow their fictional status and the defences that that might introduce?

To us, though, the most striking tendency came with Modality Talk, that is, with talk concerning the relations between the film or the filmic world, and the world beyond the film; or, more broadly, with talk touching on how the interviewee (or other audiences) may relate to the film and filmic world (this includes but can go much wider than talk about the 'reality' or 'unreality' of the film). To our surprise, in both cases it emerged that Positivity was strongly associated with a propensity to such talk, as the tables overleaf show. What is interesting about this – and what led us to examine the transcripts with particular queries in mind – was that the Disapprovers of *Crash* are evidently the least likely to want to discuss it in modality terms. This is surprising, and counter-intuitive. One might expect that those who reject the film on moral grounds might have been expected to want to raise questions of censorship, and of the possible impact of the film on the world, or to worry about a breakdown of the fiction/reality boundary. None of these appears to have been the case. Instead it is the Positives who want to talk about modal issues. So the question we asked ourselves was: what kind of issues, and how did they talk about them?

Coding: Modality

+ + 9.3	+ 0 11.5	+ − 11.8
0 + 10.1	0 0 3.6	0 − 2.1
− + 15.6	− 0 2.9	− − 5.5

Top 8: 32 (21%) + −
       30 (16%) + 0
       6 (16%) − −
       9 (16%) + +
       20 (13%) + 0
       1 (13%) + +
       8 (13%) 0 +
       24 (12%) + +

Bottom 8: 21 (2.5%) + −
          9 (2.2%) 0 0
          10 (1.8%) − −
          14 (1.5%) 0 −
          17 (1.5%) − −
          27 (1.2%) 0 +
          7 (1.1%) 0 −
          5 (0.9%) + 0

Ratio of + / 0 / − 9—6—4
Liking ratio = 50
Approval ratio = 20

3—11—7
0
-40[14]

Range = 21—0.9%   Median = 9.6   Mean = 6.6

Developing our Hypothesis

Anyone who has conducted empirical research will say, if they are honest, that there are moments when you wonder if anything of interest is going to emerge. What if the mass of materials and data turn out to be shapeless, and directionless? In our case, we faced the dilemma: what if all we could say, after all the time and energy we had invested, was that people held very different views on *Crash*? If that was all we felt we could say, this book would have had to be a list of differences. Some people think the film is good, and this is why. Others think it is bad, and here are their reasons. Informative, but no more. The gold standard, the rainbow's crock, is to discover a pattern or model which would take us beyond our collection of individuals. But this could not be by some simple act of generalisation. To do that, we would have had to be able to claim that our audience was a sampled population, representative of the population of cinema-goers, or of Bristol, or of Britain. We make no such claim. What gradually came into view, via the application of that concept, the 'viewing strategy', was a realisation that we could *explain how the Positives and Negatives related to each other*. They were not simply disagreeing with each other, they were agreeing to or refusing a role which the film proffered them.[15]

A hypothesis of this scope and importance does not emerge fully-formed. It showed its possibilities in the first place from a realisation that there was more uniformity among those who were positive about *Crash* than among those who disliked and/or condemned it. This led us to examine in detail what it was that the Positives had in common – but then to ask what the relationship might be between those things which the Positives shared in common, and the responses of the Refusers of *Crash*. Over a period of time, and several times reformulated as we tested the propositions against our transcripts, the hypothesis emerged. And as it took shape, we began to consider what its implications were. What broader accounts of the place and nature of sexuality in film and in culture might this fit within? What more general conceptualisation of films and their audiences would it suggest? About these, in the end, we did not agree, and following the collective completion of this book we have agreed among ourselves that it should be open to each one of us to go her or his own way with subsequent arguments. This book, then, goes as far as we are able in our collective summation of the outcomes of our research. We believe that this is already a substantial addition of new knowledge and new lines of understanding, all with clear social and political significance. The rest can wait.

Notes

Chapter One

1   Alexander Walker 'A movie beyond the bounds of depravity', *Evening Standard*, 3 June 1996.
2   Cited in Chris Peachment 'Crashing bores', *Daily Express*, 14 November 1996.
3   There is considerable literature on previous campaigns. The following are particularly useful: Tom Dewe Mathews (1994) *Censored – What They Didn't Allow You To See, and Why: The Story of Film Censorship in Britain*. London: Chatto & Windus; David Kerekes and David Slater (2000) *See No Evil: Banned Films and Video Controversy.* Manchester: Critical Vision; and Annette Kuhn (1988) *Cinema, Censorship, and Sexuality*, 1909–1925. London: Routledge.
4   The *Daily Mail* 'alerted every local authority in the UK to the danger of showing this film'. (*Index on Censorship*, 3, 1997)
5   'Cinema owners will help drive out *Crash*', *Daily Mail*, 23 May 1997.
6   'Boycott Sony: What YOU can do to keep this revolting film off our screens', *Daily Mail*, 21 November 1996.
7   Although we have no way of ensuring that our file of cuttings is absolutely complete, the following figures clearly demonstrate the 'rhythm' of coverage across the national and local press: May 1996 (1); June 1996 (1); July 1996 (0); August 1996 (1); September 1996 (0); October 1996 (1); November 1996 (71); December 1996 (16); January 1997 (16); February 1997 (5); March 1997 (104); April 1997 (22); May 1997 (48); June 1997 (81); July 1997 (19); August 1997 (9); September 1997 (2); October 1997 (2); November 1997 (1); December 1997 (1). The critical dates here are: June 1996, when Walker's initiating article appeared; November 1996 when, with *Crash* under consideration at the BBFC, the *Mail* began its campaign; March 1997, when the BBFC gave its verdict, and classified *Crash* uncut as an '18'; and June 1997, when the film finally reached the country's screens.
8   *Broxbourne, Cheshunt* & *Waltham Cross Herald*, 6 February 1997.
9   *Daily Mail,* 21 May 1997.
10 'Censor's yes to depraved sex film', *Daily Mail*, 19 March 1996.
11 'Distortion! Film censors cheated on expert's views to justify screening *Crash* porn film', *Daily Mail*, 23 March 1997. From being the man condemned for his poor record as 'expert', Britton then ascended the heights. He was given a series of double-page features in the *Mail on Sunday* (May 1997) in which he became the 'real-life Cracker', the 'Mind Detective' who probed crimes and located the 'evil'' within them, like some modern-day moral witch-doctor.
12 'Why do we trust this secretive clique to censor our films?', *Daily Mail*, 24 March 1996.
13 Editorial: 'Crash goes our liberty', *Staffordshire Evening Sentinel*, 14 May 1997.
14 'RAC rapped over green light for *Crash*', *Sunday Telegraph*, 10 November 1996.
15 See, for instance, Larry Lamb (1989) *Sunrise: The Remarkable Rise and Rise of the Best-selling Soaraway Sun.* Basingstoke: Macmillan; and Peter Chippindale & Chris Horrie (1990) *Stick It Up Your Punter!: the Rise and Fall of the Sun.* London: Heinemann 1990.
16 The necessary book on the rise of the *Mail* still waits to be written. Until that happens, there is useful material in the regularly updated James Curran and Jean Seaton (1997) *Power Without*

Responsibility: the Press and Broadcasting in Britain. London: Routledge, in Raymond Snoddy (1993) *The Good, the Bad and the Unacceptable.* London: Faber; and Bob Franklin (1997) *Newzak and News Media.* London: Arnold.

17 J G Ballard, 'Set for collision', *Index on Censorship*, 3, 1997, 90–7. This quote, p. 97.
18 David Cronenberg, Press conference, London Film Festival, November 1996.
19 'Porn goes into overdrive', *Evening Standard*, 6 June 1997.
20 See Martin Barker and Thomas Austin (2000) *From Antz to Titanic: Reinventing Film Analysis.* London: Pluto Press 2000, especially Chapter 1. See also Martin Barker (1998) 'Film audience research: making a virtue out of necessity', *IRIS*, 26, 131–48.
21 Editorial, *Western Daily Press*, 23 November 1996.
22 Cited in 'Film crashes into barrier over cuts', *Independent*, 21 November 1996.
23 Quoted in 'Distortion!', *Mail on Sunday*, 23 March 1997.
24 Chris Auty, Press Release, May 1997.
25 British Board of Film Classification, Press Release, 18 March 1997.
26 Christopher Tookey, Review of *Crash*, *Daily Mail*, 6 June 1997.
27 'A dangerous romance', *Daily Telegraph*, 20 March 1997.

Chapter Two

1 We conducted interviews with thirteen journalists, spread across national and local, specialist and generalist, leisure and political, for and against *Crash*. There is not the space in this book to analyse what we learnt from these interviews. We plan to undertake this in a separate Journal article.
2 A strong example of this: one local journalist whom we interviewed spoke of 'the population and the age of the residents, not so much the age, but the mentality of the residents, also … they don't want to see it, they don't want to have their minds opened, which is fair enough, they want to live in a nice little safe area but that's where I work, so I have to sort of respect … a very small town morality'.
3 Alexander Walker, 'A movie beyond the bounds of depravity', *Evening Standard*, 3 June 1996. See also his 'Porn goes into overdrive', *Evening Standard*, 5 June 1997.
4 When Walker responded to Julian Petley's criticisms in the *British Journalism Review*, he accused Petley of having given way to a current tendency to refuse moral judgements. See Julian Petley (1997) 'No redress from the PCC', *British Journalism Review*, 8, 4, 1–8; and Alexander Walker (1998) 'Walker and Petley on CRASH course', *British Journalism Review*, 9, 1, 41–4.
5 See, for instance, Comment: 'A cynical censor and a sick film', *Daily Mail*, 19 March 1997. This editorial also amends 'mainline' (with its hint at cinematic drug-like addiction) to 'mainstream'.
6 Although we do not have the space to deal with the issue in detail, it may be worth noting one interesting feature of a good deal of local responses to the controversy, as evidenced in local newspapers. It is evident that the term 'offensive' frequently changes register, from undermining morality to causing upset. In a large number of cases, where local demands emerged for banning *Crash* from cinemas in one area, it was often because friends of victims of car crashes felt that the film was tasteless, and should not be allowed in case it trivialised grief and suffering. This kind of practical transformation of Press moralising deserves attention.
7 Barbara Amiel, 'Censorship is the obscenity', *Daily Telegraph*, 14 November 1996.
8 Bel Mooney, 'I am proud to call myself a liberal, but I cannot see why freedom of expression must mean the freedom to peddle violence and pornography', *Daily Mail*, 30 November 1996.
9 In his complaint to the Press Council, Julian Petley in fact pointed up a considerable number of factual inaccuracies in the *Daily Mail*'s coverage, for instance their claim that the film had failed at international box offices, or that its British distributors were in financial difficulties. As important, though, are certain tricks of writing which, depending on near-falsehoods, sneer at those whom they are criticising. A notable example came when, without doubt partly because of the *Mail*'s own campaign, *Crash* did quite badly at the British box office. The *Mail* celebrated this, claiming it as a victory for right-mindedness: 'The cynical adage, no publicity is bad publicity has been proved wrong in the case of the depraved film *Crash*, misguidedly licensed by the British Board of Film Classification. In spite of the sensational publicity, the public has stayed away in droves. How pleasing it is to know that the public – confronted by the truth about *Crash* – had the good sense and the discernment simply to decide that they had no wish to see this sick production.' This begs the question, of course: since the 'general public' seem not to be so corrupt after all, does this not mean that all that talk of the 'endless downward spiral' was overdone?
10 Nigel Reynolds, 'Violent, nasty and morally vacuous', *Telegraph*, 9 November 1996. This was published opposite a very supportive review/article on *Crash* by JG Ballard. Our interview with Reynolds brought some interesting things to light about this. Reynolds did not see himself as a film reviewer, but picked up this task after the *Telegraph* was contacted by the film's British

distributors who were looking for ways to bring the controversy back into the light, lest the film be lost by default at the BBFC. The *Telegraph* evidently did take an editorial line on the film, and to an extent Reynolds worked to that line – but that line was that the paper should carry two sides of a controversy, and therefore set up the debate between Reynolds and Ballard. It therefore fell to Reynolds to present quite an extreme view, because 'they clearly needed a sharp contrast between the two headlines, they clearly needed to counterpose the two pieces' [Interview, June 1998].

11 Editorial, 'A dangerous romance', *Daily Telegraph*, 20 March 1997.

12 Maria Croce, 'Car kicks fail to make an impact', *Southern Daily Echo*, 6 June 1997.

13 This sense of frustration that the film ought to have been more worthy of its controversy came across also in our interview: 'I think in a way if a film is controversial I almost want to like it because I think I would defend somebody's right to see it, and so then I think if someone's gonna make a fuss over a film they might as well at least make it interesting' [Interview, May 1998].

14 Conditions of writing must play an important part here: 'They suddenly decided to release the film after the debate had occurred. And of course no one in England, or, very few people in England had had the chance to see it. And *Sight and Sound* had their deadline and they very much wanted to be able to have the review. So they called me in Los Angeles where of course it had been opening for a while' [Interview, June 1998].

15 Lesley Dick, 'Review of Crash', *Sight and Sound*, 1997, 7, 34.

16 Lord Birkett, 'President's Introduction', *Annual Report*, London: BBFC 1996/7, 1. See also the Press Release from the BBFC (18 March 1997) which talks of the 'clinical detachment' of the film, within which the 'audience is not encouraged to share the feelings of the characters'. If they had been, of course…

17 Lesley Dick, 'Review of Crash', *Sight and Sound*, 1997, 7, 34.

18 Alastair Dalton, 'Crashing bore is all talk, no action', *The Scotsman*, 20 March 1997.

19 After completing our research, we came across some work done in Belgium which in important ways parallels ours. Ernest Mathijs has researched the critical reception of Cronenberg's work for a doctoral thesis, and has presented some aspects of his findings at a conference in Nottingham. Among the issues he explores is the question of how certain Cronenberg films came to be labelled as 'cult'. Mathijs' argument is that this is not some natural property of the films themselves. Rather, the designation has to be understood as arising from the interaction of two aspects of the critical attention the films received. In the case of *Shivers* (1975), for instance, Mathijs shows that initially in several countries the film was met with critical hostility, a hostility which combined dismissal of its *intrinsic* qualities with a challenge to its *extrinsic* risks. But in response a series of counter-reviews took the film's ability to make people feel those extrinsic threats as *proof of the film's intrinsic qualities* – but at the same time thereby meant that the film had to be attended to properly (i.e. as a 'cult' film) in order that those qualities should be clearly perceived. For the development of these arguments, see Ernest Mathijs (2000a) 'Referentiekaders van filmkritiek: een onder zoek naar het gebruik van referenties in de interpretatie van David Cronenberg' ('Frames of reference in film criticism: references in the interpretation and evaluation of David Cronenberg'), *PhD Thesis*, Communications Department, Free University of Brussels. See also his 'The making of a cult reputation: frames of reference in *Shivers* criticism', Paper delivered to Conference on Cult Movies, Nottingham, November 2000.

20 Gérard Lefort, 'Driving in a sexually intoxicated state', *Libération*, 18 May 1996.

21 Pursue this a further stage. Lefort and a number of others include in their reviews direct references to French (in particular psychoanalytically inclined) theorists: Lacan, Deleuze, Guattari. These are among the resources which a national newspaper feels it can call upon in a film review. Among the concepts which reviewers derive from these psychoanalytic sources, to interrogate Crash, is the concept of the death drive. The same concept is referenced in Leslie Dick's *Sight and Sound* review but, as we have seen, it is given a different job to do, because of the very different terrain of debate.

22 Marie Queva, 'The auto-motive orgasm', *Les Echos*, 16 July 1996.

23 M-N. T, 'David Cronenberg: traffic accident', *Le Figaro*, May 21 1996.

24 M.S., 'The crash of Crash', *Le Journal du Dimanche*, 19 May 1996. Another journalist dubbed Cronenberg the 'king of disquiet' who 'loves to draw the spectator into unknown territories and disturbing fantasies' (Anon, *Le Figaro*, 17 May 1996).

25 A great deal has been written about the 'auteurism' debate. A useful introduction and overview may be found in Helen Stoddart's 'Auteurism and film authorship', in Mark Jancovich and Joanne Hollows (1995) *Approaches to Popular Film*. Manchester: Manchester University Press, 37–58.

26 Rene Rodriguez, 'Crash a head-on collision of the repugnant and the erotic', *Miami Herald*, 21 March 1997.

27 Stephen Hunter, '*Crash* is one sick movie: Cronenberg's film gives sex and violence a bad name',

Baltimore Morning Sun, 21 March 1997.

28   A good example of this kind of work is Jeffrey Richards (1997) *Film and British National Identity: From Dickens to Dad's Army*. Manchester: Manchester University Press. Richards outlines the emergence of a distinctive British national culture from the early eighteenth century, noting some key changes that it has undergone in two centuries. He then comments: '[N]ational character is not innate, it is learned, the product of the world around it ... One of the sources from which national character is learned is the mass media. Cinema and lately television, as the pre-eminent mass entertainment media of the twentieth century, have functioned as propagators of the national image, both in reflecting widely held views and constructing, extending, interrogating and perpetuating dominant cultural myths. It is instructive therefore to look at films for evidence of the promotion of images of both the national character and national identity. (pp. 26–7)'

29   For example Michael Billig's work about the Royal Family which might conceivably have gone in this direction. Billig in fact seeks only to determine what resources individual speakers lay claim to. He does not seek through that to determine the broader parameters currently existing through which, for instance, public discourses about monarchy are framed. See his *Speaking Of The Royal Family*. London: Sage (1993).

Chapter Three

1   Thomas Austin, '"Desperate to see it": straight men watching *Basic Instinct*', in Melvyn Stokes and Richard Maltby (eds) (1999) *Identifying Hollywood's Audiences: Cultural Identity and the Movies*. London: BFI, 147–61.

2   They were of course not at all alone in this. This same sense of virtual disappointment is to be found in a good deal of the press reactions to finally seeing the film. For one such example, written with an edge of mockery, see Ben Thompson, '*Crash*: did we wait so long for this?', *Independent on Sunday*, 8 June 1997: 'The cinema-going nation licked its chops in anticipation: a place beyond depravity ... what must that be like – Kidderminster? Telford? The excitement in the air was almost tangible. Now that it is finally upon us, *Crash* does not seem so very shocking or outrageous after all. The pervasive sense of anti-climax...'

3   David E. Morrison (1999) *Defining Violence: the Search for Understanding*. Luton: University of Luton Press.

4   It is quite extraordinary how little research of this kind there has been, given the long tradition of concerns about 'violence'. Apart from Morrison's work, the most important other works available are Philip Schlesinger's two books (*Women Viewing Violence*. London: BFI, 1992; and *Men Viewing Violence*. London: Broadcasting Standards Council, 1998); David Buckingham's study of young people and violence and horror (*Moving Images: Understanding Children's Emotional Responses to Television*. Manchester: Manchester University Press, 1996); and Annette Hill's study of audience responses to the 'new brutalist' movies (*Shocking Entertainment: Viewer Response to Violent Movies*. Luton: University of Luton Press, 1997). Limited though it is, such research is beginning to have an impact – if only in causing those still operating with unreconstructed 'effects' traditions to find ways – and very revealing ones, too – of fending off the challenge. It is very instructive to look at one very recent, and indeed thorough, restatement of the American behaviourist approach: W. James Potter (1999) *On Media Violence*. London: Sage. He records an extraordinary judgement on work such this, effectively denying that audiences can possibly say anything that could challenge what 'effects' researchers say, and how they choose to define 'violence'.

Chapter Four

1   See Mary's responses in Chapter 5, for what might happen when someone starts out from a position of *dislike* of Catherine.

2   For further discussion of issues around 'opinions' and 'attitudes', see (among others) Michael Billig (1991) *Ideology and Opinions*. London: Sage. For discussion of the issue of strong opinions see his *Speaking of the Royal Family*. London: Sage, 1993.

3   See Julian Petley (2000) Commentary: 'New Labour versus Horny Catbabe', *Radical Philosophy* 103, 2–5.

4   'Everyone knows what entertainment is. It is obvious. Except that as soon as we begin to talk about it we get into a muddle ... Entertainment is difficult to define *because* everyone knows what it is, because it is a commonsense idea.' (Richard Dyer (1992) *Only Entertainment*. London: Routledge, 1.) Dyer's very useful discussion about the ordinary associations of the concept of 'entertainment' is an essential background to our argument. Two things in particular emerge from his discussion: first, that 'entertainment' is marked by being non-serious, reserved to the sphere of leisure and

relaxation; secondly, that as a result the concept operates often as a blocking device, in association with the safety clause that it is *only* 'entertainment'.

5   As we explain in the Methodological Appendix, we had expected to have a problem of over-recruiting people with a high commitment to art cinema, both from a possible desire to defend the film in the face of demands for censorship, and from the fact that our screening was at the Watershed Media Centre. That this did not happen further testifies to the weakness of the art-house tradition in Britain, which we explored in Chapter 2.

Chapter Five

1   See the Methodological Appendix for an explanation of this.
2   For an example of someone 'seeing' the film differently, see the following internet review of *Crash*: 'Far from proffering some new, racy form of fucking, the movie wallows in the usual p.o.v., fixing the camera over and over on a woman's exposed loins' (Elizabeth Pincus, Review of *Crash*, www.planetout.com/pno/kiosk/popcornq/db/getfilm.html?2041). The difference interestingly highlights the way people's measurements of what they see are interwoven with their overall responses to a film. For Pincus, the camera's work is to be noted and weighed separately. But as here with Kelly, positive responses to *Crash* tend to go with incorporating its cinematic aspects within an experienced narrative unity.
3   Annette Hill (1997) *Shocking Entertainment: Viewer Response to Violent Movies*. Luton: University of Luton Press.

Chapter Six

1   There has been extensive writing on the broader history of these images. Among the most useful sources are Geoffrey Pearson (1983) *Hooligan: A History of Respectable Fears*. Basingstoke: Macmillan, and 'Falling standards: a short, sharp history of moral decline', in Martin Barker (ed.) (1984) *The Video Nasties: Freedom and Censorship in the Media*. London: Pluto Press, 88–103; Mark I. West (1988) *Children, Culture and Controversy*. Hamden, Conn.: Archon Press; and John Springhall (1998) *Youth, Popular Culture and Moral Panics: Penny Gaffs to Gangsta Rap, 1830–1996*. Basingstoke: Macmillan.

Chapter Seven

1   In the interviews, we followed the practice of quoting back to people the 'keywords' they had written down to summarise their immediate response. In at least one case [Interview 17], Patrick was surprised to hear that he had written 'dismayed', and went on not so much to defend the word, as to put a gloss on it which allowed him to establish a continuity between his now-considered view, and his first reaction.
2   For a detailed discussion of the specific ways the *Daily Mail* articulates this metaphor of 'violence', see Martin Barker (ed.) (1984) *The Video Nasties: Freedom and Censorship in the Arts*. London: Pluto Press.
3   For a useful discussion of these general characters, see David Bordwell, Janet Staiger and Kristin Thompson (1985) *The Classical Hollywood Cinema: Film Style & Mode of Production to 1960*. London: Routledge, Ch. 30 'Since 1960: the persistence of a mode of film practice'. The following is a key sentence: 'Art cinema is concerned less with action than reaction; it is a cinema of psychological effects in search of their causes' (p. 373). See also David Bordwell (1979) 'The art cinema as a mode of film practice', *Film Criticism*, 4, 1, 56–64.

Chapter Eight

1   Charlotte Brunsdon and David Morley (1978) *Everyday Television: 'Nationwide'*. London: BFI; Frank Parkin (1971) *Class Inequality and Political Order: Social Stratification in Capitalist and Communist Societies*. London: MacGibbon; David Morley (1980) *The Nationwide' Audience: Structure and Decoding*. London: BFI .
2   In a more recent study using broadly the same approach, Tamar Liebes has tried to reverse the implications. In a study of Arab and Israeli responses to news coverage of the Intifada on Israeli television, she has sought to make the 'negotiated' response the 'normal' – that is, to be welcomed – mode. What this reveals is the extent to which this model is politically driven. It also shows what is bound up in deciding who shall count as 'hesitant' or 'ambivalent' – Liebes has effectively reversed the implicit judgement made by Morley (and Parkin) in order to validate a position that one suspects she herself holds, virtually by relabelling. (Tamar Liebes (1997) *Reporting the Arab-Israeli Conflict:*

How Hegemony Works. London: Routledge.)

3   Janice A Radway (1984) *Reading The Romance: Women, Patriarchy and Popular Literature*. London: Verso.

4   Martin Barker and Kate Brooks (1997) *Knowing Audiences: 'Judge Dredd', its Friends, Fans and Foes*, Luton: University of Luton Press, esp. Ch.11.

5   Nor, crucially, was the film allowed to propose one that he had not met with before.

Chapter Nine

1   For an investigation of these attacks, see Martin Barker (2001) 'On the problems of being a trendy travesty', in Martin Barker and Julian Petley (eds) *Ill Effects: the Media/Violence Debate*. London: Rouledge, 2nd Edition.

2   Somewhat bizarrely, in one of their responses to the PCC, the *Mail*'s spokesman denied that they had ever mounted a campaign against *Crash* – a denial which is made a little strange by the fact that most of their major articles on the subject carried a logo referring to the '*Mail* campaign'. In fact Petley's complaint had never been against the fact that there was a campaign – newspapers are entitled under PCC rules to mount these, however outrageous they may be.

3   Julian Petley and Mark Kermode (1997) 'Road rage', *Sight and Sound*, 7, 7.

4   Julian Petley (1997) 'No redress from the PCC', *British Journalism Review*, 8, 4, 1–8. For an important new account of press regulation in the UK, see Tom O'Malley and Clive Soley (2000) *Regulating the Press*, London: Pluto Press.

5   On this campaign, see Stephanie Barron (ed.) (1991) *'Degenerate Art': The Fate of the Avant-Garde in Nazi Germany*. New York: Harry N Abrams.

6   See for instance James Curran and Jean Seaton (1988) *Power Without Responsibility: The Press and Broadcasting in History*. London: Routledge, 59, who quote a *Mail* editorial praising Hitler for rescuing Germany from 'its alien elements'.

7   See for instance Stuart Hall (1978) *Policing The Crisis: Mugging, the State and Law and Order*. London: Macmillan.

8   There were occasional exceptions. Several newspapers and magazines featured the controversy in terms of wider debates about censorship, for instance Toby Manning in *City Life* ('A crash course in censorship', *City Life*, 8 January 1997). More broadly, Anna Chen, reviewing *Crash* for *Socialist Review*, wrote both on the nature of the attacks on *Crash* and indeed on the ways in which the film's political challenge might provoke that attack ('Car wars', *Socialist Review*, January 1997). However, overall the public controversy was conducted on the *Mail*'s terrain.

9   Tom Dewe Mathews (1994) *Censored! What They Didn't Allow You To See And Why*. London: Chatto & Windus.

10 On this, see Martin Barker (ed.) (1994) *The Video Nasties: Freedom and Censorship in the Media*. London: Pluto Press.

11 This, of course, has the effect of recreating a distinction between 'ordinary, vulnerable' viewers and sophisticated, secure viewers which, as we will see in a moment, very much inhabited the Board's early history – albeit for different ends.

12 See the work of Ed Donnerstein and his colleagues, for example, Neil M. Malamuth and Edward I. Donnerstein (eds) (1984) *Pornography and Sexual Aggression*. Orlando: Academic Press; Edward I. Donnerstein, Daniel Linz and Steven Penrod (1987) *The Question of Pornography: Research Findings and Policy Implications*. New York: Free Press; and Russell G. Geen and Edward I. Donnerstein (eds) (1998) *Human Aggression Theories, Research, and Implications for Social Policy*. San Diego: Academic Press. There have been clear boundaries, though, to Ferman's and the Board's recognition of research. On the one hand the Board, along with the Home Office, has funded some truly atrocious research on the possible links between video violence and delinquency. See the critique of this work by David Gauntlett in Martin Barker and Julian Petley (eds) *Ill Effects*. Second Edition. On the other hand, aside from some small gestures, the Board has resolutely refused to consider what has been learnt by the kinds of qualitative research of which this book is one example.

13 On this version of media studies as inoculation, see Sara Bragg 'Just what the doctors ordered? – Media regulation, education and the "problem" of media violence', in Martin Barker and Julian Petley (eds) *Ill Effects*. Second Edition.

14 A classic history of the BBFC of this kind is James C. Robertson (1985) *The British Board of Film Censors: Film Censorship in Britain, 1895–1960*. London: Croom Helm. See also Anthony Aldgate (1995) *Censorship and the Permissive Society: British Cinema and Theatre, 1955-65*. Oxford: Clarendon Press.

15 Annette Kuhn (1988) *Cinema, Censorship and Sexuality, 1909-1925*. London: Routledge, 79.

16 See for instance James Curran 'The new revisionism in mass communication research: a reappraisal' in James Curran, David Morley and Valerie Walkerdine (eds) *Cultural Studies and Communications*.

London: Edward Arnold, 256–78.

17 Andy Ruddock (2000) *Understanding Audiences*. London: Sage.

18 See in particular Pierre Bourdieu (1984) *Distinction: A Social Critique of the Judgement of Taste*. London: Routledge.

19 For a provocative critique of such tendencies, see Chris Rojek and Bryan Turner (2000) 'Decorative sociology', *Sociological Review*, 48, 4, 629–48.

20 This is in many ways the ground of Virginia Nightingale's (1996) recent critique (*Studying Audiences: the Shock of the Real*. London: Routledge).

21 See for instance the essay by John Hartley (1987) 'Invisible fictions: television audiences, pedocracy and pleasure', *Textual Practice*, 1, 2, 121-38; see also his (1999) '"Text" and "Audience": one and the same? Methodologial tensions in media research', *Textual Practice*, 13, 3, 487–508.

22 John Tulloch has suggested to us that there may be useful resources in the field of theatre studies, in investigations of the complex relations which theatre audiences build between actors and characters.

23 The early work of the Glasgow University Media Group (1976) on the construction of news owes a good deal to these kinds of questions. See their *Bad News*. London: Routledge.

24 Alex S. Edelstein (1993) 'Thinking about the criterion variable in agenda-setting research', *Journal of Communication*, 43, Spring, 85–99. Edelstein's argument is a development from work done with two colleagues on the ways in people come to define things as 'problems'. See also Alex S. Edelstein, Youichi Ito and Hans Mathias Kepplinger (1989) *Communication and Culture: A Comparative Approach*. New York: Longman, esp. Ch. 3.

25 See their *Communication and Culture*, p. 74.

26 Some of David Buckingham's findings on children's responses seems to us of this sort, as does Ellen Seiter's recent work.

27 For an example of a piece of work which is effective for just this reason, see Annette Hill and David Gauntlett (1989) *TV Living*. London: BFI.

28 This strand has many examples, including David Morley (1980) *The 'Nationwide' Audience: Structure and Decoding*. London: Routledge; Tamar Liebes and Elihu Katz (1993) *The Export of Meaning: Cross-Cultural Readings of 'Dallas'*. Cambridge: Polity Press; Sut Jhally and Justin Lewis (1997) *Enlightened Racism: The Cosby Show*; and Tamar Liebes (1997) *Reporting the Arab-Israeli Conflict: How Hegemony Works*. London: Routledge.

29 Glasgow University Media Group (1976) *Bad News*. London: Routledge; (1980) *More Bad News*. London: Routledge; (1982) *Really Bad News*. London: Writers & Readers.

30 John Corner, Natalie Fenton and Kay Richardson (1997) *Nuclear Reactions*. London: John Libbey.

31 Guy Cumberbatch (1985) *Television and the Miners' Strike*. London: Broadcasting Research Unit. See also the resultant debate in the pages of the journal *Media, Culture & Society* during 1987–88.

32 On the general process of making such attributions, see David Bordwell (1991) *Making Meaning: Inference and Rhetoric in the Interpretation of Cinema*. Boston, Mass: Harvard University Press 1991; and Martin Barker with Thomas Austin (2000) *From Antz To Titanic: Reinventing Film Analysis*. London: Pluto Press, Ch.1. A good example of this industry of interpretation is given the *Alien* film series which has been, to our knowledge, the topic of more than a dozen analyses, of which the great majority are attributive, in the sense that the meanings are found at the same time as they are denied by the very people who found them. But they are assumed to be the meanings that others will be 'seized' by, although those seized would probably not be able to say so.

33 It may be worth recalling Ien Ang's early work on *Dallas*. She noted that those who loved the series frequently had to struggle to find a language to articulate their pleasures, while those who dismissed it had the ready vocabulary of the 'mass culture' critique to call upon. See Ien Ang (1985) *Watching "Dallas": Soap Opera and the Melodramatic Imagination*. London: Methuen.

34 In cases where 'influence' has been claimed, that claim turns out to be very problematic. See Martin Barker and Kate Brooks, *Knowing Audiences*, Ch. 4.

35 The model of such research has, surely, to be Lucien Goldmann's (1977) *The Hidden God*. London: Routledge and Kegan Paul. This once classic but now neglected study of the ways in which the cultural position of a distinct social group, the Noblesse de Robe in seventeenth-century France, took general shape from the semi-heretical religious belief and practices of Jansenism, and found specific expression in the plays of Jean Racine and the philosophy of Blaise Pascal.

36 *Screen*, 39, 2: Barbara Creed, 'Anal wounds, metallic kisses', 175–9; Michael Grant, 'Crimes of the future', 180–5; Scott Wilson and Fred Botting, 'Automatic lover', 186–92; *Screen*, 40, 2: Marq Smith, 'Wound envy: touching Cronenberg's *Crash*', 193–202.

37 *Screen*, 40, 4: Annette Kuhn, '*Crash* and film censorship in the UK', 446–50.

38 Parveen Adams (2000) 'Death drive', in Michael Grant (ed.) *The Modern Fantastic*. London: Flicks Books, 102–22.

1   A very good model in this respect is Joke Hermes' (1996) *Reading Women's Magazines,* Cambridge: Polity Press, which offers a very honest – and sometimes very funny – account of her research process.

2   It may be worth comparing our findings in this research with Greg Philo (1990) *Seeing and Believing: the Influence of Television*. London: Routledge, who used some very innovative research procedures to explore the impact of television coverage of the miners' strike. He also was working after the event, in his case a whole year after the strike ended. His findings, too, demonstrated a clear echoing presence in people's thinking of the highly standardised and anti-miners formation of news coverage.

3   The main findings of this research project were published in Martin Barker and Kate Brooks (1997) *Knowing Audiences: Judge Dredd, its Friends, Fans and Foes*. Luton: University of Luton Press. This book contains a detailed discussion of the concept of a 'viewing strategy' which was used in this present research. Barker and Brooks have also published two other essays on particular parts of the findings: 'On looking into Bourdieu's black box', in Roger Dickinson *et al.* (1998) (eds) *Approaches to Audiences: A Reader*. London: Arnold, 218–32; and *'Bleak futures by proxy'*, in Melvyn Stokes and Richard Maltby (eds) (1999) *Identifying Hollywood's Audiences: Cultural Identity and the Movies*. London: BFI, 162–74.

4   Jane Arthurs (1984) *A Question of Silence: Reading a Feminist Film*. MA dissertation, University of London.

5   Jane Arthurs (1995) 'Thelma and Louise: On the Road to Feminism?', in P. Florence and D. Reynolds, *Feminist Subjects: Multimedia. Manchester*: Manchester University Press.

6   Roger Dickinson, Olga Linné and Ramaswami Harindranath (eds) *Approaches to Audiences*. London: Edward Arnold.

7   Here we note the productive nature of this approach. Stating it crudely, we can say that in the Press the critics are much more united than the defenders; whereas among our audience the enthusiasts are more singular in their response than the critics.

8   For surveys of the different approaches to discourse analysis see Norman Fairclough (1994) *Discourse and Social Change*. Cambridge: Polity Press; and Martin Barker and Kate Brooks (1997) *Knowing Audiences: Judge Dredd, its Friends, Fans and Foes*. Luton: University of Luton Press, Ch.4.

9   See for instance Marc W. Steinberg *Fighting Words: Working-Class Formation, Collective Action,and Discourse in Early Nineteenth Century England*. Cornell: Cornell University Press; Chik Collins (1996) 'To concede or to contest? Language and class struggle', in Colin Barker & Paul Kennedy (eds) *To Make Another World: Studies in Protest and Collective Action*. Aldershot: Avebury; and Colin Barker (1997) 'Social confrontation in Manchester's quangoland: local protest over the proposed closure of Booth Hall Children's Hospital', *The North West Geographer* 1, 18–28.

10 We are not alone in having difficulty with this. In an interesting methodological note, Annette Hill discusses the problems faced by the Broadcasting Standards Council and the Independent Television Commission when they sought to measure levels of public dislike of explicit sex on television. Hill demonstrates convincingly that the differences in the measured levels of dislike between two studies are easily explained by the differences in the language of the questions asked. Many people were unwilling to identify themselves as 'offended' or 'disgusted' because of what they perceived as an implied judgement on themselves, as intolerant and Mary Whitehouse-ish. (Annette Hill (2000) 'The language of complaint', *Media, Culture & Society*, 22, 2, 233–6.) This confirms the importance of our attempt to find a way to allow people to choose their own way of expressing positivity or negativity.

11 Of our 164 respondents, 101 were male, 63 female. Their occupations (by self-designation) ranged across: students, unemployed, performers and artists in various fields, administrators, managers and company directors, accountants, media workers of several kinds, journalists and market researchers, nurses and health advisers, civil servants, sales staff, clerical and secretarial, retired, fitters and engineers, teachers and lecturers, voluntary workers, mothers, policemen, and disabled workers. Among the audience were some twelve black or Asian-origin people. At this point, 41 (33m, 8f) had declared strong opinions towards *Crash*, 58 (26m, 32f) were not sure, 65 (42m, 23f) had no settled view on the film/controversy. But almost all (150 to 14) were well aware of it. By age, they broke down as follows: 9 (2m, 7f) = <20; 61 (34m, 27f) = 20–30; 57 (42m, 15f) = 30–45; 19 (12m, 7f) = 45–60; 12 (7m, 5f) = 60>. Four men and two women did not gave their ages.

12 One pilot group of three had people with mixed responses to *Crash*, hence the thirds in this and two other Cell-Positions.

13 These quotations were presented as a collage of headlines or key phrases from British newspapers,

designed to capture the range of main responses we had found there.

14 These figures are arrived at by taking the top eight and the bottom eight percentages of talk on each topic, according to which Cell Positions these belong to. Eight was chosen as it is effectively 25 percent of the total, but in a few cases we had to go to 9 because the 8th position was a 'tie' between two, belonging to different Cell Positions. The first figure is therefore a simple count of the number of +, O and − in each column. These are then disaggregated, in order to determine what balance of Liking/Disliking, and Approving/Disapproving is found within these. For presentation purposes, every Positive counts as 10, and every Negative as −10 (Neutrals being 0, and therefore discountable for this measurement). This entails that the mid-point = 0, and maximum possible scores of 80/-80 (90 for the three cases with 'ties').

15 Subsequent to finishing the main parts of the *Crash* research, Martin Barker, with a colleague at Sussex University, Thomas Austin, has developed and elaborated this idea of a filmic role, in *From Antz to Titanic: Reinventing Film Analysis* (London: Pluto Press, 2000). The aim that this book sets itself is to show how films can be analysed in ways that are compatible with, and in principle testable by, audience research. The centre of the book turns on showing how films set up and evolve tasks – cognitive, sensuous, emotional, *et cetera* – that audiences have to agree to perform if they are to gain the pleasures available from participation.

Bibliography

Adams, Parveen (2000) 'Death drive', in Michael Grant (ed.) *The Modern Fantastic*. London: Flicks Books, 102–22.

Aldgate, Anthony (1995) *Censorship and the Permissive Society: British Cinema and Theatre, 1955–65*. Oxford: Clarendon Press.

Ang, Ien (1985) *Watching "Dallas": Soap Opera and the Melodramatic Imagination*. London: Methuen.

Arthurs, Jane (1984) *A Question of Silence: Reading a Feminist Film*. (MA dissertation) University of London.

_____ (1995) 'Thelma and Louise: On the Road to Feminism?', in P. Florence and D. Reynolds, *Feminist Subjects: Multimedia*. Manchester: Manchester University Press.

Austin, Thomas (1999) '"Desperate to see it": straight men watching *Basic Instinct*', in Melvyn Stokes and Richard Maltby (eds), *Identifying Hollywood's Audiences: Cultural Identity and the Movies*. London: BFI, 147–61.

Ballard, J. G. (1997) 'Set for collision', *Index on Censorship*, 3, 90–7.

Barker, Colin (1997) 'Social confrontation in Manchester's quangoland: local protest over the proposed closure of Booth Hall Children's Hospital', *The North West Geographer* 1, 18–28.

Barker, Colin and Paul Kennedy (eds) (1996) *To Make Another World: Studies in Protest and Collective Action*. Aldershot: Avebury.

Barker, Martin (1988) 'Television and the miners' strike', *Media, Culture & Society*, 10, 1, January, 107–12.

_____ (1998) 'Film audience research: making a virtue out of necessity', *IRIS*, 26, Autumn, 131–48.

Barker, Martin and Kate Brooks (1997) *Knowing Audiences: Judge Dredd, its Friends, Fans and Foes*. Luton: University of Luton Press.

_____ (1998) 'On looking into Bourdieu's black box', in Roger Dickinson *et al.* (eds) *Approaches to Audiences: A Reader*. London: Arnold, 218–32.

_____ (1999) 'Bleak futures by proxy', in Melvyn Stokes and Richard Maltby (eds) *Identifying Hollywood's Audiences: Cultural Identity and the Movies*. London: BFI, 162–74.

Barker, Martin, with Thomas Austin (2000) *From Antz to Titanic: Reinventing Film*

Analysis. London: Pluto Press.

Billig, Michael (1991) *Ideology and Opinions*. London: Sage.

____ (1993) *Speaking of the Royal Family*. London: Sage.

Bordwell, David (1979) 'The art cinema as a mode of film practice', *Film Criticism*, 4, 1, 56–64.

____ (1991) *Making Meaning: Inference and Rhetoric in the Interpretation of Cinema*. Boston, Massachussets: Harvard University Press.

Bordwell, David, Janet Staiger and Kristin Thompson (1985) *The Classical Hollywood Cinema: Film Style & Mode of Production to 1960*. London: Routledge.

Bourdieu, Pierre (1984) *Distinction: A Social Critique of the Judgement of Taste*. London: Routledge.

Bragg, Sara (2001) 'Just what the doctors ordered? – Media regulation, education and the "problem" of media violence', in Martin Barker and Julian Petley (eds). *Ill Effects*, 2nd Edition, London: Routledge.

Brunsdon, Charlotte and David Morley (1978) *Everyday Television: "Nationwide"*. London: BFI.

Buckingham, David (1987) *Public Secrets: "EastEnders" and its Audience*. London: BFI.

____ (1996) *Moving Images: Understanding Children's Emotional Responses to Television*. Manchester: Manchester University Press.

Chippindale, Peter and Chris Horrie (1990) *Stick It Up Your Punter!: the Rise and Fall of The Sun*. London: Heinemann.

Collins, Chik (1996) 'To concede or to contest? Language and class struggle', in Colin Barker and Paul Kennedy (eds) *To Make Another World: Studies in Protest and Collective Action*. Aldershot: Avebury, 69–90.

Corner, John, Kay Richardson and Natalie Fenton (1990) *Nuclear Reactions: Form and Response in Public Issue Television*. London: John Libbey.

Creed, Barbara (1998) 'Anal wounds, metallic kisses', *Screen*, 39, 2, Summer, 175–9.

Cumberbatch, Guy (1986) *Television and the Miners' Strike*. London: Broadcasting Research Unit.

Curran, James (1996) 'The new revisionism in mass communication research: a re-appraisal', in James Curran, David Morley and Valerie Walkerdine (eds) *Cultural Studies and Communications*. London: Edward Arnold, 256–78.

Curran, James and Jean Seaton (1997) *Power Without Responsibility: the Press and Broadcasting in Britain*. London: Routledge.

Dickinson, Roger, Olga Linné and Ramaswami Harindranath (eds) (1998) *Approaches to Audiences*. London: Edward Arnold.

Donnerstein, Edward I., Daniel Linz and Steven Penrod (1987) *The Question of Pornography: Research Findings and Policy Implications*. New York: Free Press.

Dyer, Richard (1992) *Only Entertainment*. London: Routledge.

Edelstein, Alex S. (1993) 'Thinking about the criterion variable in agenda-setting research', *Journal of Communication*, 43, Spring, 85–99.

Edelstein, Alex S., Youichi Ito and Hans Mathias Kepplinger (1989) *Communication and Culture: A Comparative Approach*. New York: Longman.

Fairclough, Norman (1994) *Discourse and Social Change*. Cambridge: Polity Press.

Franklin, Bob (1997) *Newzak and News Media*. London: Arnold.

Gauntlett, David (2001) 'The worrying influence of "media effects" studies', in Martin Barker and Julian Petley (eds) *Ill Effects*, 2nd Edition, London: Routledge.

Geen, Russell G. and Edward I. Donnerstein (eds) (1989) *Human Aggression Theories, Research, and Implications for Social Policy*. San Diego: Academic Press.

Glasgow University Media Group (1976) *Bad News*. London: Routledge.

_____ (1980) *More Bad News*. London: Routledge.

_____ (1982) *Really Bad News*. London: Writers & Readers.

Goldmann, Lucien (1964) *The Hidden God: a Study of Tragic Vision in the Pensées of Pascal and the Tragedies of Racine*. London: Routledge.

Grant, Michael (1998) 'Crimes of the future', *Screen*, 39, 2, Summer, 180–5.

Hall, Stuart (1978) *Policing The Crisis: Mugging, the State and Law and Order*. London: Macmillan.

Hartley, John (1987) 'Invisible fictions: television audiences, pedocracy, and pleasure', *Textual Practice*, 1, 2, 121–38.

_____ (1999) '"Text" and "Audience": one and the same? Methodological tensions in media research', *Textual Practice*, 13, 3, 487–508.

Hermes, Joke (1996) *Reading Women's Magazines*. Cambridge: Polity Press.

Hill, Annette (2000) 'The language of complaint', *Media, Culture & Society*, 22, 2, 233–6.

_____ (1997) *Shocking Entertainment: Viewer Response to Violent Movies*. Luton: University of Luton Press.

Hill, Annette and David Gauntlett (1998) *TV Living*. London: BFI.

Jhally, Sut and Justin Lewis (1992) *Enlightened Racism: the Cosby show, audiences and the myth of the American dream*. Boulder, CO: Westview Press.

Kerekes, David and David Slater (2000) *See No Evil: Banned Films and Video Controversy*. Manchester: Critical Vision.

Kuhn, Annette (1988) *Cinema, Censorship, and Sexuality, 1909–1925*. London: Routledge.

_____ (1999) '*Crash* and film censorship in the UK', *Screen*, 40, 4, Winter, 446–50.

Lamb, Larry (1989) *Sunrise: The Remarkable Rise and Rise of the Best-selling Soar-away Sun*. Basingstoke: Macmillan.

Liebes, Tamar and Elihu Katz (1993) *The Export of Meaning: Cross-Cultural Readings of 'Dallas'*. Cambridge: Polity Press.

Liebes, Tamar (1997) *Reporting the Arab-Israeli Conflict: How Hegemony Works*. London: Routledge.

Malamuth, Neil M. and Edward I. Donnerstein (eds) (1994) *Pornography and Sexual Aggression*. Orlando: Academic Press.

Mathews, Tom Dewe (1994) *Censored! – What They Didn't Allow You To See, and Why: The Story of Film Censorship in Britain*. London: Chatto and Windus.

Mathijs, Ernest (2000a) 'Referentiekaders van Filmkritiek: een Onderzoek naar het gebruik van referenties in de interpretatie van David Cronenberg' ('Frames of Reference in Film Criticism: References in the Interpretation and Evaluation of David Cronenberg'). PhD Thesis. Communications Department, Free University of Brussels.

_____ (2000b) 'The making of a cult reputation: frames of reference in *Shivers* criticism', Paper delivered to Conference on Cult Movies, Nottingham, November.

Morley, David (1980) *The "Nationwide" Audience: Structure and Decoding*. London: BFI.

Morrison, David with Brent McGregor, Michael Svennevig and Julie Firmstone (1999) *Defining Violence: the Search for Understanding*. Luton: University of Luton Press.

Nightingale, Virginia (1996) *Studying Audiences: the Shock of the Real*. London:

Routledge.

Parkin, Frank (1971) *Class Inequality and Political Order: Social Stratification in Capitalist and Communist Societies*. London: MacGibbon.

Pearson, Geoffrey (1984) 'Falling standards: a short, sharp history of moral decline', in Martin Barker (ed.) *The Video Nasties: Freedom and Censorship in the Media*. London: Pluto Press, 88–103.

Pearson, Geoffrey (1983) *Hooligan: A History of Respectable Fears*. Basingstoke: Macmillan.

Petley, Julian (1997) 'No redress from the PCC', *British Journalism Review*, 8, 4, 1–8.

____ (2000) Commentary: 'New Labour versus Horny Catbabe', *Radical Philosophy* 103, Sept/Oct, 2–5.

Philo, Greg (1990) *Seeing and Believing: the Influence of Television*. London: Routledge.

Potter, W. James (1999) *On Media Violence*. London: Sage.

Press, Andrea (1991) *Women watching television: Gender, Class and Generation in the American Television Experience*. Philadelphia: University of Pennsylvania Press.

Radway, Janice A. (1984) *Reading The Romance: Women, Patriarchy and Popular Literature*. London: Verso.

Richards, Jeffrey (1997) *Film and British National Identity: From Dickens to "Dad's Army"*. Manchester: Manchester University Press.

Robertson, James C. (1985) *The British Board of Film Censors: Film Censorship in Britain, 1895–1960*. London: Croom Helm.

Rojek, Chris and Bryan Turner (2000) 'Decorative sociology', *Sociological Review*, 48, 4, 629–48.

Ruddock, Andy (2000) *Understanding Audiences*. London: Sage.

Schlesinger, Philip, Richard Haynes, Raymond Boyle, Brian McNair, R. Emerson Dobash and Russell P. Dobash (1998) *Men Viewing Violence*. London: Broadcasting Standards Council.

____ (1992) *Women Viewing Violence*. London: BFI.

Seiter, Ellen (1999) *Television and New Media Audiences*. Oxford: Clarendon Press.

Smith, Marq (1999) 'Wound envy: touching Cronenberg's *Crash*', *Screen*, 40, 2, Summer, 193–202.

Snoddy, Raymond (1993) *The Good, the Bad and the Unacceptable*. London: Faber.

Sparks, Colin, 'Striking results', *Media, Culture & Society*, 9, 3, 369–77.

Springhall, John (1998) *Youth, Popular Culture and Moral Panics: Penny Gaffs to Gangsta Rap, 1830–1996*. Basingstoke: Macmillan.

Steinberg, Marc W. (1999) *Fighting Words: Working-Class Formation, Collective Action, and Discourse in Early Nineteenth Century England*. Cornell: Cornell University Press.

Stoddart, Helen (1995) 'Auteurism and film authorship', in Mark Jancovich and Joanne Hollows, *Approaches to Popular Film*, Manchester: Manchester University Press, 37-58.

Stokes, Mervyn and Richard Maltby (eds) (1999) *Identifying Hollywood's Audiences: Cultural Identity and the Movies*. London: BFI.

Walker, Alexander (1998) 'Walker and Petley on CRASH course', *British Journalism Review*, 9, 1, 41–4.

West, Mark I. (1988) *Children, Culture and Controversy*. Hamden, Connecticut: Archon Press.

Wilson, Scott and Fred Botting (1998) 'Automatic lover', *Screen*, 39, 2, Summer, 186–92.

Index

Note: because references to the film Crash occur on almost every page of the book, we have not listed these for their own sake. We have only listed those cases where a broader discussion or set of concepts is focused on and through the film.

SHORT CUTS

The SHORT CUTS series is a comprehensive library of introductory texts covering the full spectrum of Film Studies, including genres, critical concepts, film histories/movements, and film technologies.

With concise discussion of contemporary issues within historical and cultural context and the extensive use of illustrative case studies, this list of study guides is perfectly suited to building an individually-styled library for all students and enthusiasts of cinema and popular culture.

The series will grow to over forty titles; listed here are the first waves of this ambitious attempt to systematically treat all the major areas of undergraduate Film Studies.

"Tailor-made for a modular approach to film studies ... an indispensable tool for both lecturers and students."

Professor Paul Willeman, University of Ulster

November 2001

128 pages

1-903364-18-3

£11.99 pbk

COSTUME AND CINEMA
Dress Codes in Popular Film

Sarah Street

Costume and Cinema presents an overview of the literature on film costume, together with a series of detailed case studies which highlight how costume is a key signifier in film texts. Sarah Street demonstrates how costume relates in fundamental ways to the study of film narrative and mise-en-scène, in some cases constituting a language of its own. In particular the book foregrounds the related issues of adaptation and embodiment in a variety of different genres and films including *The Talented Mr Ripley, Desperately Seeking Susan, Titanic* and *The Matrix*.

Sarah Street is Reader in Screen Studies at the University of Bristol, UK. She has written widely on many aspects British cinema.

"A valuable addition to the growing literature on film and costume ... engagingly written, offering a lucid introduction to the field."

Stella Bruzzi, Royal Holloway College, University of London

PSYCHOANALYSIS AND CINEMA
The Play of Shadows

Vicky Lebeau

Psychoanalysis and Cinema examines the long and uneven history of developments in modern art, science and technology that brought pychoanalysis and the cinema together towards the end of the nineteenth century. Vicky Lebeau explores the subsequent encounters between the two: the seductions of psychoanalysis and cinema as converging, though distinct, ways of talking about dream and desire, image and illusion, shock and sexuality. Beginning with Freud's encounter with the spectacle of hysteria on display in fin-de-siècle Paris, this study offers a detailed reading of the texts and concepts which generated the field of psychoanalytic film theory.

November 200
144 page
1-903364-19-
£11.99 pb

Vicky Lebeau is Senior Lecturer in English at the University of Sussex, UK. She has published widely on the topics of psychoanalysis and visual culture.

> "A very lucid and subtle exploration of the reception of Freud's theories and their relation to psychoanalysis's contemporary developments – cinema and modernism. One of the best introductions to psychoanalytic film theory available."
>
> Elizabeth Cowie, University of Kent

NEW CHINESE CINEMA
Challenging Representations

Sheila Cornelius with Ian Haydn Smith

New Chinese Cinema examines the 'search for roots' films that emerged from China in the aftermath of the Cultural Revolution. Sheila Cornelius contextualises the films of the so-called Fifth Generation directors who came to prominence in the 1980s and 1990s such as Chen Kaige, Zhang Yimou and Tian Zhuangzhuan. Including close analysis of such pivotal films as *Farewell My Concubine*, *Raise the Red Lantern* and *The Blue Kite*, the book also examines the rise of contemporary Sixth Generation underground directors whose themes embrace the disaffection of urban youth.

December 200
144 page
1-903364-13-
£11.99 pb

Sheila Cornelius is Visiting Lecturer in Chinese Cinema at Morley College, London. Ian Haydn Smith is a freelance film critic, and the author of *The Cinema of Ang Lee* (Wallflower Press, 2002).

> "Very thorough in its coverage of the historical and cultural background to New Chinese Cinema ... clearly written and appropriately targeted at an undergraduate audience."
>
> Leon Hunt, Brunel University

MISE-EN-SCÈNE
Film Style and Interpretation

John Gibbs

*M*ise-en-scène explores and elucidates constructions of this fundamental concept in thinking about film. In uncovering the history of mise-en-scène within film criticism, and through the detailed exploration of scenes from films as *Imitation of Life* and *Lone Star*, John Gibbs makes the case for the importance of a sensitive understanding of film style, and provides an introduction to the skills of close reading. This book thus celebrates film-making and film criticism alive to the creative possibilities of visual style.

John Gibbs is Lecturer in Film and Television Studies at The London Institute, UK.

December 2001

128 pages

1-903364-06-X

£11.99 pbk

"An immensely readable and sophisticated account of a topic of central importance to the serious study of films."

Deborah Thomas, University of Sunderland

SCENARIO
The Craft of Screenwriting

Tudor Gates

*S*cenario presents a system of logical analysis of the basic structures of successful screenplays, from initial plot-lines to realised scripts. All the essential building blocks are discussed in depth: the need for a strong premise; the roles of protagonist and antagonist; the orchestration of plot, characters and dialogue leading to a clear resolution. Written by a highly-experienced and successful screenwriter, this is a book which not only instructs first-time writers how to go about their work but also serves as a valuable check-list for established authors, and for actors, directors and teachers, in their task of deconstructing and assessing the value of the material placed before them.

February 2002

144 pages

1-903364-26-4

£11.99 pbk

Tudor Gates has written, directed and produced numerous teleplays, theatre plays, and feature films (including *Barbarella*). He has also served as Chairman of the National Film Development Fund and the Joint Board for Film Industry Training.

"This is an immensely readable introduction to the craft of screenwriting and is very helpful for budding screenwriters."

Alby James, Northern Film School

ANIMATION
Genre and Authorship

Paul Wells

Animation: Genre and Authorship is an introductory study which seeks to explore the distinctive language of animation, its production processes, and the particular questions about who makes it, under what conditions and with what purpose. Arguably, animation provides the greatest opportunity for distinctive models of 'auteurism' and revises generic categories. This is the first study to look specifically at these issues, and to challenge the prominence of live action movie-making as the first form of contemporary cinema and visual culture.

Professor Paul Wells is Head of the Media Portfolio at the University of Teesside, UK. He has published *The Horror Genre: From Beelzebub to Blair Witch* (Wallflower Press, 2000).

February 2002
144 pages
1-903364-20-8
£11.99 pbk

BRITISH SOCIAL REALISM
From Documentary to Brit Grit

Samantha Lay

British Social Realism details and explores the rich tradition of social realism in British cinema from its beginnings in the documentary movement of the 1930s to its more stylistically eclectic and generically-hybrid contemporary forms. Samantha Lay examines the movements, moments and cycles of British social realist texts through a detailed consideration of practice, politics, form, style and content, using case studies of key texts including *Listen To Britain, Saturday Night and Sunday Morning, Letter To Brezhnev*, and *Nil By Mouth*. The book considers the challenges for social realist film practice and production in Britain, now and in the future.

Samantha Lay is Lecturer in Film and Media Studies at West Herts College, UK.

May 2002
144 pages
1-903364-41-8
£11.99 pbk

WOMEN'S CINEMA
The Contested Screen

Alison Butler

May 2001
144 pages
1-903364-27-2
£11.99 pbk

Women's Cinema provides an introduction to critical debates around women's film-making and relates those debates to a variety of cinematic practices. Taking her cue from the ground-breaking theories of Claire Johnston and the critical tradition she inspired, Alison Butler argues that women's cinema is a minor cinema which exists inside other cinemas, inflecting and contesting the codes and systems of the major cinematic traditions from within. Using canonical directors and less established names as examples, ranging from Chantal Akerman to Moufida Tlatli, the book argues that women's cinema is unified in spite of its diversity by the ways in which it reworks cinematic conventions.

Alison Butler is Lecturer in Film Studies at the University of Reading, UK.

THE WESTERN GENRE
From Lordsburg to Big Whiskey

John Saunders

2001
144 pages
1-903364-12-4
£11.99 pbk

The Western Genre offers close readings of the definitive American film movement as represented by such leading exponents as John Ford, Howard Hawks and Sam Peckinpah. In his consideration of such iconic motifs as the Outlaw Hero and the Lone Rider, John Saunders traces the development of perennial aspects of the genre, its continuity and, importantly, its change. Representations of morality and masculinity are also foregrounded in consideration of the genre's major stars John Wayne and Clint Eastwood, and the book includes a number of detailed analyses of such landmark films as *Shane*, *Rio Bravo*, *The Wild Bunch* and *Unforgiven*.

John Saunders is Senior Lecturer in film and literature at the University of Newcastle, UK.

"A clear exposition of the major thematic currents of the genre providing attentive and illuminating reading of major examples."

Ed Buscombe, Editor of the *BFI Companion to the Western*

DISASTER MOVIES
The Cinema of Catastrophe

Stephen Keane

Disaster Movies provides a comprehensive introduction to the history and development of the disaster genre. From 1950s sci-fi B-movies to high concept 1990s millennial movies, Stephen Keane looks at the ways in which the representation of disaster and its aftermath are borne out of both contextual considerations and the increasing commercial demands of contemporary Hollywood. Through detailed analyses of such films as *Airport*, *The Poseidon Adventure*, *Independence Day* and *Titanic*, the book explores the continual reworking of this, to-date, undervalued genre.

200
144 page
1-903364-05-
£11.99 pb

Stephen Keane is Lecturer in Film at Bretton Hall College, University of Leeds, UK.

> "Providing detailed consideration of key movies within their social and cultural context, this concise introduction serves its purpose well and should prove a useful teaching tool."
>
> Nick Roddick

READING HOLLYWOOD
Spaces and Meanings in American Film

Deborah Thomas

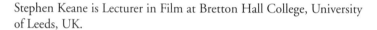

Reading Hollywood examines the treatment of space and narrative in a selection of classic films including *My Darling Clementine*, *Its a Wonderful Life* and *Vertigo*. Deborah Thomas employs a variety of arguments in exploring the reading of space and its meaning in Hollywood cinema, and film generally. Topics covered include the importance of space in defining genre (such as the necessity of an urban landscape for a gangster film to be a gangster film); the ambiguity of offscreen space and spectatorship (how an audience reads an unseen but inferred setting) and the use of spatially disruptive cinematic techniques such as flashback to construct meaning.

200
144 page
1-903364-01-
£11.99 pb

Deborah Thomas is Reader in Film Studies at the University of Sunderland, UK, and a member of the editorial board of *Movie*.

> "Amongst the finest introductions to Hollywood in particular and film studies in general ... subtler, more complex, yet more readable than most of its rivals, many of which it will displace."
>
> Professor Robin Wood

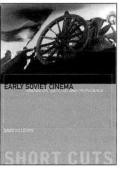

EARLY SOVIET CINEMA
Innovation, Ideology and Propaganda

David Gillespie

Early Soviet Cinema examines the aesthetics of Soviet cinema during its golden age of the 1920s, against a background of cultural ferment and the construction of a new socialist society. Separate chapters are devoted to the work of Sergei Eisenstein, Lev Kuleshov, Vsevolod Pudovkin, Dziga Vertov and Alexander Dovzhenko. David Gillespie places primary focus on the text, with analysis concentrating on the artistic qualities, rather than the political implications, of each film.

David Gillespie teaches Russian Language and Culture at the University of Bath, UK.

2000
144 pages
1-903364-04-3
£11.99 pbk

"An excellent book ... lively and informative. It fills a significant gap and deserves to be on reading lists wherever courses on Soviet cinema are run."

Graham Roberts, University of Surrey

SCIENCE FICTION CINEMA
From Outerspace to Cyberspace

Geoff King and Tanya Krzywinska

From lurid comic-book blockbusters to dark dystopian visions, science fiction is seen as both a powerful cultural barometer of our times and the product of particular industrial and commercial frameworks. The authors outline the major themes of the genre and explore issues such as the meaning of special effects and the influence of science fiction cinema on the entertainment media of the digital age. The book concludes with an extensive case-study of *Star Wars Episode I: The Phantom Menace*.

Both authors lecture in Film and Television Studies at Brunel University, London. Geoff King has written on contemporary Hollywood cinema and cultural studies. Tanya Krzywinska has written on explicit sex films and the cinema of the occult.

2000
144 pages
1-903364-03-5
£11.99 pbk

"The best overview of English-language science-fiction cinema published to date ... thorough, clearly written and full of excellent examples. Highly recommended."

Steve Neale, Sheffield Hallam University

THE STAR SYSTEM
Hollywood's Production of Popular Identities

Paul McDonald

The Star System looks at the development and changing organisation of the star system in the American film industry. Tracing the popularity of star performers from the early 'cinema of attractions' to the internet universe, Paul McDonald explores the ways in which Hollywood has made and sold its stars. Through focusing on particular historical periods, the key conditions influencing the star system in silent cinema, the studio era and the New Hollywood are discussed and illustrated by cases studies of Mary Pickford, Bette Davis, James Cagney, Julia Roberts, Tom Cruise, and Will Smith.

2000
144 pages
1·903364·02·7
£11.99 pbk

Paul McDonald is Senior Lecturer in Film and Television Studies at the University of Surrey, Roehampton, UK.

"A very good introduction to the topic filling an existing gap in the needs of teachers and students of the subject."

Roberta Pearson, University of Wales, Cardiff

THE HORROR GENRE
From Beelzebub to Blair Witch

Paul Wells

The Horror Genre is a comprehensive introduction to the history and key themes of the genre. The main issues and debates raised by horror, and the approaches and theories that have been applied to horror texts are all featured. In addressing the evolution of the horror film in social and historical context, Paul Wells explores how it has reflected and commented upon particular historical periods, and asks how it may respond to the new millennium by citing recent innovations in the genres development, such as the urban myth narrative underpinning *Candyman* and *The Blair Witch Project*.

2000
144 pages
1·903364·00·0
£11.99 pbk

Paul Wells is Head of the Media Portfolio at the University of Teesside, UK. He is the author of *Animation: Genre and Authorship* (Wallflower Press, 2002)

"A valuable contribution to the body of teaching texts available ... a book for all undergraduates starting on the subject."

Linda Ruth Williams, University of Southampton